Simple Repairs

GALAHAD BOOKS · NEW YORK CITY

Copyright © 1974 Publications International, Ltd.

All rights reserved under International and Pan American copyright

This publication may not be reproduced or quoted in whole or in part by mimeograph or any other printed means, or for presentation on radio or television without written permission from the publisher.

Library of Congress Catalog Card Number: 74-29623

ISBN 0-88365-271-4

Manufactured in the United States of America

Published by arrangement with Publications International, Ltd.

Contents

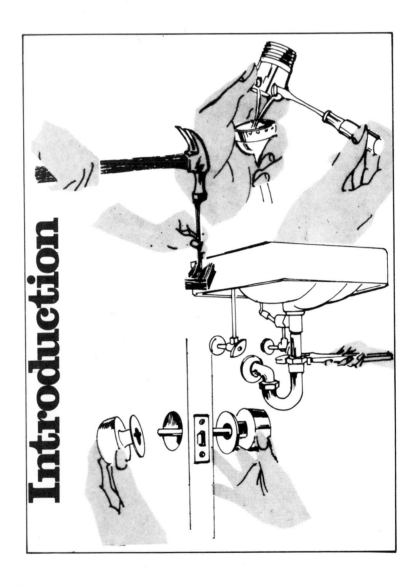

Introduction

THERE IS ONE situation with which you are probably all too familiar. The scenario goes something like this: The repairman — be he a plumber, electrician, glazier, carpenter, etc. — has just walked out your door after a service call. You stand at the door, mouth agape, stunned at the charges enumerated on the bill he has handed you for his services. You

4

know that he worked on your faulty pipes, toilet, wiring, windows, etc., for only a short time — and you sense that what he did required nothing more than you could do if you only knew how to do it.

Actually, your belief in your own ability to perform simple repairs — and to save a great deal of money by doing so — is well founded. Perhaps the majority of malfunctions that occur in an apartment or in a house do not demand that you have many years of training or enormous varieties of tools in order to repair the defects. Instead, they require that you know certain basic principles regarding your home's plumbing and electrical systems and that you have a relatively small number of high quality tools and a comprehensive guide to performing simple repairs yourself.

What To Do And What Not To Do

THIS VOLUME of CONSUMER GUIDE Magazine has a two-fold purpose. First, we want to indicate to you how many simple yet money-saving repairs you can perform yourself. Second, we want to make clear that there are areas of home repair into which you should not venture. There are, indeed, repairs that do require a great deal of technical expertise. If you do not possess such expertise, you endanger your safety and you threaten to make matters worse by tackling projects beyond your capabilities. This is not to say that *Simple Repairs* covers every project you are capable of doing; you will have to decide whether a given plumbing or electrical or household repair is within your knowledge and ability to perform safely and properly. We feel duty-bound, however, to point out the dangers inherent in going beyond these simple repairs to more complex ones; and we suggest — at several points throughout the book — that you call in a professional when his knowledge and training are required.

It is, nevertheless, the positive side — what you can do — that we wish to emphasize. To that end, we have structured the plumbing and electrical segments of the book to aid you in diagnosing the problem and then in making the appropriate repair. Two very important chapters — "How Your Plumbing System Works" and "How Your Home Is Wired" — introduce main sections. They are must reading for anyone who contemplates performing do-it-yourself home repairs.

The plumbing and electricity in your home are systems; a breakdown can occur in a particular fixture, but you should never forget that the broken fixture is just one link in a complicated yet comprehensible system. For example, suppose that one of your drains is clogged. If you want to clear the clog by using a rubber

5

plunger (plumber's friend), you must seal off all the outlets (such as overflow vents) that connect to the clogged drain. Otherwise, the pressure that you create with your vigorous and forceful pumping of the plunger will all be lost through the outlet, and never get anywhere near the clog. Moreover, the other outlet can be a part of another plumbing fixture, even one that is a good distance from the one on which you are working. Therefore, you must think in terms of systems — how all the fixtures and conduits in your home relate to one another to provide the services you expect.

Other Preparatory Chapters

ONCE YOU READ and understand the chapters covering the plumbing and electrical systems in your home, do not jump right into a needed repair project. Instead, take some time to acquaint yourself with the other preparatory chapters in each section.

"Plumbing Tools" and "What To Do In An Emergency" are designed to introduce you to the tools of the trade and how to use them when a disaster strikes. You do not want to put off reading these chapters until your basement floor is covered with water six feet deep. Read them now, even though you cannot even foresee any plumbing complications or breakdowns impending. Then, make sure that you have the basic tools required to handle the plumbing emergencies that can and do arise. The tools themselves are not expensive, and many of them can be used for other household repairs and do-it-yourself projects.

Similarly, the chapters on "Electrical Wire" and "How To Work Safely With Electricity" are ones that you should read, even though there may be nothing that needs fixing in your electrical system at present. Were you to make a mistake while working on a plumbing project, you could make a mess and ruin a pipe or a fixture; but if you make a mistake while performing an electrical task, you could make that the last repair project you ever attempt.

Actually, you have nothing to fear when working with electricity — as long as you follow certain basic rules. The most important thing to remember is that you must never come in physical contact with a live circuit. The first thing to do, therefore, when embarking upon nearly any electrical repair is to deenergize the circuit on which you plan to work. Pull the fuse or trip the circuit breaker to its off position, and protect yourself from someone accidentally energizing the circuit while you are working on it. Remove the fuse and put it in your pocket, or place a piece of tape over the turned-off circuit breaker and write "Hands Off" on the

6

tape with a felt-tipped pen. With the circuit dead, you might need a flashlight (or a trouble light with a cord long enough to reach the nearest live outlet) to see what you are doing, but at least you assure your safety from coming in contact with a potentially harmful live circuit.

Learning how to work with electricity — and plumbing too — not only saves you money, but it also adds immeasurably to your self-confidence. No longer will you be completely dependent upon technicians and service personnel. Even when you cannot perform a specific repair yourself, you will be able to explain the problem accurately to the professional repairman. Such an explanation can save you money in two ways: (1) by reducing the time a serviceman must spend in your home, and (2) by convincing him that he cannot charge you for procedures that are not required by the repair at hand.

Speaking Of Specifics

NOW THAT YOU know how the plumbing and electrical systems function and how to work on them safely, you are ready to tackle the specific repair projects that need doing around your house. Some of the chapter titles themselves may strike a responsive chord in you. Perhaps you thought that nothing could be done to cure a certain malfunction — nothing, that is, short of spending a small fortune to replace substantial segments of your plumbing and/or electrical systems.

Take the problem of noisy plumbing for example. If you think that you have no choice but to put up with pipes that clang or faucets that squeal, you are in for a pleasant surprise. In fact, for a truly nominal investment you can steady those pipes or stop that squeal. Moreover, do you think that condensation on pipes or tanks is irreparable? Nothing could be further from the truth. We tell you how, and all you must do is tackle the project for yourself.

Likewise, many people are aware that a broken doorbell or a lamp that no longer functions need not remain in that condition, but they do not know how to make the necessary repairs, nor do they comprehend just how easy those repairs can be. The parts needed to make the repair are easily accessible at any hardware store, and their cost is not worth a moment's hesitation when you consider that you will have a doorbell or lamp as good as new at a fraction of what it would cost to have a professional repairman do the job.

The same holds true for other household repairs. You will be amazed at how little it costs, for example, to replace a broken window yourself. The hardware dealer will cut the glass to the

7

precise size you need, or you can save even more money — if you have several windows to replace — by learning how to cut glass and then buying it in large sheets. The installation of the new window takes no great expertise; merely follow our directions. Similarly, you have no idea how easily you can silence a squeaky floor. All it takes is a little know-how, and you find that you no longer have to tolerate what you once thought could never be changed.

We know, however, that once the do-it-yourself bug bites you will not be content merely to repair the broken items around your house. You may, for example, look at that old-fashioned leg-supported bathtub and wish that you could afford to replace it. If you follow the instructions provided in "Remodeling and Modernizing," you can be sure that the job is done properly and save yourself a bundle of cash at the same time. Perhaps your plumbing project plans are a little less grandiose, and all you want to do is add a garbage disposer, a new toilet seat, or a water cutoff to an existing fixture. Find the appropriate chapter under the general heading "Simple Plumbing Repairs," and you are well on your way to making significant improvements to your home at minimal costs.

You can, of course, improve your electrical system as well. Perhaps you always wanted to have an air conditioner, but your house or apartment lacked the 240-volt receptacle and wiring required for the larger air conditioning units. Or, you purchase a beautiful electric wall clock, but then are distressed to see the cord dangling down several feet to the baseboard outlet. Or, you wish that you had a lamp fixture where there never was one before, and that you could turn that lamp on and off at more than one location. All of these projects are well within your abilities, and none requires parts that you cannot obtain from your local hardware dealer.

Conclusion

IT SHOULD BE clear by now that this volume of CONSUMER GUIDE Magazine is meant to uphold our constant purpose: to help you derive maximum value for your money. Two of the ways we can help you are to keep the serviceman away from your door, and to show you how you can improve your home at modest expense. If you save yourself just one service call or make only one improvement for which you would normally call upon a professional plumber, electrician, etc., then you more than pay for the cost of this book — and you make CONSUMER GUIDE Magazine's purpose a reality.

8

Simple Plumbing Repairs

Plumbing is, in concept, a simple system. Clean water comes into your home, and waste water drains out of it. Breakdowns in the system can and do occur, however. Clogs, drips, and cracks in plumbing fixtures and pipes can be annoying and sometimes disastrous. But you can fix your own plumbing problems, and save yourself a great deal of money.

9

How Your Plumbing System Works

ALTHOUGH THE entire plumbing system may seem like a mystery, it is more misunderstood than mysterious. The plumbing in your house operates on some very basic laws of nature — laws like gravity, water pressure, and the fact that water seeks its own level.

There are two separate and distinct plumbing systems in your home — one for incoming, and one for outgoing. Total separation is an absolute must between these two plumbing systems. Let's take a look at the way a typical home receives and disposes of water.

Water Supply System

NO MATTER what the source of water to your house may be, it is delivered under pressure. If you live in a typical city, the community water department pumps water into a storage tank or water tower, and usually gravity provides the pressure because the tower is higher than the outlets in the homes. In some cases, pump pressure is needed.

The water to your home is supplied through a water main. The water main usually goes through a water meter which is located very near the point where the supply line enters your property. The meter may be underground outside the house with a metal cover for access, or it may be inside at the point where the supply pipe comes in the house. The meter records the number of gallons brought into the house. If you can see it easily, look at the meter's

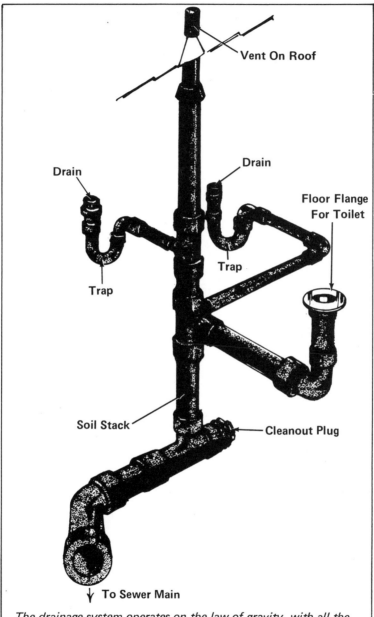

Vent On Roof

Drain

Drain

Floor Flange For Toilet

Trap

Trap

Soil Stack

Cleanout Plug

To Sewer Main

The drainage system operates on the law of gravity, with all the waste pipes going downhill. Water drains out of the house and into a sewer line.

11

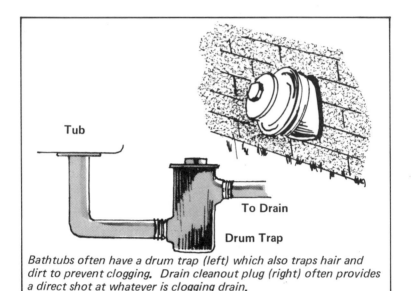

Tub

To Drain

Drum Trap

Bathtubs often have a drum trap (left) which also traps hair and dirt to prevent clogging. Drain cleanout plug (right) often provides a direct shot at whatever is clogging drain.

dials spin when you have several outlets open at one time.

If you have your own well, you are probably using a pump to supply the water and add the pressure. Except for the fact that you lack a meter, all the rest of the information here concerning your water supply is the same.

Very close to the meter is a main cutoff valve which shuts off all the water coming into the house. You must know how to find and use the main cutoff in a plumbing emergency. The cutoff may be a stop and waste valve that drains the water from the pipes as well as shuts off the supply. Most fixtures have — or should have — individual shut-off valves.

All water comes into your house as cold water. It is piped directly to all fixtures that use unheated water through the cold water main; offshoots to individual fixtures are called branches. The water can travel upstairs, around corners, or wherever needed because it is under pressure. The pipes that run vertically and extend upward a story or more are called risers.

One part of the cold water system carries water to the heater. From the water heater, a hot water main carries hot water to all the fixtures, outlets, or appliances that require hot water.

All faucets, hot or cold, should have some sort of air chamber. The air chamber serves as a cushion to stop the shock waves that

12

occur when water under pressure is moving rapidly and is suddenly shut off.

Water Pressure

YOU CAN, no doubt, see the value of water pressure, but too much of a good thing can be bad. Too much pressure causes your pipes to bang around, and it may even cause joints and connections to break. Too much pressure is also a water waster. In addition, it can strain your fixtures and cause faucets to leak. Pressure that fluctuates, of course, can be uncomfortable in the shower.

Residential water pressure that reaches or exceeds 60 psi (pounds per square inch) is too much of a good thing. You can test the pressure in your house by attaching a pressure gauge to any threaded faucet. If the gauge shows 60 psi or more, you ought to in-

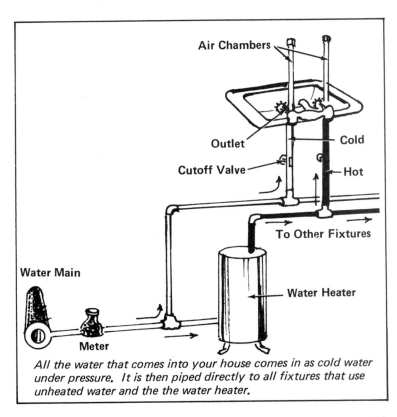

All the water that comes into your house comes in as cold water under pressure. It is then piped directly to all fixtures that use unheated water and the the water heater.

13

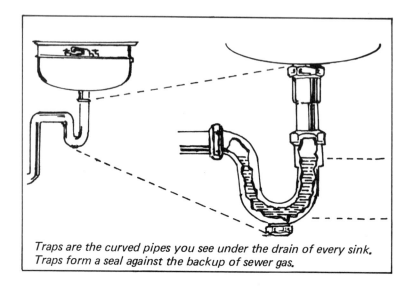

Traps are the curved pipes you see under the drain of every sink. Traps form a seal against the backup of sewer gas.

stall a pressure-reducing valve. Of course, be sure to test the pressure at several times during the day to find a good average. In addition, make sure that no water is running in your home besides the outlet with the gauge attached.

A pressure-reducing valve is a fairly inexpensive unit, and installation is an easy do-it-yourself project. Most of the valves work best when installed on a horizontal pipe, and the valve has union fittings for an easy connection. You can set the valve to provide the pressure that best suits your needs. Once set, the valve lowers the pressure to the setting, and steadies it at that level.

While too much pressure can be tamed for a little investment, too little pressure is something you may have to accept. Trying to increase pressure may require such major endeavors as building your own water tower or completely replacing all the pipes in your home.

Drain System

NOW THAT we have all that water in the house, how do we get rid of it after we use it? The answer is called a drainage system.

The drainage system operates on the law of gravity, with all the waste pipes going downhill. The water drains out of the house and into a sewer line that continues the downhill flow, carrying away the waste and used water. There is more to the system than that,

14

however. There are vents, traps, and cleanouts.

The vents are open pipes that stick out the roof of the house and allow air to enter the drain pipes. The vents sometimes are just extensions of a drain pipe. Proper venting is a must. The introduction of air pressure helps the water to flow out. Air from the vents also prevents a syphoning action at the traps.

The curved pipes you can see under the drain of every sink are called traps. When a basin is emptied, the water flows out with enough force to push through the trap and out through the drain pipe. When it runs out, however, there is still water left in the trap to protect you; the trap water provides a seal against the backup of sewer gas. If you had no seal there, bad odors and dangerous gases could enter your home. Every fixture must have a trap.

If the vents were not there — or if they were clogged up — the lack of air in the drain could cause the rush of water going out to syphon out too much of the water in the trap, leaving a gap. The gap means that there is no longer a seal, and the sewer gas backs up into your house.

Toilets are self trapped, and do not require an additional trap in the drain. Frequently, bathtubs have a drum trap which provides the same safeguards, but also traps hair and dirt to prevent clogging. In some kitchens, grease traps collect grease that goes down the sink. Grease and hair are the prime offenders in the clogging department, but the clean-out plugs on these traps allow for a direct shot at any clogs.

Fixtures

THE BRIDGE between the two systems — supply and drainage — is the point of having the plumbing in the first place: the fixture. Plumbing jargon refers to any outlet — whether it be an outside hydrant or a twelve-cycle automatic washing machine — as a fixture.

Those are the basics of the plumbing in your house. The fact that it is usually hidden in the walls, under the floors, and beneath the ground may make the plumbing seem mysterious, but it is really a simple and logical system. Now that you know how it works, take a look at the pipes in your basement or crawl space. The larger heavy pipes are for drainage. You should also be able to pick out the supply lines. Try to locate the clean-out plugs. If you can see up on your roof, you will have no trouble picking out the vent stacks. It is always a good idea, moreover, to tag as many different lines as possible so that you can know what each pipe does should an emergency arise.

Knowing how the plumbing systems work should make the diagnosis of your next plumbing problem a little easier.

15

What To Do In An Emergency

IT IS A sad fact but a true one: By the time you get a call through to the plumber, a burst pipe can pour thousands of gallons of water into your house. Untamed water, of course, can do thousands of dollars in damage to your house and its furnishings. Now, while there is no emergency, is the time to learn what to do in the event of a major plumbing disaster.

Water Cutoffs

THE FIRST thing everyone should know is how to shut off the flow of water. Take the entire family on a tour of your home to see where the cutoffs are located. Each sink, basin, tub, and appliance should have its own cutoff, but you will find that many do not have them. Everyone must, therefore, know the location of the main cutoff.

Usually located very close to where the water supply enters the house, the main cutoff may be a gate valve or it may be an "L"-shaped rod. If the meter is in the basement, you could have a meter valve that requires a wrench to turn. An underground meter would have the same type of valve, but a buried pipe means that you must dig to find the cutoff.

Once you locate the main cutoff valve, find out exactly how it works and, most importantly, if it works. Little-used valves have a way of corroding, and it is better to find out now that the valve needs replacement than when you are struggling in a panic situa-

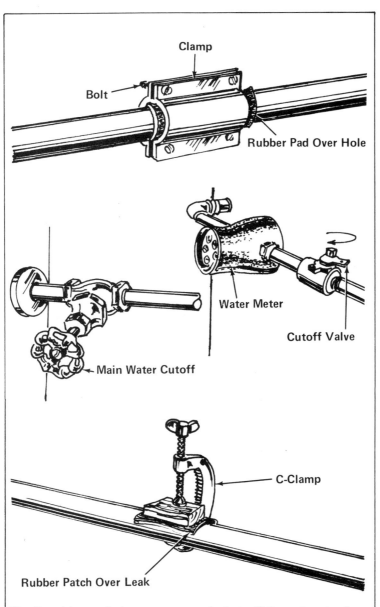

Clamp

Bolt

Rubber Pad Over Hole

Water Meter

Cutoff Valve

Main Water Cutoff

C-Clamp

Rubber Patch Over Leak

The first thing to do in an emergency is shut off the water supply. Find the main cutoff valve, which may be one you can turn by hand (middle, left) or it may require a wrench (middle, right). Once the water is off, you can put a patch (top and bottom) over leak.

tion. In the case of the "L"-shaped rod, the actual valve is usually underground. If the valve malfunctions, you must dig down and treat the valve with penetrating oil to free it.

Make sure that you know which way to turn the valve to shut off the water. It might even be a good idea to tag the cutoff with a drawing that indicates what the valve is and which way to turn it. You can use the occasion to acquaint the family with gas and electricity cutoffs as well. As for preventive maintenance, it is a good idea to turn the water cutoff valve off and then on again once every six months or so to keep it in working order.

Flooding

ONE WORD OF caution: Remember that the flooding waters can come in contact with electrical components. Make sure that you do not complete the fatal triangle. If there is any chance of electrical contact, always throw the main switch to your household current before you go wading around in the water.

If the cause of the flood is a burst pipe, there are temporary patches that you can make. Unfortunately, the chances are that if the pipe is bad enough to spring a leak, the entire pipe is probably in bad shape; you may fix one spot and see the pipe burst somewhere else. Nevertheless, you must know what to do in an emergency or until the pipe is replaced.

There are pipe repair kits available at the hardware store. Some have a rubber pad that goes over the hole in the pipe. The metal plates then bolt tightly together to compress the rubber pad against the hole. A quick and easy way to stop a leak, this sort of repair can even be permanent if the pipe is otherwise sound. Therefore, it would be a good idea to have such a kit on hand for emergencies. You can rig up a kit of your own by cutting a patch of rubber from an old inner tube and using a C-clamp or hose clamp to press the pad in place. When using the C-clamp, you may wish to place a block of wood against the pad to spread the clamping pressure.

Waterproof tape can often do an adequate temporary patching job. Start wrapping the tape two or three inches from the hole and extend it the same distance beyond. Dry the pipe before you start wrapping the tape.

For tiny leaks in pipes, you can use one of the sticks of special compound that are available at hardware stores. You just rub the stick over the hole, and the leak stops. One brand, Krak-Stik, can even stop small leaks while the water is still running in the pipe. For permanent patching, epoxy metal can do the job. Just be sure to follow the directions, and allow for the full curing time.

18

If the flood emanates from a leaky tank, try one of the self-tapping plugs that are designed to go into the hole. When tightened down, the screw applies enough pressure to stop the leak. Here again, however, if the tank rotted through in one place, it may well do so in another. The plugs, nonetheless, may buy you enough time to shop around for the best replacement tank while preventing damage to your home.

Other Emergencies

A CLOGGED drain can seem to be an emergency, but all you need do is to make sure that no additional water is poured in until you are able to unclog the drain. In some cases, other outlets are on the same common drain and water poured into any of them could cause an overflow.

The most important thing to remember in a plumbing emergency is to keep a cool head. Stop the flow of rising water to minimize damage. Once you get the water shut off, there is no reason to panic; you even have time to figure out your next move. You may decide that the time has come to call in professional help, but you may conclude that this emergency is merely one of the many plumbing projects that you can tackle yourself.

Plumbing Tools

ANY FIX-IT project is much easier and the results much better when performed with the proper tools. Some of the tools that you need for repairing drains, faucets, toilets, and pipes are useful in many other areas besides plumbing. The ones you elect to purchase depend on how deeply you are involved in performing home repairs in general and plumbing projects in particular.

One word of advice, however: Whatever tools you decide to buy should be the best you can afford. The price difference between top quality tools and inferior ones is generally insignificant. The relatively small difference is, however, a fairly good indicator of tool quality. Often a good tool will last a lifetime, whereas a poor tool may not make it through the project for which you bought it. Stick with known brands or with private brands from known tool manufacturers.

Wrenches

YOU WILL need a wrench for most faucet repairs and for various other connections. A medium-sized adjustable wrench serves well because it can be used on different sized nuts. One adjustable wrench will do the same thing as will a set of open end wrenches. Of course, you can frequently use a pair of long-handled pliers instead of a wrench to do the job.

Working on pipe requires heavier wrenches, known as pipe or

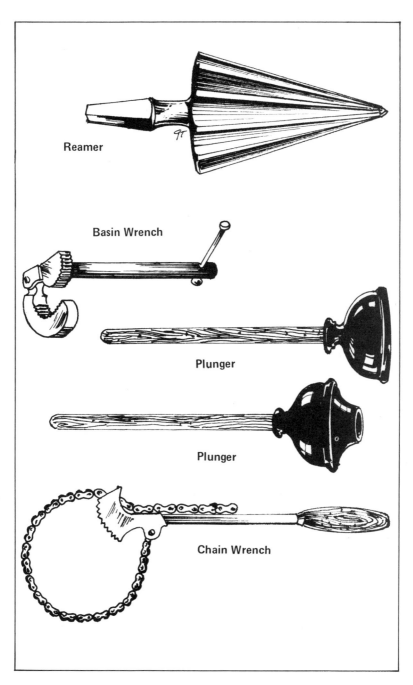

Reamer

Basin Wrench

Plunger

Plunger

Chain Wrench

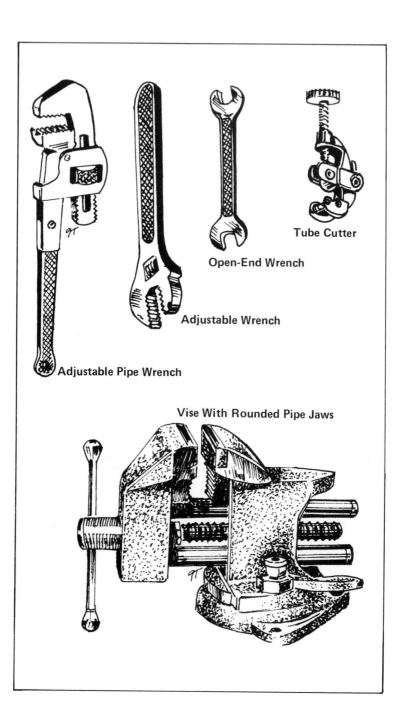

Open-End Wrench

Tube Cutter

Adjustable Wrench

Adjustable Pipe Wrench

Vise With Rounded Pipe Jaws

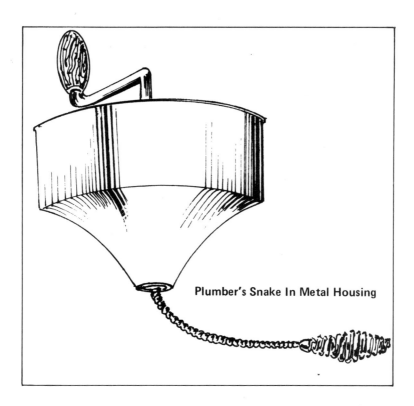

Plumber's Snake In Metal Housing

Stillson wrenches; these wrenches are generally used in pairs — one holds while the other turns. A chain pipe wrench is ideal for larger pipes, and a strap wrench — which works on the same principle as the chain wrench — can be used on polished pipe without marring the finish.

A basin wrench allows you to get up in tight spots under sinks and basins. The jaws not only adjust to different sizes, but they also flip over to the opposite side for turning in the opposite direction. A special type of socket is needed to remove the packing nut from recessed tub and shower fixtures. If you do not already own a socket wrench set, it does not pay to buy one just for this job; but you can find many tasks in which a socket wrench set is useful, in addition to your do-it-yourself plumbing chores.

A special wrench used for very large hexagonal slip nuts is called the adjustable slip and locknut wrench. Its more popular name is the "spudwrench." The adjustable type is much more versatile than its cousin, the solid spud wrench, which has wrenches of different

23

sizes at either end.

Drain Tools

A MUST for every household is the plumber's friend, also referred to as a plunger or force cup. Get a long-handled plunger, and be sure that the suction cup is large enough to cover the drain opening.

Plumber's snakes or augers come in various lengths; you should possess both a short one and a long one. The newer types come encased in a metal housing and are, therefore, much less messy. The closet auger is made for toilets. A plumber's tape or ribbon is much like a long clock spring.

Pipe Tools

COPPER TUBING and copper pipe require some special tools. Avoid using a hacksaw to cut copper connections. Instead, get a tube cutter in a small size for work in close quarters. You will be amazed at how many plumbing chores are performed in close quarters.

Since many copper connections are soldered, you will need a propane torch. A propane torch, of course, is a handy tool for many other do-it-yourself chores. For flared fittings, you must have a flaring tool.

When working with iron pipe, you need a vise to hold the pipe. A combination vise has a section with jaws for pipe, but yoke and chain vises are made especially for pipe work. Cutting iron pipe is best done with a pipe cutter tool similar in appearance to the tube cutter. Whenever you cut iron pipe, however, be sure to use a cutting oil. In addition, you must be prepared to remove the burrs created by the cutting. Outside burrs will come off if you file them, but for inside burrs you will need a reamer.

Much iron pipe is threaded, and generally you can purchase what you need already threaded. If you get deeply involved in plumbing projects, however, you may wish to do your own threading. If so, you will need the special dies made for threading pipe. Referred to as NPT dies, they come in sizes for all standard pipe diameters. Be sure, once again, to use cutting oil during the threading process.

Speaking of oil, you should always have penetrating oil around when tackling a plumbing repair job. You can always find a use for penetrating oil.

Many larger drain pipes are made of cast iron. The joints are made leak-proof by inserting a treated rope — called oakum — into the joint and then pouring molten lead over the oakum to seal it. For performing such tasks, you must have a caulking tool for poking the

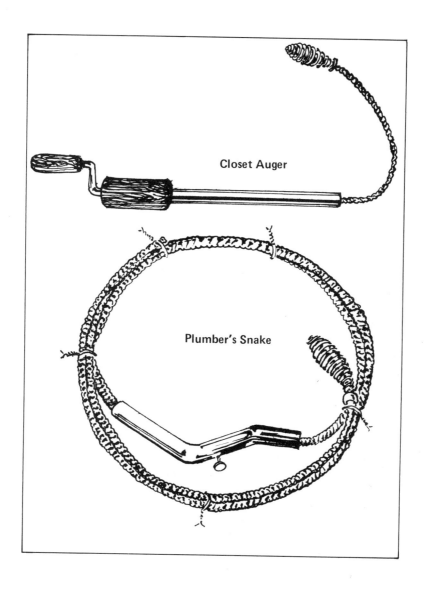

Closet Auger

Plumber's Snake

oakum in, a melting pot, and a ladle for pouring the molten lead. With horizontal pipes, you may wonder how you can ever pour the molten lead in without its running out on the ground. The answer is an asbestos joint runner.

You can cut plastic pipe with a hacksaw, but be sure to have a miter box handy to aid in making straight cuts.

25

Fixing Clogged Drains

WHEN A DRAIN stops draining, you have a problem. Sometimes, the drain starts to appear a little sluggish, giving you a warning of what is to come. That is the best time to attack the problem. Most people, unfortunately, wait until no water runs out before they take corrective action. Then they find themselves with a full-scale war on their hands.

The Plumber's Friend

THE FIRST weapon of the counter-attack, generally, is the plumber's friend. Otherwise known as the rubber plunger, this tool can create tremendous movement within the pipe. Although you need not have any specialized training to use a plunger, most people use it incorrectly. They pump up and down two or three times, and then step back to see what happens. When the water does not go whooshing out the drain, they abandon the plumber's friend for other devices or for professional repairmen.

To be effective, you first must make sure that the suction cup is big enough to cover the drain opening. Next, the water in the sink or tub must come up to at least a couple of inches over the bottom of the plunger. In addition, you must block off all other outlets between the drain and the blockage. Here is a list of the outlets you may need to block:

Kitchen Sinks: In most cases, a single kitchen sink is ready for

26

the plunger as is, but if it is part of a double sink, you must block up the drain on the other side. Moreover, there may be an additional drain connected to the same line, and if water starts backing up in another such outlet, you must block that one as well.

Bathroom Basins: Nearly all wash basins have an overflow vent (if you cannot see one, look under the rim at the top for a hidden vent). Frequently, a home with two bathrooms has basins back to back in adjacent rooms. In such instances, you must block the other basin at both the drain and the overflow vent.

Bathtubs: Most tubs have an overflow vent. Often, the lever to close the drain is held to a plate that covers the overflow vent. Shower facilities seldom have vents.

Laundry Tubs: Your laundry tub may have two and sometimes three overflow vents. You must cover them all. With a double tub arrangement, you must cover the drain in the other side, as well as all vents on both sides.

With all other outlets covered, you are ready to put the plumber's friend to work for you. Place the cup over the drain with the handle sticking straight up. Start your pushing in a slow, steady, up-and-down motion. You will soon begin to feel the water move in and out, and you can establish a rhythm to your strokes. This back-and-forth pressure of the water can build up a fairly potent force to dislodge whatever is blocking your drain.

Continue the up-and-down motion for about 15 to 20 strokes. Then lift up the plunger. Hopefully, the water will now go rushing out. If not, try the same routine again two or three more times before going on to another method. One good thing about the plumber's friend — it is good exercise; even if it fails to open the drain, it provides a great way to work off the frustration caused by the drain being clogged.

Chemical Drain Cleaners

THE NEXT STEP some people try is chemical warfare. There are a number of drain opening chemicals on the market, in both dry and liquid forms. In either case, you should be aware that any chemical that can eat up a drain blockage can also eat up your skin. When you use the chemicals according to the manufacturer's directions, you need not be afraid; but be sure to read the warnings on the label.

Some chemical drain openers are used differently than others. Only certain types of drain cleaners are suitable for use in a kitchen disposer unit. Before you put any chemical down your kitchen

27

drain, make sure that it is specified for such a purpose. Soda, for example, is a completely safe chemical that many people use regularly to prevent drain blockages. It also leaves drains in a better smelling condition.

Many people, in fact, believe that chemical warfare is best suited as a preventative measure, to be used before the drains are actually clogged. Regular applications of drain cleaners — some people use chemicals every month, while some wait for the first signs of sluggish drainage — will probably prevent any clog from forming in your drains.

No matter what type of chemical you use and when you use it, be sure to read and follow the directions and precautions printed on the label. Moreover, if you use chemicals and they do not work, be especially careful to avoid contact with the water in the drain when you resort to other weapons in the drain opening arsenal. The chemically treated water held by the blockage is harmful to the skin, and you must be very cautious when using other plumbing tools on a drain that contains such water.

The Plumber's Snake

THE SNAKE, whose proper name is the plumber's auger, is a very flexible metal coil that is fed down into the clogged drain until it reaches the blockage. It has a head that works its way through the blockage to loosen the clog. The snake is so flexible that it can negotiate all sorts of turns and bends in the pipe; you can make your task much easier, though, if you remove the trap first.

The trap is a bad stretch of curves in the pipe directly under the sink, designed to block the backup of sewer gas. Some traps have a clean-out plug that you can remove to save your snake some unnecessary twisting. Other traps do not have such a plug, but you can remove the trap itself by turning two slip nuts counterclockwise. When the nuts are free of the trap, slide them along the pipe away from the trap. There is a rubber washer under each nut; do not lose these washers.

Remember: All that water in the sink will come rushing out when you remove the trap. Have a bucket ready, and be sure not to empty the bucket back into the sink. You may laugh, but this happens more often than you might imagine.

Frequently, the trap itself is the location of the blockage. If so, you need not even use the snake. You can gouge out the guck with a piece of wire. Inspect what comes out because the trap can hide lost jewelry or contact lenses that were accidentally dropped down the drain.

If the trap is not the problem, you now have a straighter shot

28

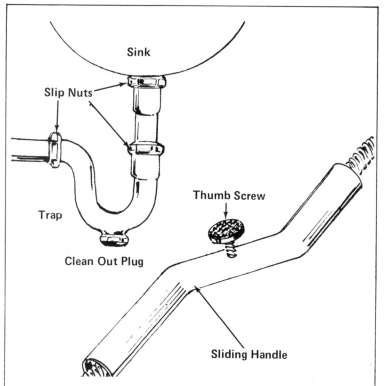

Under many sinks you will find a trap with a cleanout plug. Remove the plug to save your plumber's snake some unnecessary twisting. Feed snake in until it stops; then move sliding handle (lower right) to within a few inches of the opening.

for your snake into the pipes. Feed the snake in until it stops. Most likely you have not yet struck the blockage but rather a turn in the pipe. If the snake has a handle, push it up to within a few inches of the opening; then turn the thumb screw tight against the snake to anchor the handle.

Now start turning the handle as you push and pull the snake in and out. It may seem like it will never get past the turn, but be patient! Eventually the snake will make the turn. When it does, loosen the thumb bolt and slide the handle out of the way. Keep feeding the snake into the pipe. You may hit two or three turns before you hit the blockage; each turn requires the same procedure.

29

When you finally do hit the blockage, it will feel different from the other times the snake stopped. Once again, fasten down the handle and turn as before. Work the snake back and forth as you turn it. The snake head will grab some of the blockage, pull it back out, and push the rest on through. It may take some time and effort to get the snake through the blockage. When it does go on through, work the snake back and forth, continuing to turn the tool so that you loosen all the blockage. Just to be safe, run the snake a few feet on into the pipe to spread the debris and move it along.

When you remove the snake, have your bucket under the pipe to catch the bits of blockage that the snake may bring with it. In addition, the snake itself will be wet and dirty as it emerges; feed it into a corrugated box to keep the dirt off the floor and to prevent the snake from springing against and damaging your fixtures and furnishings.

After you pull the snake out, replace the trap. Apply pipe joint compound to the threads of the slip nuts, and check the joints with the first water that you run through to see if they leak. Now, turn the hot water on full force for several minutes to clean out all of the debris which once blocked your drain.

Another place to use your plumber's snake is through cleanout plugs like those found in a basement, in the crawl space under the house, or on an outside wall. Cleanout plugs generally give you a straighter shot into pipes. The feed and twist procedure is the same. You may, however, find that the covers to these plugs are difficult to remove. Penetrating oil is often effective in such cases.

Sometimes, instead of a snake, you can feed a garden hose into an outside cleanout plug. The pipe is big enough to accommodate a hose, and while the hose may not be as flexible as a snake, it has two advantages: (1) Most people have little use for a 50-foot snake, but they do have a hose that long; and (2) when you reach the blockage, you can blast through it with a full stream of water. After you break the blockage, you can flush out the debris by turning on the water.

A word of caution regarding cleanout plugs: If the pipes are full of water, opening the plug will allow all the water to run out. Therefore, do not remove the plug; instead, turn it just far enough to allow water to come out around the threads. Catch the water with a bucket.

There are vents on the roof of your house that are connected directly to the drain system. For a clog that is deep, you may find that you have a straighter shot at it by running the snake or a plumber's ribbon down the vent. Using this vent also makes sense when the pipes are full of water, when the cleanout plug is in the

30

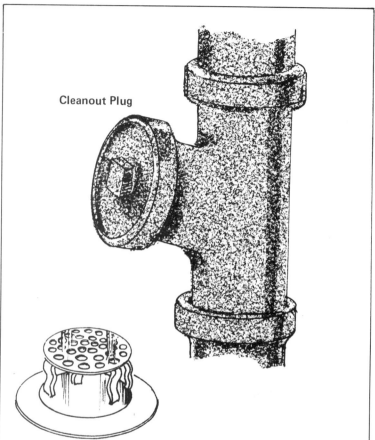

Cleanout Plug

Cleanout plugs (upper right) give you a straighter shot for clearing out clogs with a plumber's snake. Sink strainers (lower left) are held in place by springs; remove such strainers before using chemical or aerosol drain openers.

basement, and when removing the plug could result in a minor flood. Generally, the vent is not the most direct route, but keep it in the back of your mind just in case the situation demands its use.

When the main drain or a floor drain in the basement gets stopped up, the cause of the blockage may be roots that have grown in at the joints. There are chemicals that eat away at roots, or you can rent an electric rooter which goes into the pipe and cuts away roots from the walls of the pipe as it moves along.

31

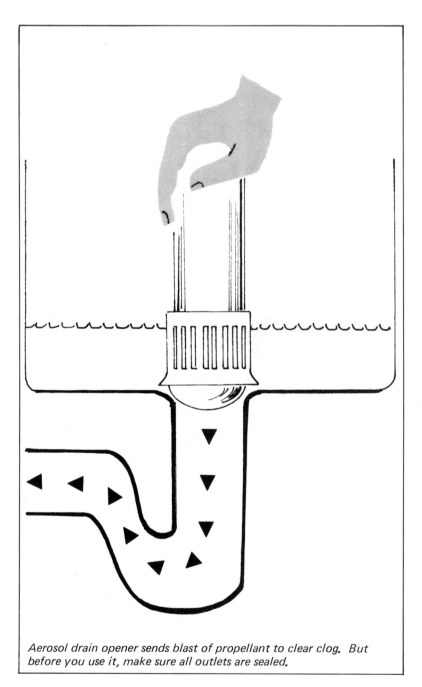

Aerosol drain opener sends blast of propellant to clear clog. But before you use it, make sure all outlets are sealed.

Aerosol Drain Cleaners

THE NEWEST home remedy for a clogged drain is the aerosol unclogger — the first entry being marketed under the name "Drain Power." It is a plastic cannister with a domed head. You place the dome in the drain and push downward on the end; this sends a blast of propellant that forces water in the pipe down against the blockage.

If you are going to use an aerosol to clear your drains, you must make sure that the blast is directed toward the blockage; a force like this is naturally going to seek the path of least resistance. Therefore, if there is an overflow vent or any other easy way for the pressure to escape, it will do so. Block vents, the other side of a double sink, and any other openings on the same common drain just as you would when using a plumber's friend.

Here is the basic procedure for using an aerosol drain cleaner:

1. Remove any visible debris from around the drain opening.
2. Locate all other outlets and block them off.
3. Remove any built-in stoppers or strainers. Some strainers are held in place by a bolt that can be removed easily with a screwdriver. Others are held in by spring tension; they can be snapped out.
4. If there is no water standing in the sink, put the stopper in and fill the sink or tub to a level of about two inches. If the blockage is such that the water cannot run out quickly, you need not close the drain.
5. With all vents closed, replace the stopper with the domed end of the cannister.
6. Push down sharply on the end of the can for one second only — no more.
7. Remove the can from the drain slowly. If the blast did what it should, the water in the sink will swirl on out. You may see a white mist rise up from the drain opening after unclogging occurs; the mist is just water vapor.
8. Run the hot water for about a minute to clear out the loosened debris.

The propellent itself is harmless, but if you have used chemical drain cleaners before using the aerosol, you can get splashed with corrosive. Make sure that the chemicals have been completely flushed out before using an aerosol cleaner.

The aerosol type of drain opener does not work on clogged toilets, nor on a sink or tub that has a nonremovable strainer.

33

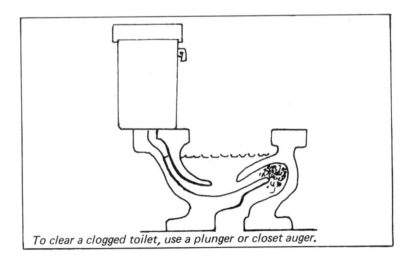

To clear a clogged toilet, use a plunger or closet auger.

Clogged Toilets

THE STOPPED-UP toilet can generally be cleared with the plumber's friend (plunger). The routine is the same as with a clogged sink. Make sure that there is water over the rubber suction cup, and then work the handle up and down. If the water has drained out, do not flush to get the water you need to cover the plunger. Flushing a clogged toilet will just cause the bowl to overflow; instead, haul in a pan of water from another source.

When you decide that you have had enough arm exercise, it is time to go on to the next step. Usually the blockage is not very far away, and sometimes you can hook the blockage with a wire coat hanger. The coat hanger is really a substitute for the plumbing tool that is called for here. The tool is a snake, but a different version from the snake used in drains. It is a shorter model, and it has a crank. The tool is called a closet auger.

Once the auger reaches the blockage, turn the crank until it feels tight. This means that the snake has twisted its way into the blockage. Usually, a pull backwards will bring out whatever is clogging the toilet, but if not (after several attempts), try to push a regular plumber's snake through the blockage.

As a last resort, you may have to remove the toilet from the floor and turn it upside down. This gives you a straight shot at the blockage. Naturally, you should give all the other methods as much opportunity as possible before resorting to so drastic a measure as actually removing the toilet.

34

Simple Plumbing Repairs

Stopping Leaks In Pipes And Joints

I N OUR discussion of emergencies, we touched on some things to do to stop leaks. Those were the quick steps to take that might not be permanent, but would at least save the carpets. Now we should make a closer examination of the proper ways to do away with leaks.

Joints

WHAT TO do for a leaking pipe joint depends on the type of joint it is. If it is copper pipe or tubing that is sweat soldered, turn to the chapter on sweat soldering.

A threaded joint may need only retightening, but a leak at a point where there is no union in the pipe section cannot be stopped so easily because there is no way to turn the pipe. Rather than removing the leaking section and replacing it with two shorter sections joined by a union, you may elect to apply epoxy metal to the joint to stop the leak. You must cut off the water, dry the metal completely, and then follow the directions for applying the epoxy.

You can stop threaded fittings from leaking by merely coating the threads with pipe joint compound. If the threaded connection contains a washer, examine it to see if it is still intact. The washer could need replacing.

Leaky joints in plastic pipe usually have to be cut out and new pieces added. Once the solvent which is used to fuse the pipes together has been applied to join two pieces of plastic pipe, there is

35

no way to get them apart. You may, in fact, have to add several connections to make up for the pipe that is cut away.

One sure way to solve a leaking joint problem is to install a new type of fitting called a Click & Seal. Made of a special Dupont nylon in eight widely used versions, Click & Seal fittings require no solvents, no solder, and no tools. They can be used to connect plastic, copper, or other metal pipes. They are also usable with either hot or cold water. When buying these fittings, use the outside diameter of the pipe to get the proper size.

The Click & Seal connection is made by merely pushing the pipe into the fitting and tightening by hand. Looking inside a fitting, you see only four parts: the nut, grab ring, U cup, and body. When the pipe is pushed into the fitting, it goes all the way into the cup. The lock ring has a sharp angled surface that holds the pipe or tubing in position while the nut is tightened. Water flows into the fitting, fills up the U cup, and presses the cup against the tubing. That is the secret of the seal: the higher the pressure, the tighter the seal.

Click & Seal fittings are approved by the National Sanitation Foundation for both hot and cold water use and by the United States Food and Drug Administration for carrying potables.

Pipe Leaks

THE SUREST way to repair a leaking pipe is to remove the section that has the leak and replace it with a new section. But if you are already thinking that all you need to do is unscrew the pipe from its fittings and remove it, think again. If you turn the pipe to remove it from the fitting at one end, it is being tightened into the fitting at the other end.

The solution to this impossible situation is to cut into the pipe in the middle. You must be exceedingly careful, however, in sawing and removing so as not to put undue strain on other parts of the system. For galvanized iron pipe, cut off the water (if you have not already had to do so), and drain the water out of the system. Opening taps below the pipe will drain it, or you can use the drain valve built into the system.

Use a fine-toothed hacksaw blade for cutting. Before you start the sawing, make sure that the pipe is properly braced. Otherwise, your sawing motion could cause movement that might break a seal at a joint. Saw right straight through. Remember, since the two stubs are going to be heavy, have them propped up to prevent them from sagging and pulling on the joints.

Now, by gripping the fitting with one wrench and the pipe with another, you can turn the pipe stub out of its fittings. Remove the other stub the same way. You are ready to install the new sections.

36

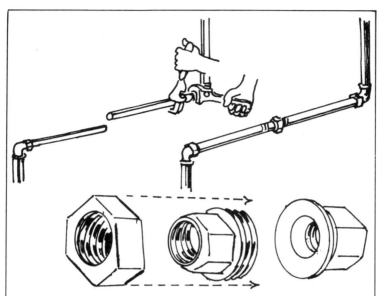

To remove a leaky section of pipe, you must cut the pipe in the middle, and then turn the stubs out of the fittings. Grip the fitting with one wrench (top) and pipe with another. Connect new pipe sections with a union (middle). Exploded view shows how union's threaded sections are held together by nut.

Replace the bad section with two new sections, connected in the middle by a fitting called a union. A union fitting has two female threaded sections that are pulled together by turning a special nut in the middle. This allows you to fasten the pipes together without having to turn the pipes themselves.

Measure the sections carefully to be sure of a proper fit, and make sure that you take the length of the union into account. The two new sections of pipe must be threaded on both ends, and — as with all threaded metal connections — pipe joint compound or teflon tape should be used to assure a watertight bond.

With copper pipe, you can cut out a section with a tube cutter, then solder in a copper-to-copper union as well as a coupling to reconnect the new section. Although you only would need one section as a replacement, you will still do better using a union.

The emergency pipe repair kit can be used as a permanent repair for any kind of pipe. If the leak is a result of corrosion, however, chances are that the whole section of pipe needs replacing.

How To Fix Dripping Faucets

THE MOST common plumbing problem — the dripping faucet — is easy to remedy, and yet it is often left unrepaired. To many people it must seem that a tiny drip is not worth the effort required to fix it, but if someone were to offer you $50 to fix the dripping faucet, would you still think it not worth the effort? Amazing as it sounds, that single drop of water mounts up to so many gallons in a year that, in some cases, the drip can cost you about $50 in wasted water. If you have several such faucet thieves around, you are literally putting a great deal of money down the drain.

Take a look at the drawing showing the inner workings of a typical faucet. When the handle is in the off position, the washer is pressed tightly against the seat, holding the water there. Obviously, if the washer does not do its job, a little water can seep through; and that seepage — the drip — can wind up costing you plenty of money. To stop the drip, probably all you need do is replace the washer.

How To Change A Washer

THE FIRST thing to do when changing a washer is to turn off the water supply to the faucet. Generally, you will find a cutoff under each faucet that resembles the one pictured here. If you cannot find such a "local" cutoff, however, you must go to the main cutoff and stop the flow of water throughout your house. With the

38

water flow stopped, you can proceed to change the washer.

No matter what the faucet looks like outside, if it has two separate handles for hot and cold water, it operates on the same basic principle. Start by taking off the handle. Many faucets have a metal or plastic button on top of the handle to designate "Hot" or "Cold." These buttons usually snap out, but some are threaded. Once you get the button out, you will see the handle screw, which is usually removed quite easily. Some handles, however, are held by a tiny set screw on the back instead of a handle screw going down from the top; loosen the set screw or the handle screw and slide the handle off. If any of the screws (and/or nuts) are exceptionally hard to turn, use a little penetrating oil to free them.

Sliding the handle off reveals the packing nut underneath. Loosen the packing nut — sometimes called the bonnet — with either a large pair of channel lock pliers or an adjustable wrench. If the packing nut on your faucet is made of chrome (most nuts that are visible when you view the assembled faucet are made of chrome),

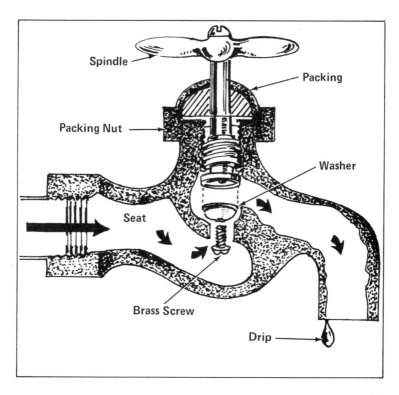

39

take special care not to scar the metal. It is a good idea to place tape around the packing nut to absorb the chewing effect of your pliers or wrench.

With the packing nut off, remove the spindle (sometimes called the stem) by twisting it in the same direction you would turn on the tap. Now you can see the washer at the base of the spindle. To remove the washer, turn the brass screw that holds it to the spindle in a counterclockwise direction. Penetrating oil will make a stubborn brass screw much easier to remove, but even if the screw is impossible to remove, do not despair; you can replace the entire spindle for very little money. If you do get the brass screw out, check to see if it needs replacement along with the washer.

You can, of course, buy replacement washers in an assortment pack that contains about a hundred washers of all shapes and sizes. Usually, however, you find that you can use only three or four out of the pack, and the rest are wasted. It is more economical, therefore, to buy the size washers you need for your faucets. If you cannot see the size on the old washer, take the spindle with you to the hardware store to be sure that you purchase the proper size. Washers that "almost fit" will "almost stop the drip." In addition, pay attention to whether the washer is beveled or flat, and make sure that the replacement is an exact duplicate.

There are some washers that do not work on a hot water tap. Perhaps you have experienced a hot water tap from which water flows at the desired rate until the water gets hot and then slows down to a trickle. The reason that happens is that the washer expands when it gets hot, closing the opening and slowing the hot water flow. Therefore, be sure to specify whether the washer you need is for the hot or for the cold water side. Some washers will work for either.

Screw the new washer to the bottom of the spindle, and screw the spindle back into the faucet (the same direction that you turn the handle to stop the water flow). With the spindle in place, install the packing nut, again being careful not to scar the metal. The only remaining task is to replace the handle by screwing it to the faucet with either the handle screw or the rear set screw. Your faucet is now completely reassembled, and your wasted water should be entirely eliminated.

Other Drips

SOMETIMES you replace a washer and there is still a drip. If that happens, it means that the washer is not properly seating. Improper seating usually results from a former defective washer that al-

40

FAUCET ASSEMBLY

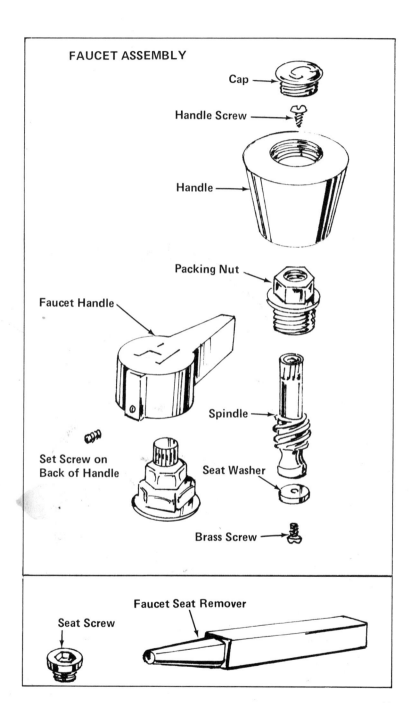

Cap

Handle Screw

Handle

Packing Nut

Faucet Handle

Spindle

Set Screw on
Back of Handle

Seat Washer

Brass Screw

Faucet Seat Remover

Seat Screw

41

lowed the metal spindle to grind against the seat and leave it uneven. Or, the chemicals in water can deposit a residue that prevents the washer from fitting tightly against the seat. You can purchase a reseating tool (quite inexpensive) that can correct the situation, but be sure not to use the tool too long or with too much force. The faucet seat is made of soft metal, and it is easy to grind the seat down too far.

If you were to grind the seat down too far, however, it would still not be the end of the world. Many seats are removable and, therefore, replaceable. Removal calls for a special tool that is inserted into the seat and turned counterclockwise. Once you get the old seat out, be sure you get an exact replacement for it. For seats that are impossible to remove, there are seat sleeves available that slide into place and can often do the job.

That should take care of all the drip problems that concern the faucet's spout. Some faucets, however, leak around the handle when the water is running. The first repair procedure is to make sure that the packing nut is on tight. If the nut is not the problem, then the second thing to do is replace the packing. Packing can be a solid piece, an "O" ring, or it may resemble something like burned spaghetti that is wrapped around the spindle under the packing nut. To replace the packing, remove the handle and slip the packing nut and the packing up off the spindle. It is a good idea, after you install the new packing, to smear a light coat of petroleum jelly over the threads of the spindle, as well as over the threads of the packing nut.

A single-lever faucet that leaks is simple to fix, but there are so many different types that you must rely on the manufacturer for the appropriate faucet repair kit. The kit contains replacement parts along with detailed instructions and diagrams. The only problem you may have is in locating such a kit. If the hardware dealer does not carry the one that matches your faucet, a plumbing supply house is your next best bet.

About the only other faucet failure occurs on kitchen installations where the spout swings from side to side. Kitchen faucets have an "O" ring — sometimes more than one — inside that keeps the water from oozing out around the spout. If this rubber ring wears out, you will notice water at the base of the spout each time the faucet is used. To replace the ring or rings, remove the threaded coupling nut that holds the spout in place. Cover the nut with tape before removal to prevent scratching. Now, you can work the spout up and out of its socket to reveal the ring(s). Replace the ring or rings, reassemble the kitchen faucet, and the problem is solved.

42

Taking Care Of Toilet Tank Troubles

C LOGGING IS, perhaps, the most serious toilet problem, but it is far from the only trouble "John" can cause. The tank can make all sorts of weird noises, or it can run water continuously. These troubles are not only annoying; they also can waste a great deal of your money. Fortunately, most of the toilet tank troubles can be eliminated easily.

Before you can solve the problems that plague your toilet, however, you must know exactly how this most vital of plumbing fixtures operates. These are the steps through which the toilet goes when it is flushed:

1. You trip the handle on the outside of the tank.
2. The handle raises the trip lever inside the tank.
3. The lift wires, connected to the trip lever, are lifted as the trip lever rises.
4. The tank ball, fastened to the bottom lift wire, rises.
5. The water in the tank rushes out past the raised tank ball and into the bowl below.
6. The rush of water raises the bowl's level above that of the water in the drain spout. Since water seeks its own level, the water from the tank pushes the bowl water out into the drain and causes a syphoning action that cleans everything out of the bowl. When all the water is gone from the bowl and air is drawn into the drain spout, the syphoning stops.
7. Meanwhile, the tank ball is no longer supported by the water

43

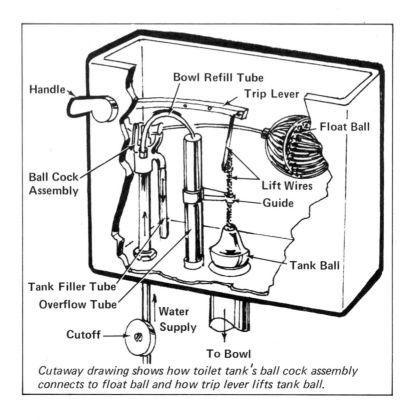

Cutaway drawing shows how toilet tank's ball cock assembly connects to float ball and how trip lever lifts tank ball.

in the tank. Consequently, the ball falls back in place, covering the flush valve opening.

8. In addition, while the water was rushing out of the tank, the float ball (which floats on top of the water) dropped down. The dropping float ball pulled down on the float arm, raising the valve plunger and permitting new water to flow into the tank.

9. As the water level rises in the tank, the float ball rises until the float arm gets high enough to lower the valve plunger and shut off the water. If the water should fail to shut off for some reason, there is an overflow tube that carries the water down into the bowl to prevent the tank from overflowing.

Toilets That Run Continuously

NOW THAT YOU know how the toilet works, you will find it easy

44

to figure out how to fix a continuously running toilet. Lift the lid off the tank. When you look inside, you will see that your tank looks very much like the one we have been describing. Now, you can start to search for the source of your toilet tank troubles.

Lift up on the float arm. If the flow of water stops, the problem is that the float ball does not rise far enough to lower the valve plunger. Check to be sure that the float ball does not rub against the side of the tank; that can be one reason why it does not rise far enough. If it is rubbing, bend the float arm slightly to move the ball away from the back of the tank.

If the ball does not touch the tank, the problem may be in the ball itself. Continue to hold the float arm, and remove the ball by turning it counterclockwise. Shake the ball to see if there is water inside (the weight of the water may be preventing the ball from rising normally). If so, replace the float ball with a new one. If not, replace the old ball and bend the float rod down very gently to lower the level which the float ball must reach to cut off the entry of water.

If the problem is not in the float arm at all — the water did not stop running when you lifted the arm — you should next check the condition of the tank ball. Water seeping out around the opening to the toilet bowl is a good indication that the tank ball itself is starting to wear out.

Shut off the water at the toilet's cutoff valve, and then flush the toilet to empty the tank. Now you can examine the tank ball. Install a new one if required. If you find nothing wrong with the tank ball itself, however, check the lip of the flush valve opening. Many times, residue from chemicals in the water can build up and form a rough edge that prevents the ball from seating properly. Abrasive action is needed to clear away the debris; wet-dry emery paper, steel wool, or even a knife blade will do the job. As preventive maintenance, you can retard the formation of this residue by dropping leftover slivers of soap into the toilet tank.

If there is no residue on the flush valve opening and nothing defective in the tank ball, check to see if the lift wires let the tank ball fall down straight into the hole. The guide may be out of line or the wires may be bent. Make sure that the lift arm is not rubbing against anything and that the lift wire is not installed in the wrong hole of the lift arm, causing the tank ball to fall at an angle.

At this point, if neither the float ball nor tank ball are at fault, the problem is in the ball cock assembly (which looks much more complicated than it really is). Make sure that the cutoff valve is in the off position, and you are ready to go to work.

With most ball cock assemblies, you will find a pair of thumb screws that hold the valve plunger. If the unit in your toilet tank has

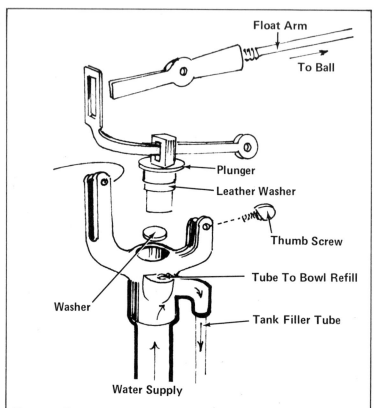

Float Arm

To Ball

Plunger

Leather Washer

Thumb Screw

Tube To Bowl Refill

Washer

Tank Filler Tube

Water Supply

If your toilet runs continuously, there is a good chance that the ball cock assembly is defective. Replace any faulty washers, but if still defective you must replace the whole unit.

a different linkage arm arrangement, however, do not despair. You should have no trouble in figuring out how to remove the valve plunger. Even if you discover that the unit is sealed and there is no way to get inside — or that once inside you find part of the metal damaged — you can buy an entirely new ball cock assembly for a few dollars.

Once you remove the valve plunger, you will see one or two washers and sometimes an "O" ring. One washer may even be a split-leather job. Of course, if any of the washers are faulty, water will continually go past the plunger, causing the toilet to run without ceasing. Examine all the washers and replace any faulty ones.

46

How To Replace A Ball Cock Assembly

SHOULD YOU discover that the ball cock assembly is damaged, you can replace it easily and at little expense. The first thing to do, of course, is to get all the water out of the tank so that you can remove the old unit and install the new one.

Shut off the water coming into the tank at the toilet cutoff valve. Flush the tank, and then remove whatever water remains in the tank with a large sponge. Unscrew the float arm from the ball cock unit, and remove the refill tube from the overflow tube (the refill tube may be clipped on, or it may just be bent in place).

Now, look underneath the tank. Where the water pipe meets the tank, you will see a coupling nut. Loosen both the coupling nut and the lock nut that is right above it. Lift out the ball cock assembly from the tank, being sure to save all the washers from connections both inside and outside the tank. Chances are that all the necessary washers will be included with the new unit you buy, but just to be safe hang onto the old parts until you are ready to install the new ball cock assembly.

When buying the new assembly, you have a choice between plastic or metal units. Plastic costs less and will not corrode, but it is not as sturdy as metal and usually cannot be repaired because plastic assemblies are generally sealed units. Although you can consider purchasing a different type of unit than the one you are replacing, make sure that the new ball cock assembly has a threaded shank the same size as the one you removed.

The new types of ball cock units eliminate the float arm and ball. The most popular model is called the Fluidmaster, which floats a plastic cup up to cut off the water as the tank is filled. You can set the water level in the tank by adjusting the setting of the plastic cup on the rod.

The Fluidmaster type of ball cock assembly offers one big advantage. The unit lets the water run full force until it reaches the proper level; then the water shuts off immediately. By doing so, the Fluidmaster eliminates the long drawn-out groaning that some toilets go through as the conventional float arm gradually closes the valve.

Whatever type of replacement unit you purchase, insert it in the hole in the tank with the inside washer in place. Tighten the lock nut on the outside only enough to make the washer inside fit watertight against the hole. Once you tighten the coupling nut and reinstall the float arm, you're in business. Turn the water back on at the toilet cutoff valve, and check the joints closely to be sure that there are no leaks. Also check to make sure that the float ball does not rub against the back of the tank.

Another new replacement for ball cock assembly is a unit called

47

the Fillmaster Fill Valve, which — like the Fluidmaster — eliminates the float ball and float arm. A very small unit, the Fillmaster rests almost on the bottom of the tank, and its diaphragm-powered valve senses the level of the water from down there. Moreover, since it requires no tools, it is an easy unit to install. You may need a couple of common tools for the removal of the old ball cock assembly, but after that, all you do is follow these steps:

1. Cut off the water.
2. Flush, and then sponge out the remaining water from the tank.
3. Remove the old ball cock assembly.
4. Slip the following parts over the supply pipe under the tank: coupling nut, friction washer, cone washer, and mounting nut. Put these parts — all included with the Fillmaster Fill Valve — on in that order.
5. Put the unit in place in the tank, fitting the threaded shank over the supply pipe. Make sure that the gasket shank fits down into the hole.
6. Now you are ready to put it all together. Do not use any pipe joint compound. Start the mounting nut on the threaded shank section, and hand tighten only.
7. Push the washers into place, and hand tighten the coupling nut.
8. Attach one end of the refill tube to the overflow pipe, and place the other end on the stem of the Fillmaster unit. You are now ready to turn the water back on, and the tank will start filling. The Fillmaster is preset to a level of about eight inches, but you can adjust the level with the knob marked "ADJ."

The plastic Fillmaster Fill Valve unit carries a lifetime guarantee, but the guarantee requires that you mail the faulty unit back to the factory. Unless you save your old ball cock assembly, your toilet is out of commission until the mail delivers the new unit. While we wish that it carried a better guarantee, we do recommend Fillmaster Fill Valve if you are considering modernizing or replacing a defective ball cock assembly.

Inadequate Flushing

IF TOO LITTLE water goes into the bowl to flush it clean, the first thing to check is the water level in the tank. Bend the float arm up a little if the water level fails to reach within 1½ inches from the top of the overflow tube.

If the water level in the tank is correct, the next thing to check is the tank ball. A ball that drops too soon will prevent a sufficient amount of the tank water from running out into the bowl. The ball may be dropping too soon because the guide is too low. Raise the guide, but make sure that it stays straight with the line the lift wires must take to drop the tank ball straight into the hole.

If the tank ball is not the problem either, check the small ports around the underside of the bowl's rim. The ports can get clogged with the residue from chemicals in the water. A small purse mirror can be very handy in helping you see the holes. If the ports are indeed clogged, ream them out with a piece of a wire coat hanger or — if you have one — an offset Phillips screwdriver.

Toilet Tank Tips

USE PENETRATING oil when you encounter a stubborn nut. If you have to strain, your wrench can slip off the nut and crack the tank. Similarly, avoid overtightening the nuts that are fastened to the tank. By applying too much pressure, you can also crack the tank.

When you remove the tank top to work on your toilet, put it on the floor in a place where it will not be in your way. If you were to knock it off from the bowl or from the sink onto the floor — or if you were to step on the tank top while it was on the floor — you could find yourself having to buy a new one.

With all this knowledge, you should have no trouble in keeping "John" working — and doing so in his normal quiet manner.

Thawing Frozen Pipes

WHEN WINTER sets in, the water in unprotected pipes can freeze. Of course, it is a great inconvenience not to have water, but that is only a temporary problem. The expansion caused by freezing can rupture the pipe, and then you really have a major plumbing problem on your hands.

The best time to fight frozen pipes is before the freeze sets in. By taking the proper preventative steps, you may never have to worry about thawing frozen pipes. Here are some freeze-fighting tips:

1. If you are building a new house or adding pipes underground, be sure to bury them below the frost line if possible. Since this depth is different in different parts of the country, check with your local United States Weather Bureau to learn about the frost line in your community.
2. Make sure that new pipes are as well insulated as is practical. Run the pipes along your home's inner walls instead of along the outside walls.
3. Install frost-free faucets outside, and when the cold weather sets in, cut off the outside faucets and open the tap to drain the exposed pipe and faucet.
4. If you have a stretch of pipe that is subject to freezing, invest in heat tape (sometimes called heat cable). You can buy tape that has an automatic thermostat to start the heat when the temperature outside drops to about 35 degrees.

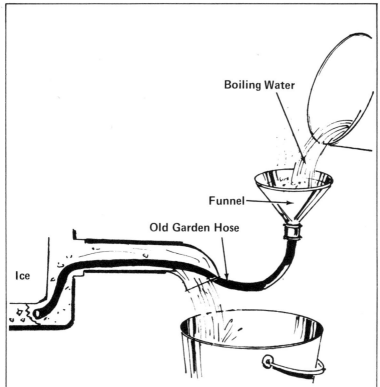

Boiling Water

Funnel

Old Garden Hose

Ice

The best way to thaw a frozen drain pipe is to insert a short length of garden hose until it reaches the ice, and then pour in hot water. Be careful not to scald yourself.

Thawing Frozen Pipes

THE SUGGESTIONS above will be of little value or consolation when you wake up to find a pipe frozen solid. Here are some hints on thawing frozen pipes: (1) Before applying any heat to the pipe, open the tap so that the steam produced by the thawing can escape. (2) Start your heat at the tap and work back toward the source of the freeze. This way, as the ice melts, the water and/or steam will come out the open tap. If you were to start in the middle, the expansion as the ice melts and becomes steam could build up enough pressure to burst the pipe.

One very popular and safe heat source for thawing pipes is sim-

51

ply hot water. The heat can be concentrated by wrapping the pipe with a heavy towel or burlap bag; the towel holds the heat and lets it surround the pipe. Pour very hot water over the towel. Since most of the water runs off, be sure to have a bucket on hand to avoid one heck of a mess.

A less messy way to heat pipes is with a propane torch, but you must be extremely careful to insure that the heat does not ignite a wall behind the pipe. A scrap of asbestos siding or some other fireproof material behind the flame can help, but never leave the flame in one spot. Keep it moving back and forth. Above all, pass over any soldered joints very quickly; otherwise, you could cause an even bigger problem than you already have.

Other heat sources include heat lamps and electric irons. Both are very slow, but they are safe.

Frozen Drain Pipe

IN THE CASE of a frozen drain pipe, the best way to go is to put hot water down the drain. Sometimes, however, you may need to get the water closer to the actual ice blockage. In such cases, remove the trap and insert a short length of garden hose into the pipe. When the hose gets to the solid ice and can no longer be pushed through, raise the outside end and — with the aid of a funnel — feed the hot water in.

This is the best way to get the hot water to the problem area. Of course, until the ice melts and drains down the pipe, the hot water you insert will back up at you. Have a bucket ready under the pipe, and be careful not to scald yourself when the back-flow process begins.

Water Heater Maintenance

THE HOT WATER system is pretty much taken for granted — as long as there is always plenty of hot water for everyone. Water heaters rank high among appliances for length of service; many heaters carry a ten-year warranty, and some last years beyond that. Yet, no matter what type heater you have — gas, electric, or oil — you can get additional years of top performance if you maintain the unit properly. Follow the manufacturer's recommendations; the best maintenance guide is the owner's manual you received when the unit was installed.

The Biggest Enemy: Sediment

SINCE SEDIMENT is one of the biggest enemies of any type of heater, most of the units made in the past twenty-five years are equipped with a drain valve, which is a faucet at the bottom of the tank. Sediment can help start rust and corrosion, clog the pipes, and make the tap water dirty.

By regularly draining a little water from the tank, you can remove the sediment before it does any harm. The best time to drain for sediment is in the morning before anyone uses the hot water. The sediment has had all night to settle in the bottom of the tank. Use a small container, and drain just a cup or so. If the water shows sediment, keep draining until the water runs clear. By testing the water every month or so, you can soon establish a timetable for water heater drainage. Regular use of the drain valve will allow your

53

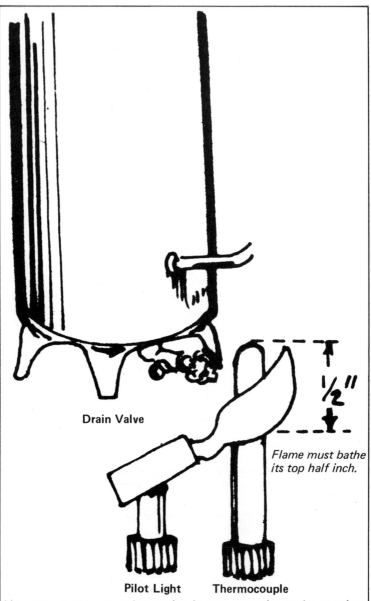

Drain Valve

$\frac{1}{2}''$

Flame must bathe its top half inch.

Pilot Light   Thermocouple

You can prevent rust and corrosion in your water heater by opening the drain valve at the buttom of the tank, and draining water out until it runs clear. If your pilot light does not stay on, you may have to replace the thermocouple.

54

heater to provide longer and more efficient performance.

There is one type of heater that has a magnesium rod in the tank. The idea is that chemicals in the water will attack the rod rather than other parts of the hot water system, but after a while the rod becomes so corroded that it can no longer hold any more; the excess then darkens the hot water. If your hot water heater has this type of rod, the first sign of dirty water tells you that the rod probably needs replacement.

Other Heater Headaches

IF YOU HEAR rumbling in the hot water tank and noise in the hot water lines, the unit is probably developing steam. You can solve the problem and eliminate the noise by merely adjusting the thermostat to a slightly cooler setting.

Most of the other possible problems you may encounter with a hot water heater unit are not really plumbing concerns. When there is suddenly no hot water, you may be able to take care of the problem with a simple check of the heater. If the unit is electric, check to see if a fuse is blown or a circuit breaker switch is tripped. If it is a gas heater, check to see if the pilot has gone out. Relighting instructions are on a metal plate on the side of the unit near the pilot. Read and follow the instructions. Many people fail to depress the pilot relight button for the full time specified. If the instructions tell you to keep the button down for 30 seconds, 5 seconds will not work.

If the pilot fails to light, clean the pilot orifice. Often, minute particles can clog the pilot and prevent its proper functioning. If the problem is not particles, however, you may have to replace the thermocouple, which is a safety device that is next to the pilot. As long as there is heat from the pilot against the thermocouple head, the gas stays on. When the heat goes, the system shuts off. When you replace the thermocouple, get a unit with the same length line as the one you are removing. Save all the little parts that hold the thermocouple in place, and be sure to position the unit so that the flame will bathe about its top half inch. In most cases, the new thermocouple comes on a card that has detailed installation instructions on the back.

About the only other plumbing related ill your water heater can suffer is a leak. Detective work will help you find the leak. If the problem requires draining the tank to make the repair, cut off the heat source and do not turn it back on until the tank is refilled.

Silencing Noisy Plumbing

THERE ARE several different mysterious noises that can come forth from the plumbing in your home. Many systems emit knocking sounds whenever the water is turned on. Generally but incorrectly referred to as "water hammer," this noise probably results from the pipes hitting against something.

To correct this noisy situation, you first must track down the source of the knocking. Turn on the water and start looking for pipe movement. If the moving pipe is between walls, you can still eliminate the noise without tearing out the wall by placing stops at each end where the pipe emerges. If the moving pipes are exposed and accessible, adopt one of the following methods to stop the racket.

Most often, the noisy pipe is held to the wall by a tube strap or a U-clamp. If there is sufficient room within the strap, the pipe can move and create noise. Slit a piece of old garden hose or cut a patch of rubber, insert it in the strap or clamp, and the noise should vanish.

Supply pipes and drain pipes that run right next to each other can knock. Your best solution to this problem is soldering the two pipes together. Often, pipes in a basement or crawl space are suspended from the joists by perforated pipe straps. This is a proper installation, but a long run of pipe may be able to move in the straps and hit something. If you install a block at the end of the long run — in the direction of the water flow — you will eliminate the pipe's movement.

Pipes that strike against a masonry wall can be held away from that wall with a wood block inserted between the pipe and the wall. Attach the pipe to the block by means of a pipe strap, and nail the block to the wall with masonry nails or with a screw installed in a masonry wall anchor.

When securing a pipe with any type of bracket, be sure that you do not anchor the pipe so as to restrict its ability to expand and contract according to changes in temperature. Use a rubber buffer between the pipe and the clip to give the pipe the freedom it needs to function properly. You can make such buffers from garden hose, radiator hose, foam rubber, rubber cut from old inner tubes, or kitchen sponges.

Water Hammer

ANOTHER TYPE of noise occurs when the water is shut off suddenly. The force of the fast-moving water rushing through the pipe is brought to a quick halt, and that creates a sort of shock wave which causes a hammering noise. This plumbing defect is called "water hammer."

Properly installed plumbing possesses air chambers that compress when the shock wave hits, preventing any hammering. If you had formerly experienced no hammering and then it suddenly starts, most likely your air chambers have become waterlogged. The air chambers can fail because water under pressure gradually absorbs the air; when there is an insufficient air cushion remaining,

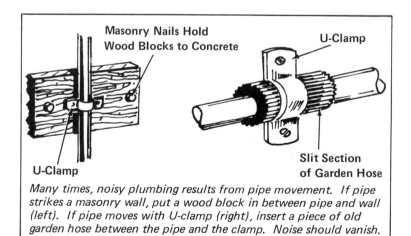

Many times, noisy plumbing results from pipe movement. If pipe strikes a masonry wall, put a wood block in between pipe and wall (left). If pipe moves with U-clamp (right), insert a piece of old garden hose between the pipe and the clamp. Noise should vanish.

57

the noise begins.

You can remedy the problem by cutting off the water beyond the chamber (perhaps at the main cutoff), opening the offending faucet, and letting the faucet drain thoroughly. If all the water can drain from the chamber, air will go back in to fill up the chamber and restore the cushion.

The chamber is merely a capped length of pipe. If chemicals from the water create a residue, you may have to remove the cap and ream out the scale in order to let the pipe drain. The capped pipe should be a tiny bit larger than the supply pipe to which it is attached in order to preclude such clogging. If the air chamber is located below the outlet, you may have to drain the main supply lines to allow the chamber to fill with air again.

There are several devices on the market that serve the purpose of the air chamber. Many of these have a valve that provides an easy way to let the air re-enter. If your plumbing system does not have air chambers, you either have to learn to live with the hammer or to install the needed air chambers. If there is no room to make the installation (without tearing into a wall), go to your plumbing supply dealer and find out about the devices that substitute for air chambers in such problem areas.

Other Noises

FAUCETS THAT scream, whistle, or chatter may have washers of the incorrect size that do not allow enough room for the water to pass, or they can indicate that the pipe has become restricted by the formation of scale. If your house is newly constructed, most likely you have either an inadequate pipe size or an improperly designed faucet.

If the problem is the washer, you should have no trouble replacing the washer and ending the noise. Before you go out and buy a new washer, however, make sure that the present washer is held securely to the spindle. In addition, check the washer seat to make sure that it is not partially closed with residue.

Pipe that has become restricted with scale or mineral deposits is a big problem. Cleaning supply pipes that are clogged is an almost impossible task. In some cases, a water filter can prevent this type of clogging, but usually you must replace the clogged pipe to stop the noise. You can, however, muffle the noise considerably by wrapping the pipes with sound-damping insulation.

Another possible cause for the restriction of water flow is a sagging pipe. Sometimes, the straps that hold a long run of pipe can come loose, and the weight of the pipe and water bend the pipe. If the bend does not put a kink in the pipe, you can straighten the pipe

58

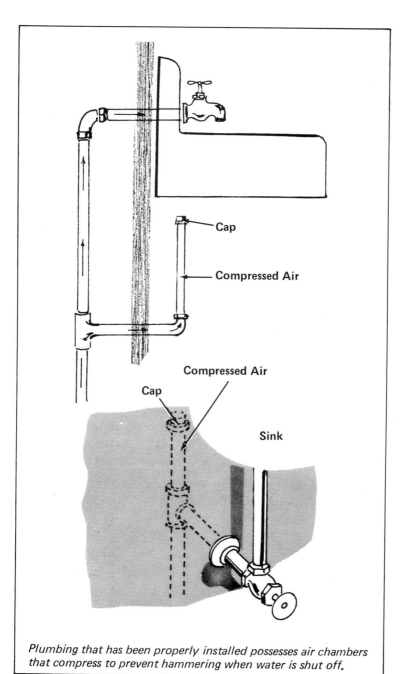

Cap

Compressed Air

Compressed Air

Cap

Sink

Plumbing that has been properly installed possesses air chambers that compress to prevent hammering when water is shut off.

and reestablish the support with new straps. If, however, the pipe has developed a bad kink (especially in copper pipe), you may have to replace that part of the pipe.

A faucet can make a terrible squealing noise as the handle is turned. The squeal is caused by the metal threads of the spindle (stem) binding against the faucet's threads. Remove the spindle and coat both sets of threads with petroleum jelly. The lubrication should both eliminate the noise and make the faucet easier to turn.

If the spindle and faucet threads have become worn, there will be vibration and noise in the faucet. Replace the spindle, and the noise should vanish. If there is still play in the spindle after you install a new one, the threads inside the faucet are worn and that requires a new faucet. Fortunately, the spindle usually goes first, but even if the entire faucet wears out, replacement is an easy and inexpensive do-it-yourself project.

Hot water pipes can create a racket when the water heater is set too high. The steam that results from the water being too hot can knock and rumble in both the heater and sometimes in the pipes. By turning the heat setting down, you'll solve this particular problem.

Drain pipes rarely cause noise, but they can emit a sucking sound as the water first leaves a sink or basin. The sucking indicates a clogged vent or, perhaps, a nonexistent vent. An improper or absent vent should be remedied because the water seal could be syphoned from the trap, allowing sewer gas to back up into your home. A plumber's snake or ribbon run through the vent will eliminate the clogging. If there is no vent on the drain, install an anti-syphon trap (available at the hardware store) to quiet the noise and prevent any sewer gas problem. The traps are inexpensive to buy and easy to install.

If you are adding new plumbing, make sure that your pipes are of adequate size. Many times, the minimum size acceptable to the local building code is not big enough to render quiet plumbing. Install air chambers, and run the pipes in such a way as to prevent their striking each other or nearby walls. If you follow these simple procedures, you should be able to cure most plumbing noises before you ever hear them.

60

How To Sweat Solder Copper Pipes

COPPER PIPES are often jointed by a process known as sweat soldering. It is the most popular method because it is effective and inexpensive. If not done right, however, sweat soldering certainly is not effective — and it can be disastrously expensive.

Sweat soldering is accomplished with a torch instead of with an iron or a gun as in conventional soldering. Formerly, a blow torch was the heat source, but now most people use the easier and safer propane torch for sweat soldering. In addition to the propane torch, you will need paste flux, emery cloth, and solid core solder.

Preparing The Pipe

THE KEYS TO assuring good sweat soldered joints are: (1) clean copper, (2) pipes that are totally dry, and (3) proper heat. If the joint is a newly cut pipe or tube, be sure to remove all the burrs from both inside and out. Check the fittings to be sure the joint will be tight. If you bend or crush the tube in the cutting process, start over with a new cut. The fittings should be very close.

Next, you must clean all the metal surfaces that will be involved in the joint. Emery cloth strips are easy to use for this task because they can be wrapped around the tubing or pipe and used like a shoeshine rag; but fine steel wool or fine sandpaper will do. Make the metal shine, but do not overdo it. The last thing you want is to take away so much metal that you destroy a tight fit.

61

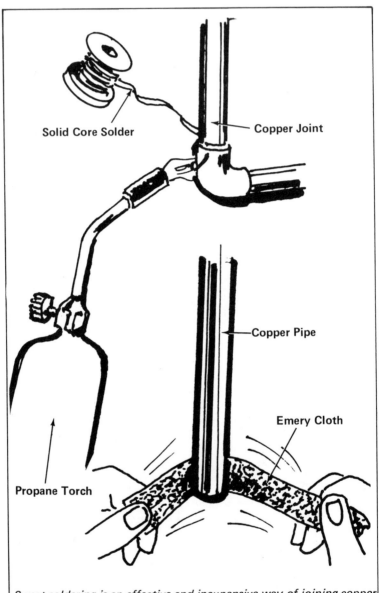

Solid Core Solder

Copper Joint

Copper Pipe

Emery Cloth

Propane Torch

Sweat soldering is an effective and inexpensive way of joining copper pipes, but it must be done properly. Clean all pipe surfaces with emery cloth before soldering. Actual soldering process involves playing torch flame over fitting, and then holding wire solder in contact with hot metal.

62

Be sure to use the emery cloth inside the fitting into which the pipe is supposed to go.

Coat these cleaned surfaces with flux — a paste especially compounded for copper soldering. Spread it on both the pipe and the fitting, and when you insert the pipe, rotate it a bit to distribute the flux paste.

Before you actually start putting the pieces together, make sure that there is no moisture in the pipes. Residual moisture will turn to steam when heated, leaving you with a weak or leaky joint. If the pipe is vertical, you can use a rag to remove any moisture; but if it is part of a horizontal run, use this trick. Wad up a ball of bread, poke it into the pipe, and push it back beyond the area where you will be soldering. The bread will absorb any drops of moisture that might foul up your soldering. When the job is done the water will dissolve the bread, and the crumbs will come out through the nearest open tap.

How To Sweat Solder

NEXT COMES the actual soldering. Light your torch, and get the wire solder ready in your other hand. Play the flame over the fitting — overlapping the edge and onto the pipe — but do not put the flame on the solder. Avoid aiming the flame at an angle that would direct it into the joint.

As you continue to heat the fitting, bring the end of the wire solder into regular contact with the lip of the fitting. Soon, the metal will be hot enough to melt the solder, and then an amazing thing will happen. Not only will the solder melt, it will also be sucked up into the joint under the fitting. This happens due to a law of nature called capillary action, and it will occur even if the pipe runs vertically up into the fitting.

Keep playing the flame on the fitting and melting the solder until you can see that the entire joint is filled — obvious when the solder forms a bead around the lip. If you desire neater looking joints, take a quick swipe around the lip with a piece of coarse toweling to wipe away excess solder. Do this right away before the solder has a chance to harden, but be careful not to touch the hot metal with your hand.

There are some precautions you must observe regarding the propane torch. If the fitting is very close to a wall or ceiling, insert a scrap of asbestos or a piece of aluminum foil behind the pipe or tube to prevent the flame from charring or even starting a fire. When you finish a solder joint, turn off the torch; be especially careful not to melt already soldered joints nearby. Wrap a wet rag around the good joint to dissipate the heat before the flame can do any damage. Exercise the same caution when soldering very close to a valve that could suffer internal damage from the heat.

Some sweat solderers are so proud of their work that they rush to turn on the water and see how great a job they have done. They are making a big mistake. The joint should be allowed to cool naturally; water cooling can cause the joint to weaken or even crack.

If you find a leak in the joint when you turn on the water, do not apply more solder. Instead, cut off the water, melt the solder, and remove the fitting. Dry and reclean the tubing, and then reflux. In other words, start the job over from scratch. There are times when you can get away with not starting over, but you will learn that it is usually easier, quicker, and more effective to do the sweat soldering job as though you had not done it before.

After you sweat solder a few joints, you can do it like a pro. In fact, why not practice a bit now to gain your expertise before you are faced with a genuine soldering situation? For a little pocket change, you can buy a few short lengths of copper pipe and some fittings. Use the solid core solder specified for plumbing work, and use the paste type plumbing flux. Get out your torch and sweat a few pieces together. When you get the hang of it, you may wish to dismantle all your supply pipes just for the fun of restoring the fittings, but try to resist the temptation.

Replacing A Toilet

PERHAPS YOU are tired of the way the old John looks, or maybe you have not been careful enough in working around it and have cracked the bowl. Or maybe you just have a commode that leaks around the bottom where it goes into the floor. Any of these situations calls for the removal and reinstallation or replacement of the unit. This may seem like a major operation, but in most cases, it is really not that bad.

Removal

THE FIRST step in removing the water closet is to shut off the water supply to the unit. Then you have to remove all the water in both the tank and the bowl. Flush, and then use a sponge inside the tank to soak up whatever water is left. Try bailing out the remaining water in the bowl with a small container; you will not be able to get it all, but try.

In older toilets, the tank is connected to the bowl by a large pipe called a "spud." This may be an advantage if you just need to remove the old bowl in order to repair a leak or to get rid of a clog that cannot be removed any other way. The spud may make it possible to remove the bowl without removing the tank. The spud is connected at both ends by a slip nut similar to those that hold a sink trap. The nuts on a toilet, however, are much bigger and require a spud wrench for removal. Once you loosen the slip nuts, slide them onto the spud; in most cases, you will have just enough

65

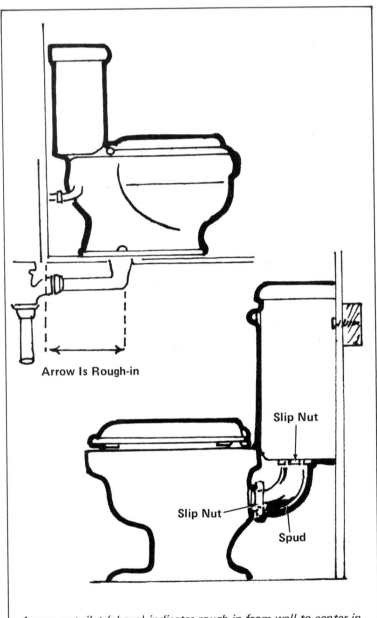

Arrow Is Rough-in

Slip Nut

Slip Nut

Spud

Arrow on toilet (above) indicates rough-in from wall to center in flange. Toilet tank (below) is bolted to brace behind wall and connects to bowl with a "spud."

66

room to remove this pipe which, in turn, gives you room enough to remove the bowl while the tank is still suspended from the wall.

If your toilet is not connected with a spud — or if you want to remove the tank anyway — check to see if the tank is connected to the wall. The old type might well be, but most newer models are not. If the tank unit is connected to the wall, remove the pair of big-headed hanger bolts from inside the tank. Next, look down in the bottom of the tank for a pair of bolts that hold the tank to the bowl unit. Remove these bolts as well, but if you intend to reinstall the tank, be sure not to lose the rubber gaskets that are under all the bolts.

With the tank out of the way, you are ready to attack the bowl. Remove the seat and lid; they just get in the way. The next step is to remove the caps over the hold-down bolts at the base of the bowl. There may be two such caps, or there may be four. Usually ceramic to match the bowl, these caps are often held on by compound and can be pried off, while others are threaded and screw off. If you do not know which kind they are, wrap the caps with masking tape and try first to unscrew them. If the caps seem not to want to come off, they are not threaded; take a putty knife and pry them off. Brush away the dried compound.

Remove the nuts or bolts that are exposed when you get the caps off. You may have to use penetrating oil. With the hold-downs removed, lift the bowl straight up. If you could not bail out all the water, have a bucket handy and pour the remaining water into it. Since you are now looking down into the soil pipe, plug up the hole to prevent any backup of sewer gas. A towel with a string tied on

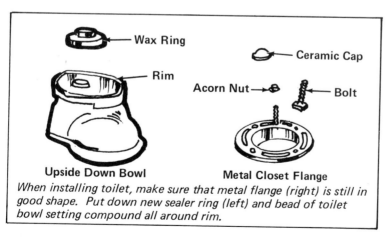

Upside Down Bowl   Metal Closet Flange

When installing toilet, make sure that metal flange (right) is still in good shape. Put down new sealer ring (left) and bead of toilet bowl setting compound all around rim.

67

makes a good plug that cannot get away from you.

If you are just repairing or unclogging, turn the bowl upside down; but be very careful with the tank and bowl unit because one bad blow could crack the porcelain. It is a good idea to use an old piece of carpet as a work surface for these units.

Installation

REINSTALLING an old unit and putting in a new toilet are done the same way. Scrape away all the old putty or other sealing material from the bottom of the bowl and from the metal floor flange. Inspect the metal floor flange to make sure that it is still in good shape, and check the threaded bolts that come up from the flange to be sure that the threads are not stripped. If anything is amiss, replace the bolts or the floor flange; all of these parts are inexpensive to replace, and there is no point in trying to get by with parts whose quality is in doubt.

The next step is to put down a new sealer ring. The best and easiest type is the wax toilet bowl gasket — which comes with a plastic sleeve in the wax — available at any hardware store. There are also rubber rings, but the wax is easiest; both are better by far than the old method of forming a ring from plumber's putty. In most cases, you do better to put the wax ring in place in the bottom of the bowl while the unit is upside down. The plastic sleeve faces up since it goes into the soil pipe.

Coat the rim of the bowl base with toilet bowl setting compound, applying a uniform layer about 1/8 of an inch thick. Toilet bowl setting compound is a sort of caulking that can be purchased at hardware or plumbing supply houses. Turn the bowl right-side-up and place it down over the flange, guiding the bolts in place through the opening in the base of the bowl unit. Press down firmly, and give the bowl a slight twist to be sure that the wax ring seats against the flange.

Check to be sure that the bowl is level. If it is off even a slight bit, apply weight on the high part to level it. In some cases, you may need to insert wedges to shim up the bowl; but make sure that you do not lift the bowl enough to affect the seal of the wax ring. You can hide the wedges with additional toilet bowl setting compound.

Once you get the bowl square with the wall behind, you are ready to install the nuts to hold the bowl to the floor. Do not overtighten the hold-down bolts or you can crack the unit. Hand tightening is all that is needed. Coat the bolts with toilet bowl setting compound, and reinstall the caps to hide the bolts.

Now you are ready to reattach the tank to the bowl. If the tank is joined directly to the bowl, there is a gasket or spud washer be-

68

tween the bowl and tank. Inspect it to be sure that the gasket or washer is still in good shape. Replace the bolts and their washers so that the tank is again attached to the bowl. If the tank is mounted on the wall, rebolt it. If tank and bowl are separated by the curved spud, reinstall the slip nuts after applying pipe joint compound to the threads. Check all the washers and gaskets to be sure that they are still sound. Turn the water back on, and if you did everything right, your job is done.

Toilet Tips

WHEN YOU have to dismantle most of the unit anyway, it might be good to consider any other toilet alterations needed. For example, if your toilet water supply does not have a cutoff, why not add one now? Most hardware stores carry a kit that has all the materials you need to replace your old supply pipe with one that has a cutoff.

If the ball cock assembly is giving you fits, consider putting in a new one; you do part of the job anyway when you disconnect the tank for removal.

If you must replace the toilet, you can modernize; but your new unit must fit into the space from the outlet to the wall. This is called the "rough-in" and is measured from the wall in back of the toilet to the center of the floor flange. It is possible to leave space behind the unit, but it is impossible to get a larger toilet into the smaller space occupied by your former unit.

As you can see from these procedures, removing and reinstalling or replacing a toilet is not an extremely difficult job. In many communities, however, it is one that the official plumbing code prohibits anyone but a licensed plumber from doing. Check first; if the job does not violate the code and if you feel confident in your plumbing skill and knowledge, go ahead and tackle old John.

Changing The Toilet Seat

THERE ARE so many styles of replacement toilet seats on the market that you should find it easy to match any bathroom color scheme or motif. Since most toilets are standard size, you will have no difficulty in getting a new seat and lid that fit. If your toilet is extra wide or very old, however, you may not be able to use a standard size replacement. You would probably have to place a special order with a firm that deals in plumbing fixtures.

How To Replace The Seat

THE PROBLEM for most people is not in getting the new seat, but in removing the old one. Removal sounds simple. Remove the two nuts and lift the old unit up and out. What could go wrong? Wait until you try to loosen those two nuts. Usually, they are rusted or corroded, and sometimes they are recessed and practically inaccessible. Penetrating oil should help loosen the nuts. Give the oil plenty of time to work, and do not use too much muscle on the stubborn nuts. If your wrench were to slip, you could crack the tank or bowl or whatever else the wrench were to strike.

The inaccessible nuts may require a deep throated socket wrench, but if all else fails, a hacksaw inserted under the hinge can saw through the bolts. Start sawing, however, only after you are convinced that nothing is going to break the nuts loose. Again, be extremely cautious so as not to hit anything with the hacksaw.

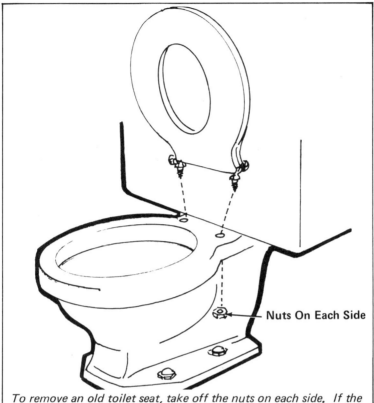

Nuts On Each Side

To remove an old toilet seat, take off the nuts on each side. If the nuts are stubborn, use penetrating oil; if you still cannot remove them, saw them off very carefully with a hacksaw.

Once the old seat is off, the new one goes on simply by replacing the bolts and tightening the nuts. Be careful not to overtighten the nuts. If the lid and seat are still in good condition, but the little rubber bumpers are shot, your hardware dealer can sell you replacements. Some of these bumpers are screw-ins, while others are nailed in. Try to install the new ones in new holes that are close enough to the old holes so that the new bumpers cover the old holes.

If you live in an apartment and put on a new mod seat and lid unit, be sure to keep the old one. When you are ready to leave, put the old toilet seat back on and take your fancy new one along with you to your next abode.

Adding A Cutoff

THE PLUMBER who installs any fixture without providing a cutoff at the fixture does the homeowner a disservice. After a few plumbing crises, you may want to invest some time and a little money in adding cutoffs or — as they are more properly called — supply stop valves.

Whether it be at a sink, basin, or appliance, the cutoff principle is the same. The section of pipe running from the floor or wall to the fixture must be removed, leaving a section sticking out that is called a stub-out. The kind of stub-out you have dictates the fittings you need. A threaded pipe naturally takes a threaded cutoff, while a copper pipe uses an adapter that you sweat solder, leaving a threaded end to which you attach the cutoff. If the stub-out comes from the wall, you need an angled stop to turn the flow at a right angle; a floor stub-out utilizes a straight stop.

Once you decide which stop you need, you need to get the water supply up to the fixture. Flexible chrome-plated copper tubes that come in several lengths make the job easy. The tubes mean that you need not cut or piece together pipe to connect the stop to the fixture.

The copper tubes are called "speedees." They come with three different types of ends. The flat flange end is for toilet tank connections; bayonet ends are for lavatories; while the threaded-tipped speedee is for kitchen sinks. The speedee and the stop are usually joined by a flared connection, a compression fitting, or compression ring fitting.

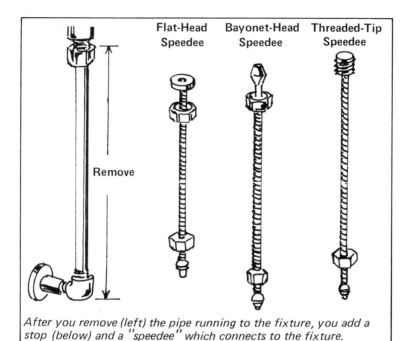

Flat-Head Speedee | Bayonet-Head Speedee | Threaded-Tip Speedee

Remove

After you remove (left) the pipe running to the fixture, you add a stop (below) and a "speedee" which connects to the fixture.

There are complete kits you can purchase that contain the stop and speedee already joined; the kits also include all the connectors, rings, and other items you need to make the connection. They also have instructions to help you do the job right. While there are more economical ways to install a cutoff, there are no easier ways; and unless you have a number of cutoffs to install, the kit is the best way to add a cutoff to your plumbing system.

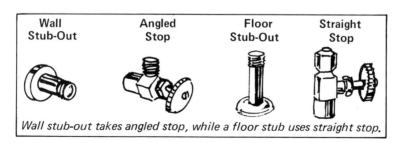

Wall Stub-Out | Angled Stop | Floor Stub-Out | Straight Stop

Wall stub-out takes angled stop, while a floor stub uses straight stop.

73

Simple Plumbing Repairs

Adding
A Faucet

PROBABLY, THERE have been several occasions when you wished that you had a water outlet right in the middle of a pipe that runs up a basement wall or even inside a wall. Perhaps you would like to add a drinking fountain, or possibly a washing machine, or even a faucet to your home bar. Most likely you think that you have to cut into the pipe and install fittings that will take a faucet, but you are in for a pleasant surprise! Adding a faucet may be the easiest plumbing task of them all.

The secret is a gadget called the saddle tee — composed of a plate that is curved to fit the back of the pipe and is bolted to a front plate which is threaded to accept a faucet. The threads come in several sizes to accommodate popular connections, and the plates are made for several sizes of pipe. The front connector is backed by a washer or gasket and has a hole through which the water from the pipe will flow.

How To Install A Saddle Tee

PLACE THE saddle tee on the pipe at the point where you would like to have the faucet. Tighten the bolts to hold the two plates together securely, and turn off the water supply to that pipe. Drill a hole straight through the hole in the front connector plate and on through the front side of the pipe. A power drill is much faster than a hand drill for making this hole, but it can sometimes go through both the front and the back of the pipe before you can stop it.

74

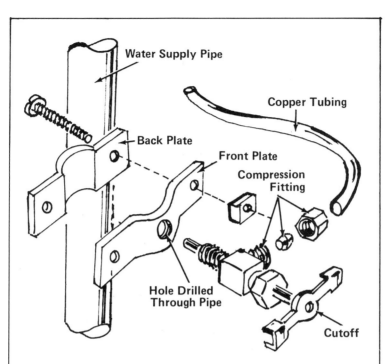

Water Supply Pipe

Copper Tubing

Back Plate

Front Plate

Compression Fitting

Hole Drilled Through Pipe

Cutoff

You can save yourself some money by hooking up the water supply to the ice making device in your new refrigerator.

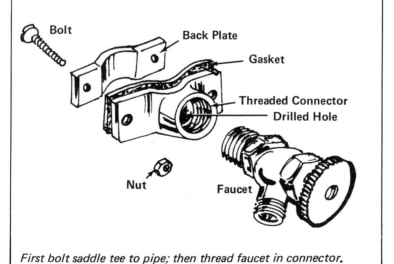

Bolt

Back Plate

Gasket

Threaded Connector

Drilled Hole

Nut

Faucet

First bolt saddle tee to pipe; then thread faucet in connector.

75

Therefore, use a hand drill unless you enjoy patching holes in pipe. Use a bit that will make a hole in the pipe as big as the hole in the front connector plate.

After you drill the hole through the pipe, remove all the metal filings from the threaded opening. Never blow the chips out; they might end up in your eye. A squeeze bottle is the best way of providing the air to blow out the metal.

Now you are ready to install the faucet. Apply pipe joint compound to the threads, and turn the faucet into the threaded connector. If you have done everything correctly, you can turn on the water supply again and enjoy a faucet that works great despite the fact that it took practically no time to install.

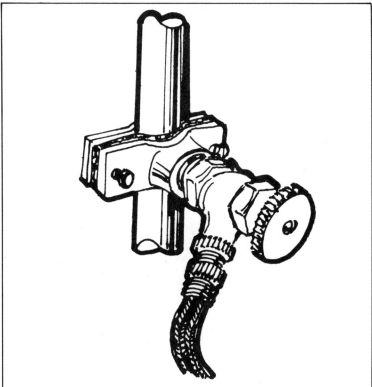

Your completed saddle tee installation should look just like this one; attached hose can lead to any appliance requiring a water supply. Note that correct installation includes cutoff.

Supplying Water To Your Ice Maker

ONE OF THE best uses for the saddle tee is to bring the water supply to the ice making device in your new refrigerator. The principle is the same, but you can buy a kit that contains the saddle tee and the connector to which the copper tubing is fitted. The kit and the tubing (which carries the water) cost only a few dollars, and yet this installation can run from $15 on up when you have it done professionally.

Make sure that you include a water cutoff in your installation. You may never have to use it, but a cutoff is a big help if you ever need to do any work on your ice maker connection. Once you install the tubing, bend it so that it cannot vibrate against anything; otherwise, you will hear some strange noises coming from your refrigerator.

Saddle tees, which are made for use on copper or iron pipes and for hot or cold water, can also be used for connecting a branch pipe or for any other threaded connection or fixture. For a dishwasher or clothes washer installation, you would probably need to tap into both hot and cold water pipes. Then, use a threaded faucet to which a hose could be screwed to carry the water into the appliance.

Most amateur plumbers are reluctant at first to drill into a pipe, but once you drill the first hole you will realize how simple the saddle tee makes what you thought would be a difficult installation.

Simple Plumbing Repairs

Eliminating Condensation On Pipes And Tanks

THE POPULAR name for condensation is "sweating." Sometimes, so much water drips from tanks or pipes that it can cause as much damage as if there were a leak involved. The sweating occurs when the water inside the tank or pipe is much colder than the surrounding air, a situation that is true just about year round in many homes. In summer, the air is naturally hot and in the winter your home heating system does the job. Since the water in the cold water pipes usually comes from below ground, it is always fairly cool.

Sweating Pipe

IN THE CASE of the sweating pipe, there are two ways to control the moisture problem. One way is to place pans strategically on the floor, but the better way is to insulate the pipes. There are several types of drip tape in rolls of self-sticking material that can adhere easily to the pipes. Wind the tape around the pipe to completely cover it, including the fittings.

There are also no-drip compounds that you can brush on the pipe to form a coating of insulation. Although an easy task to do, often you will have to brush on a second coat.

Another sweat fighter is asbestos tape. Use special asbestos cement for best results. The tape can be soaked in the cement until it becomes like paper mache for molding around odd-shaped fittings.

78

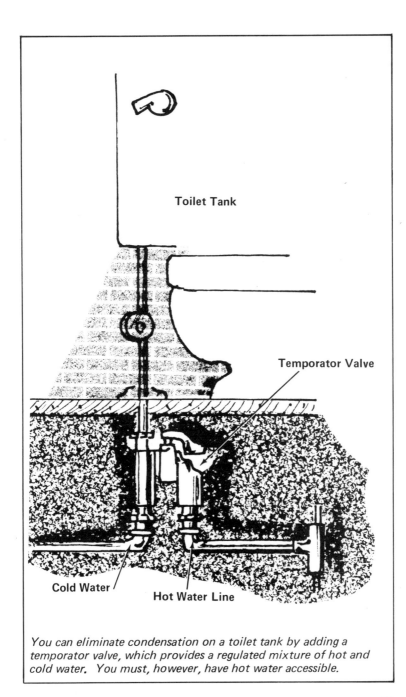

Toilet Tank

Temporator Valve

Cold Water

Hot Water Line

You can eliminate condensation on a toilet tank by adding a temporator valve, which provides a regulated mixture of hot and cold water. You must, however, have hot water accessible.

Ready-made asbestos pipe jackets are available, and they are excellent for straight runs of pipe.

Sweating Tanks

TOILET TANKS also sweat and drip off onto the floor. There are jackets that can be fitted over the tank to absorb the moisture, and there are also drip pans that fit under the tank to catch the droplets. A better solution is to install a new gadget called a temporator valve. By providing a regulated mixture of hot and cold water, the device eliminates toilet tank sweating. It requires, however, that you bring a hot water line to the valve. If there is no hot water line close by, it may be inconvenient to run one to the toilet. Moreover, the temporator valve does not prevent the water from cooling between flushings, and the condensation can still occur.

If your toilet tank sweats, the unit could develop a leak that you might not recognize for some time. You might not notice the seeping water, but there is an easy way to check for leaks. Pour enough bluing into the tank to give the water a noticeable blue color; you can also use one of the toilet bowl cleaners that fits inside the tank and turns the water blue. If there is a leak, the moisture on the floor will show traces of blue.

There is another method that has actually been used by some people, but which others may consider a bit weird. This method involves buying one of the small heater units designed for a fish tank. Rig the heater to fit into the tank, and you should never again be troubled by a sweating toilet tank.

It is worth your time, effort, and expense to take care of condensation problems. The moisture that drips from sweating pipes and tanks can damage floors, encourage mildew, and do a host of other bad things to your home.

80

Working With Pipes

THE TYPE of pipe in your house was probably not your own choice, and your choice of replacement or additional pipe is limited to what your local plumbing code says you can use. Nevertheless, we want to acquaint you with all the more popular types of pipe and how each type is used. The fact that we recommend a particular type of pipe, and you then find that the local code forbids it, does not mean that someone is in error. Sometimes, local soil conditions or chemicals in the water can make a crucial difference in the material used in your plumbing. Our aim here is not to try to convince you that a particular pipe is best, but rather to survey the field and tell you how to work with each type.

Copper Pipe

RIGID COPPER pipe is probably the most popular pipe currently in use. It is on the approved list in almost every local plumbing code. Copper is lightweight and, therefore, quite easy to handle. It is easy to work with (once you master the technique of sweat soldering), and copper will probably outlast you and your house under normal conditions. It resists corrosion and scaling, and due to its smooth inside surface, it offers little resistance to water. This means that a smaller size copper pipe can handle the same job as larger pipes in some other metals.

Not all copper pipe is the same; it comes in three thicknesses for plumbing purposes. Type K is the heavy wall and is used mainly underground. Type L is medium weight and is used for interior plumbing. Type M, the lightest weight, is also used for interior plumbing, but there are some local codes that will not accept it. Nonetheless, Type M is adequate for most inside home plumbing. There is an additional type of copper pipe known as DWV (drain, waste, vent) that is permitted in some areas for those three uses only. DWV has an even thinner wall than Type M, but since drains are under no pressure, wall thickness is not a crucial consideration.

Flexible Copper Tubing

MOST OF the same qualities of rigid copper pipe are found in the flexible tubing, which offers a big advantage in that it can be bent around corners and snaked through walls and over ceilings with great ease. The biggest advantage, however, is in the fact that the flexible tubing comes in rolls of up to 60 feet, and often requires no joints except the connections on each end. The fewer joints, of course, the fewer chances for a leak.

You can form gradual bends by hand, using a knee to help create the curve. For sharp turns, use a spring-like affair called a tube bender. What you have to avoid doing in the tubing is putting a kink in it. The tube need not stay perfectly round, but a kink will result in restricted water flow. Keep in mind that the larger the size of the tube, the easier it is to get a kink. Flexible tubing comes in Type K and Type L only.

Copper pipes or tubes can be joined in several ways. Sweat soldering is the most widely used and the least expensive method. The other two accepted ways, flared connections and compression fittings, are used mainly on flexible tubing.

Flared Connections

FLARED CONNECTIONS require a flaring tool and special flare type fittings. In addition, the tubing must be cut completely square. The fitting comes in two parts: the flange nut and the fitting. The first step is to put the flange nut on over the tube; be sure that the open end of the nut faces out.

Next, you must flare the end of the tube. Insert the tubing into the proper sized hole in the flaring tool, and turn the tool down to flare the end. One type of flaring tool has a beveled point that is tapped into the tube with a hammer until the flare is formed. This type of flaring tool necessitates a little practice because if you get a wobbly flare, you must cut off the end and start over. When the flare is made, inspect it to be sure that it is even, has no burrs, and that the

82

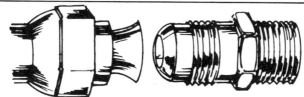

Flared fittings consist of two parts: the flange nut and the fitting. Put flange nut over tube with open end facing out.

surface is completely clean.

Now you can put the beveled fitting into the tube, pull the flange nut up, and start turning it down tight. Start the nut by hand to be sure you get the threads started properly. When the nut is hand tight, use a pair of open end wrenches to finish the connection, turning the flange nut with one and holding the fitting with the other.

The advantages to a flared fitting are: (1) It can be taken apart easily with a pair of open end wrenches; and (2) it can be used where soldering could not be easily done because of a fire hazard or because of uncontrollably wet conditions. The disadvantage is that flared fittings are much more expensive than the ones you sweat solder.

Compression Fittings

A COMPRESSION fitting consists of the same two parts as a flared fitting, but it also has a compression ring. The cut must be completely square. Place the flange nut on the tubing, slip the ring over the tube, and insert the tube into the fitting as far as it will go. Start tightening the nut by hand and continue until it is hand tightened. Then use two open end wrenches, one to turn the nut and the other to hold the fitting. This action seals the ring against the fitting and, at the same time, squeezes it against the tube.

The compression fitting offers the same advantages as the flared fitting, but requires no flaring tools — in fact, no tools at all except the wrenches. Like the flared fitting, however, the compression fitting is more expensive than sweat soldered fittings.

Cutting Copper

AVOID SAWING copper pipe or tubing. Whenever possible use a tube cutter. When you work on the larger sized copper for drains, of course, you must use a hacksaw; in such instances, use the finest

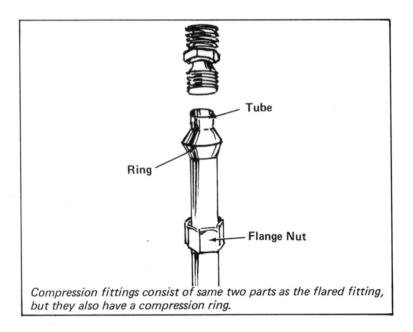

Tube

Ring

Flange Nut

Compression fittings consist of same two parts as the flared fitting, but they also have a compression ring.

toothed hacksaw blades and cut as straight as possible. If the cut is not as straight as it could be, dress the edge with a file. When you must put the pipe in a vise to hold it, clamp the vise far enough away from the cut so that if the vise dents the pipe, you still come out with a round end. Remove the burrs, both inside and out.

Galvanized Pipe

IT USED to be that galvanized pipe was all that was used for the water supply lines in homes. Although copper has to a great extent replaced it, galvanized pipe does offer some advantages. One big advantage is price. Another is the fact that galvanzied steel pipe is much tougher than copper. If pipes run through a garage or basement and are exposed to possible blows from cars, tools, etc., galvanized has it all over copper.

On the other hand, galvanized pipe is much more expensive to repair. It takes so much longer to cut, thread, and join galvanized pipe than it does for copper that labor costs will eat you up if you ever have to call a plumber. Another disadvantage is that galvanized pipe is subject to corrosion from alkaline water or from acids in the water. Lime and scale deposits build up in the pipe and

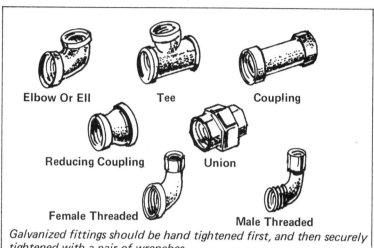

Elbow Or Ell   Tee   Coupling

Reducing Coupling   Union

Female Threaded   Male Threaded

Galvanized fittings should be hand tightened first, and then securely tightened with a pair of wrenches.

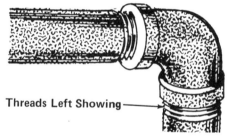

Threads Left Showing

When connecting galvanized pipe to fittings, turn until only about three threads still show outside the fitting.

restrict the flow of water. Moreover, even at its best, the flow in galvanized pipe is not as good as in copper because the inside surface is not as slick, and the fittings are such that they reduce the flow.

Galvanized pipe is joined by threaded joints. Cutting is usually done with a hacksaw, and the pipe must be held in a vise. A pipe cutter makes the job much easier, but it is not the kind of tool that you or your neighbors normally have on hand. If you do, be sure to use cutting oil during the process. After each cut, the new end must be deburred and then threaded.

Threading is done with a pipe die. When you are ready to join the

85

pipe to its fitting, smear the threads with pipe joint compound to help seal the joint. Teflon tape placed around the threads of the pipe and down into the grooves makes the joint watertight. Fittings should be hand tightened, and then securely tightened with a pair of pipe wrenches. Turn until there are only about three threads still showing outside the fitting.

In addition to the standard fittings for galvanized pipe, there are short lengths of pipe available that are threaded on both ends. They are called nipples and come in lengths from one to twelve inches.

Plastic Pipe

ALTHOUGH MANY building codes do not yet accept plastic pipe, plastic provides many advantages. In fact, it is difficult to say which quality is its most advantageous. Plastic pipe is not subject to the corrosion, scaling, or rust to which metal succumbs. Plastic is virtually self cleaning; it will not rot and usually does not sweat; it can withstand freezing much better than metal, and its light weight makes it easier to handle. Plastic pipe is a joy to cut, and joining two pipes is almost as simple as gluing photos in an album. To cap all these advantages, plastic is very inexpensive; it costs less than even galvanized pipe. If you are allowed to use plastic pipe, we urge you do so.

The disadvantage is in plastic pipe's lack of code approval for many plumbing installations. Not all types of plastic are usable for a hot water system, but you should have no trouble finding the type that is. The three most popular types are PVC (polyvinyl chloride), ABS (acrylo-nitrile butadiene-styrene), and CPVC (chlorinated polyvinyl chloride). These are all rigid types of pipe; there is also a flexible type called polyethylene. Only the CPVC is capable of taking hot water, but all three will handle cold. If your code allows CPVC for hot water, it will also specify a change in the pressure control valve on your hot water heater.

Cutting is done with a fine-toothed saw; a hacksaw is as good as any and better than most. To get a square cut — which is very important — place the pipe in an inexpensive wooden miter box, using the right-angle slots. Sawing plastic requires very little effort, and light sanding removes burrs both inside and out.

Joining plastic pipe is accomplished via a process called solvent welding. All it involves is brushing a special solvent cement on the end of the pipe and inside the fitting, and then putting the pipe and fitting together. A twist spreads the solvent, and then you must position the fitting in place quickly because the solvent goes right to work. It actually fuses the two parts together. In the case of CPVC, there is a two-part solvent weld system, with the first part

86

being a sort of flux. With any plastic weld, it is best to hold the fitting in place for about fifteen seconds to prevent any slippage. After that, the weld is set.

Since plastic may be allowed under your local plumbing code for some installations and not for others, you should know how to connect it with other types of pipe. For example, most codes allow plastic pipe for underground sprinkler systems. Somewhere, the plastic must be tied into your existing plumbing — copper or galvanized. You can make the connection with an adapter. Flexible polyethelene pipe is joined to special fittings by a worm gear hose clamp. There are adapters that also allow for connecting polyethelene pipe into existing plumbing systems.

Cast Iron

THE LEADER in soil and easte pipes is the old favorite cast iron. Very durable and practically corrosion free, cast iron can be tied into other types of drain pipes. In most communities, copper drains of the DWV type are used for waste branches, and cast iron is used for soil and waste stacks and for the main drains. It can go underground with no problems. Cast-iron pipe comes in two weights, service and extra heavy. Unless the local plumbing code forbids it, opt for the lighter service weight.

Cast-iron pipe is joined in three ways. The old style bell and spigot type joint is still used widely. One end of the pipe has a bell shaped hub into which the slightly ridged end of the connecting pipe fits. There is space to spare between the two sections of pipe. Into this space you pack a sort of oily rope called oakum. Wrap the

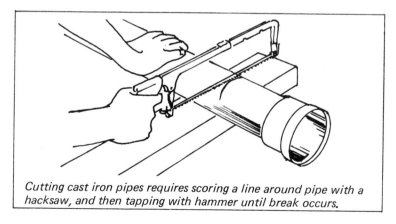

Cutting cast iron pipes requires scoring a line around pipe with a hacksaw, and then tapping with hammer until break occurs.

87

oakum around the pipe, and then poke it down into the space. When you have oakum filling the void up to about an inch (different codes may specify an exact depth), you pour molten lead over the oakum. As soon as the lead hardens, work it down tight against the oakum and the sides of the pipe.

There is a special gadget needed for pouring lead into a horizontal joint; the gadget is called a joint runner. Horizontal joints are treated, in all other ways, the same as the vertical joints. Use the same procedure whether you connect two sections of pipe or a pipe to a fitting.

Gasket-type iron pipe connections also use a belled hub, but the other pipe end is hubless. The connection is held together with a neoprene gasket that is inserted into the bell. Then (with the aid of a lubricant), you force the plain end of the other pipe into the hub, and a watertight joint is the result.

The newest and easiest cast-iron joining system is called no-hub. The ends of all pipes and fittings are plain, and they are joined by a neoprene sleeve that is held in place by a shield tightened by clamps similar to worm gear hose clamps. No-hub connections are easy to put together, and they have the advantage of being easy to take apart. The only disadvantage is that some local codes forbid no-hub connections; other codes do not allow them below ground. Where a no-hub connection is allowed, use it. It is compatible with other cast-iron pipe after the hub or spigot end has been cut off.

Cutting cast iron requires some special procedures. Mark the line to be cut with chalk. Probably, the best way to cut is to score the pipe all the way around with a hacksaw. Make the cut square, and saw to a depth of about 1/16 of an inch. Then, if you are using the

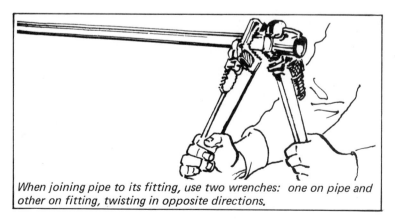

When joining pipe to its fitting, use two wrenches: one on pipe and other on fitting, twisting in opposite directions.

88

lighter service weight pipe, place the pipe over a scrap block of wood, and let the scored line overhang slightly. Using a hefty hammer, start tapping the part that is to come off. The pipe should eventually come off with a clean break. If you are using the heavier cast-iron pipe, you would do better to cut on through the line with a cold chisel. Since cutting cast-iron pipe is hard work, plan ahead and arrange for as few cuts as possible.

Other Types of Pipe

THERE ARE other types of pipe which find more limited use in homes. Lead pipe is rarely used anymore except as a closet bend — the pipe that joins the toilet to the soil pipe. Steel drain pipes are used when weight is a factor because they are much lighter weight than cast iron. Steel drain pipes can never be used underground, however, because the weight of the dirt could collapse them.

Fiber pipe is used for some underground drainage systems, and the perforated type is used in the drain fields of a septic tank system for releasing liquids into the soil. Vitrified clay or tile drains are also used underground. Because of their smooth interior, they allow the waste to flow readily. A faulty joint, however, in a vitrified clay or tile type drain is an invitation for roots to grow in and cause trouble.

Measuring Pipe

TO ORDER pipe for replacement or for a new installation, you must measure properly, which is easy when you know the ground rules. You must learn to take into account two factors over and above the measurement of the pipe that you can see: "fitting gain," or the amount of length added by the fitting; and "make-up," the amount of the pipe on each end that goes into the fitting. Since the pipes in most fittings do not butt against each other, the fitting gain must be added to the overall run, and the make-up to the individual pieces of pipe. Since threaded fittings are so standardized, there is a table showing the screw-in distance, making it a simple matter to measure each fitting.

Copper pipe goes into the fitting, and in most copper fittings you can see from the outside just how far the pipe goes in. Bell and spigot cast-iron pipe requires that you measure the distance from the bell lip down to the place where the spigot will rest. Since the no-hub fittings butt against each other, there is no gain or make-up to consider. With flexible copper tubing, precise measuring is not critical because with enough length, you can make the tubing fit with a little gentle bending.

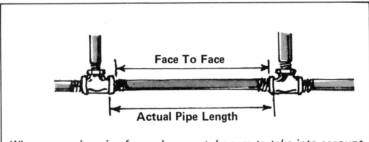

Face To Face

Actual Pipe Length

When measuring pipe for replacement, be sure to take into account the "fitting gain" and the "make-up."

Pipe Hints

HERE ARE some general hints that may make your work a pipe dream instead of a nightmare. Make sure that all drain lines are pitched so that the downward flow will carry out the waste. A quarter inch per foot is the norm. In addition, be sure that all runs of pipe are properly supported by either hangers, straps, notches in the studs or joists, or by whatever method is best for the given situation. If you have notched joists, compensate for the strength you may have removed from the joist; nail a brace strip under the pipe. Notches in studs should be reinforced with metal mending plates. Also, if possible, run the pipe across the upper half of studs; notching higher up weakens them less. When putting in new pipes, a hole drilled in a joist or stud weakens the member less than a notch does.

If you must tear into floors or walls to correct pipe problems, consider running a new line over some other course. Even pipe along the outside of an interior wall can be boxed over easier than ripping into some walls. Frequently, pipes can be hidden by running them through a closet. Keep joints to a minimum; each joint is a possible leak. Most importantly, always check the local code before you change any pipe.

Simple Plumbing Repairs

Fixing Or Installing A Garbage Disposer

IF YOU HAVE a garbage disposer in your kitchen sink, you probably feed it all sorts of leftovers. Usually it eats everything you serve. It is able to digest everything from corn cobs to coffee grounds. Eventually, however, you try some new things and the disposer gets indigestion.

Most people think the blades in a disposer are sharp and cut up the garbage, but that is not true. The blades are attached to a flat wheel that is turned by the motor. The blades are called impellers, and they do not cut. Their function is to batter the garbage and sling it against the shredder and cutter surfaces. All this action renders the waste matter into small particles that can then be washed down the drain.

The most common failing of a disposer occurs when you put something down that the unit cannot digest. If particles of hard matter get lodged between moving parts, the unit stops. With most home units, all you need to get the disposer eating again is to insert the end of your broom handle — with the unit turned off — in the disposer. Angle it against one of the impeller blades and pry; use the broom handle as a lever. When you feel it give, withdraw the broom and try the unit again. You may have to repeat this procedure several times to get the particles out of the way.

If you have a disposer that has a reset button, it probably tripped when the overload occurred; push the reset button once you clear the blockage. Some models have a sort of crank that fits into a socket in the bottom of the unit. The crank lets you back up the

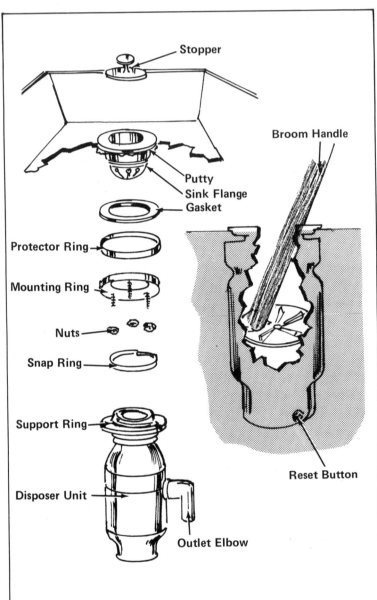

Stopper

Broom Handle

Putty
Sink Flange
Gasket

Protector Ring

Mounting Ring

Nuts

Snap Ring

Support Ring

Reset Button

Disposer Unit

Outlet Elbow

Installation of a garbage disposer certainly constitutes a feasible do-it-yourself project. If your unit ever stalls, try sticking a broom handle in with the unit off. Use the handle as a lever and pry against the impeller blades to free lodged particles.

92

plate inside the disposer to loosen the clog. Really deluxe models have an automatic reversing mechanism. When an overload occurs on such a machine, you clear it by reversing the movement inside the disposer. You can usually operate the automatic reversing mechanism by merely flipping the switch off and then on again.

Preventive Maintenance

WHILE IT MAY sound impressive to grab the old broom stick and get the disposer whirring again, this problem need never even arise. Proper care and feeding of the disposer will keep it going, and — at the same time — be kinder to your drains. There are several things that should never go down the disposer: plastic, aluminum foil, bottle caps, pull-top rings, string, cigarette filters, rags, and paper. Other items — such as bones, seafood shells, and glass — may be ground up but really should be put into the garbage pail. You may get away with putting some of these things down once or twice or maybe even for months, but eventually you will damage the disposer or clog the drains — or both.

Another tip to keep your disposer working as it should is to always use cold water when the unit is on. Many people think that very hot water is better when grease is involved. The cold water, however, lets the grease get ground into tiny solid bits that wash down the drain. The hot water, on the other hand, melts the grease, letting it coat parts of the disposer unit as well as the drains.

Never put regular drain cleaning chemicals down your kitchen disposer. There are drain cleaners that are specially made for disposers. These cleaners contain a petroleum distillate base that can degrease, unclog, clean, and deodorize the disposer without damaging the unit. Make sure that any drain cleaner you plan to use in your disposer is labeled for use in disposers, and also be sure to follow the directions.

As grease builds up on the walls of the disposer, food particles collect there and unpleasant odors result. Sometimes, ice cubes fed to the disposer can help to scrape off the residue on the walls. Fill the disposer about three quarters full of cubes, turn the unit on, and do not be frightened by the noise that ensues. When all the ice is chewed up, flush the unit with cold water. Then, drop in a lemon half and let the unit chew it up; the nice lemon smell will replace the bad odor.

Adding A Disposer To Your Home

HAVING A disposer makes it doubly important that you keep your drains grease free. If you do not, the small particles of waste will

93

stick to the grease and gradually build up a clog. If you decide to add a disposer to your home, therefore, you must thoroughly clean out the drain lines with a plumber's snake before you install the unit.

Installation of a disposer certainly constitutes a feasible do-it-yourself project. Detailed instructions come with the unit, but just to indicate how easy the job is, here are the steps in a typical installation:

(1) Remove the drain pipe under the sink.

(2) Remove the old sink flange, as well as the sealing material and any gaskets from the sink.

(3) Place a bed of plumber's putty around the opening and around the underside of the sink flange unit.

(4) Insert the flange into the opening and press it down into place. Once it is in place, do not rotate the flange; otherwise, you could break the seal.

(5) Remove the excess putty from around the flange.

(6) Now you are ready to go below the sink. Slip the gasket over the underside of the sink flange, followed by the protector ring with the flat side up. The mounting ring — which has three threaded pins inserted in it — follows the protector ring.

(7) While holding these parts in place above the groove on the flange, push the snap ring up along the flange until it snaps into the groove. One word of caution about the snap ring: If you spread it, it can become too loose to hold in place around the groove. You may find it slow to push the snap ring in place, but it will go. Make sure it fits firmly in the groove.

(8) The threaded pins have screw slots which must be uniformly tightened against the protector ring to hold it and the gasket snugly against the bottom of the flange.

(9) Now, lift the disposer unit and put it in place. Match the holes in the disposer with the threaded pins, but before tightening the nuts that hold the unit in place, rotate the disposer so that the outlet pipe faces in the right direction. Tighten the nuts.

(10) Now you are ready to hook up the drain. Use slip nuts and remember that the parts of the trap can be maneuvered around so that they will fit together. If this is a replacement unit, you will have no problem. If it is a new installation, you may have to buy and install some extra pipe sections. A common trap for both the disposer and the other side of the sink is acceptable.

(11) Test the installation and the unit for leaks.

(12) Before you plug in the unit, reach inside to see whether you dropped any tools in there. Now you can start throwing the garbage down the sink.

94

Replacing Tub And Sink Stoppers

I N YOUR bathtub, you flip up a lever at the end of the tub, and the drain down in the bottom of the tub closes. In your sink, you raise the basin's lifter handle between the two faucet handles, and that action pulls down the stopper in the drain. You take these things for granted until a plumbing problem occurs and you need to get into the drain. Then, how do you get that stopper out of your way?

The most common lavatory basin stopper is the pop-up hollow-cylinder kind. The pop-up unit attaches to a rod that sticks out into the drain pipe, and the top of the cylinder is closed to keep the water in the basin when the cylinder is down.

The basin is closed by pulling up on the lifter, which is connected to a lever that, in turn, pivots a ball that causes the rod in the drain to go down and close the drain. You can remove a pop-up stopper easily by applying a slight downward pressure and twisting. Most twist clockwise, but some go the other way. You should remove this type unit about every month or so because it catches hair and needs to be cleaned. There are several versions of the pop-up hollow-cylinder basin stopper, but you can tell at a glance how minor the differences are.

Another type of stopper is called the trip lever system. It has no visible stopper and usually has a strainer over the drain opening. The trip lever closes the drain by lowering a metal plug into such a position that it blocks the drain. The plate that holds the trip lever is open to accommodate any overflow. Remove a trip lever system by

95

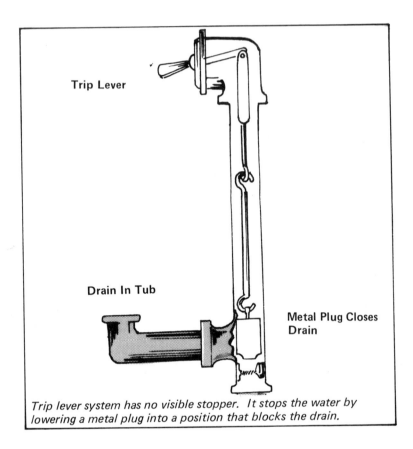

Trip Lever

Drain In Tub

Metal Plug Closes Drain

Trip lever system has no visible stopper. It stops the water by lowering a metal plug into a position that blocks the drain.

taking out the two screws in the plate, and then lifting the entire assembly straight out. It goes back in the same way.

Any time the basin or tub does not hold water, the stopper is suspect. If the stopper has become corroded or dirty around the lip that should seal when the stopper is closed, there may be room for water to seep out. This corrosion or dirt may not even be visible, but removal and cleaning of the stopper will probably stop the seepage. Some pop-ups can be cleaned while the unit is still in the drain.

There are two basic types of stoppers that are directly connected to the strainer. One employs a screw nut to hold the unit to the sink. The other utilizes a retainer with screws that are turned tight to secure the unit. When replacing either type, you first must remove the old unit. Unhook the trap from the tailpiece underneath. Chances

96

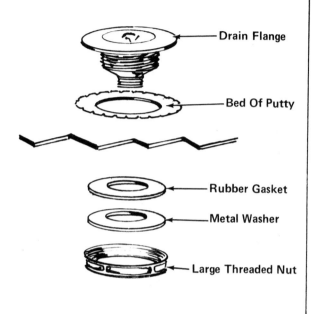

Drain Flange

Bed Of Putty

Rubber Gasket

Metal Washer

Large Threaded Nut

Other Type Of Stopper

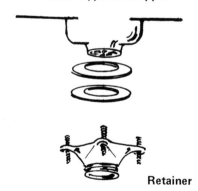

Retainer

Most likely, the drain plug in your sink is held on by a large threaded nut. Remove the nut and tap the tailpiece upward to remove the unit. Always use fresh putty when replacing the drain.

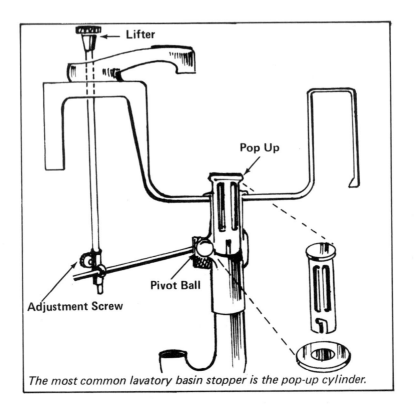

Lifter

Pop Up

Pivot Ball

Adjustment Screw

The most common lavatory basin stopper is the pop-up cylinder.

are that the drain flange inside the sink is held on by a large nut. Remove the nut and tap the tailpiece upward; the unit should pop loose. Remove all the old putty from where the flange was in the sink, and you are ready to install the new unit. With either type unit, use fresh putty around the opening in the sink.

With the screw nut stopper unit (probably similar to the old one you took off) you put the flange in the hole, and from the bottom you place the rubber gasket and the metal washer in place, followed by the threaded nut. This nut is tightened until the strainer is waterproof.

The other type goes on in just about the same way, but when the retainer is turned onto the unit, tighten the three screws against the friction ring until the strainer is watertight. With both stoppers, the tailpiece is connected by a slip nut. Reattach the trap, remove the excess putty, and you have a new strainer installed with no strain at all.

98

Remodeling And Modernizing

OLD PLUMBING can be modernized both inside and out. Adding new modern fixtures can change the outward appearance, and putting in new pipes can enhance your plumbing system's efficiency and give you greater peace of mind. If you have had a few problems with the plumbing, you probably have already learned much of the mystery behind the walls. As the need arises, you will change over to new pipes. Therefore, we can talk now about modernizing for looks.

Changing old fixtures for new designs is usually not much of a hassle. Chances are, you have lived with the old fixtures for some time; this is not an emergency situation in which you must make a snap decision. Take your time and investigate all the possible new types of fixtures. This is not the kind of change you make very often; therefore, consider buying the best. The small amount extra you spend to get top quality will average out to only pennies per year over the long haul.

In addition to replacing the old fixtures, you may want to consider adding new plumbing facilities to your home. A half bath in the basement can save many trips up and down the stairs. Converting a large closet or an under-the-staircase space into a guest powder room might make sense. If you have a workshop, would it be handy to have a sink nearby for clean up? A family with active kids might do well to add a drain to a back entry porch for cleaning off muddy shoes and clothes. An automatic dishwasher, of course, can make the homemaker's chores much more pleasant.

The facilities you can add to your home — if you are willing to tackle plumbing projects — are almost limitless. You may have to add some new pipes and drains, but that is certainly a feasible do-it-yourself endeavor. Check the plumbing code in your community to find out what you can do legally, and then decide what you are capable of doing. You may wish to contract with a plumber for part of the job and do the rest yourself. Select a plumber who will cooperate with you along these lines, and when you find the right one, make sure that you cooperate with him as well.

Plumbing Codes

ALMOST EVERY community has a plumbing code. These are rules which govern materials and procedures for plumbing work. In some places, the code specifies that only a licensed plumber can perform certain plumbing installations. The only way to find out what you can and cannot do is to read your local plumbing code. If you live in a city, there should be a building inspector's office that has copies of the code. If such an office is not available, check city, county, or state offices until you find the code.

All codes set forth minimum standards for procedures and materials. The local code may be quite strict regarding the required materials and procedures. Some cities, for example, have codes that allow no plastic pipe to be used. Eventually, plastic will be acceptable everywhere, but for now be sure to check your local authority to see what standards are set forth. Pipe size is another area where the local code may be very specific.

The local code is law; any others are guides to show generally accepted minimum standards. Anything that is not covered in the local code should be looked up in the broader codes to ascertain the acceptable minimum standards.

The same people who have copies of the code are the ones to see about plumbing permits. The cost of a permit ranges from free to a few dollars. Many times this authority will inspect your plumbing projects to insure that what was done was done according to the code. Actually, having an inspector who will approve your plans and check afterwards to see that the work was done properly is a big plus.

Although some local codes are antiquated, the idea behind codes is good. Plumbing must be done right; otherwise, the health of your family and the well-being of your entire neighborhood could be endangered. Even though the work is being done inside and the city inspector may never know that you are remodeling, be sure to get a permit if one is required. Making certain that your project is being done according to the code will pay off in the long run.

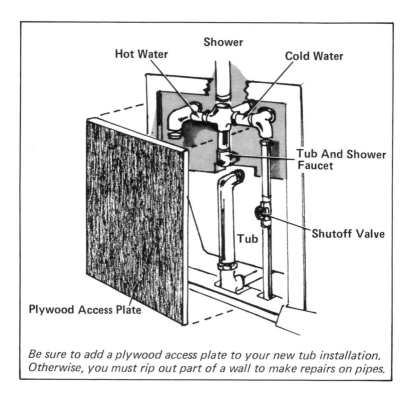

Be sure to add a plywood access plate to your new tub installation. Otherwise, you must rip out part of a wall to make repairs on pipes.

Changing Faucets

SOMETIMES, YOUR tubs and sinks can take on an entirely new character by merely changing the handles. There are two ways to go about making such a change; you can just replace the handles, or you may wish to put in an entire unit that includes a new spout as well as handles.

People seldom think how easily they can rid themselves of old handles that may be out of style and pockmarked from corrosion. In fact, the changeover is so simple as to be worth only very brief mention. Just figure out how the handle is attached and remove it. Then, purchase a new one that will fit the stem. When replacing shower handles that come out from the wall, you may also wish to change the cover plates that hide the holes in the wall.

Changing entire faucet units gets into a little more work, but it is still a relatively easy do-it-yourself project. Suppose, for example, that you decide to replace the old unit in your kitchen sink with a

101

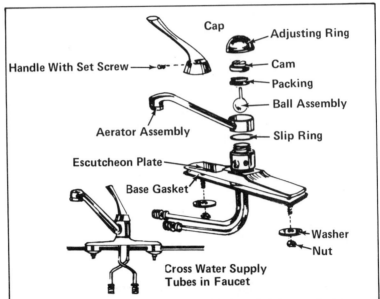

Cap

Adjusting Ring

Handle With Set Screw

Cam

Packing

Ball Assembly

Aerator Assembly

Slip Ring

Escutcheon Plate

Base Gasket

Washer

Nut

Cross Water Supply Tubes in Faucet

Installing a single-handle faucet on a kitchen sink is easy, but be sure to get a unit that covers old holes and to cross copper tubes before reconnecting supply lines.

holes left by the old unit. While finding a unit that will cover properly is no big problem, some older sinks are different. Many of the new faucet units are adjustable to fit many types of sinks.

Once you pick out the new model faucet you want, follow these steps for a correct installation:

1. Cut off the water supply to both the hot and cold faucets.
2. Disconnect the old faucet from the supply lines. It will probably be a threaded connection, but no matter how it is connected, you should have no trouble removing it.
3. The old unit is probably held in place by nuts underneath the sink. With the faucet out of the way, clean the area around and under where the new unit will go.
4. Place the gasket in position over the supply tubes and the lugs of the new unit.
5. Feed the tubes down into the center hole, and position the threaded lugs into the outer holes.

102

6. Go below under the sink and install the washers and nuts to secure the unit squarely in place.
7. The copper tubes now need to be bent in a cross pattern. The reason they are crossed is because the hot water comes into the right side, as you face the unit, and the cold from the left. This is the reverse of the way you expect your faucet to operate: cold from the right, hot from the left. Bending must be done very gently; take great care not to kink the tubing.
8. Once the tubes are crossed, you are ready to reconnect the supply lines. Make sure that the cold and hot lines are connected to the correct tubes on the unit. When you attach the lines, use pipe joint compound and be sure to use two wrenches. One must hold the shank of the fitting on the tube, while the other turns the nut on the water supply line. If you fail to hold the tube, you could twist it and stop the flow of water. If you need different sized connectors, an adapter can do the job.

Once the connection is made on both sides, you can turn the water supply back on. Installing a new faucet unit is just that simple. New lavatory faucets are installed about the same way. Once you purchase a unit to cover the existing holes, you should have little difficulty with the installation.

Shower and tub faucets are a little more complicated because you may not be able to get at the unit inside the wall. Whoever built your home should have provided an access panel to allow entry to the pipes at the tub, but if you do not have such a panel, now is a good time to cut into the wall and add one. If you do have an access panel, you merely cut off the water, remove the handles on the tub side, and then disconnect the old faucet unit from the back. The old pipe with the shower head will unscrew from its pipe inside the wall, as will the tub spout. Now you are ready to install all the new parts.

Fortunately, all the new faucet units are made for do-it-yourself installation and come with very easy to follow instructions. Even if the unit you select is slightly different from what we describe, you still should have no trouble attaching it to your pipes. In most cases, the installation of new faucet units does wonders for the appearance of the old fixtures, but even better than that is the fact that all the leaks and drips and problems you had with the old units suddenly vanish.

Replacing Tubs Or Showers

IF YOUR bathtub is up on legs so high that you feel like you must

When replacing old-fashioned tub (above), everything goes but three pipes. Then you add tub supports and framing for new walls (below).

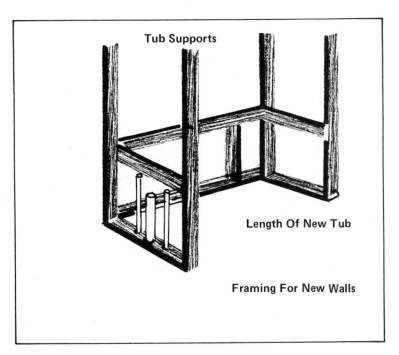

Tub Supports

Length Of New Tub

Framing For New Walls

104

pole vault to get into the tub, you might wish to look into a more modern facility. In addition to hooking up the plumbing, however, you probably will have to do some carpentry work, some tiling, and maybe some painting.

Be sure to pick out a new tub that will fit in the area occupied by the old one. If you opt for a tub that is bigger than the allotted space, you have to move some walls or part of a wall. Since tubs are made in several different widths and lengths, however, you can get one to fit just about any normal space. After you decide on style and size, check the existing rough-in to see precisely where the supply lines and drains are in relation to the distance from the wall and the floor. You must know how much alteration is required to fit the old pipes to the new tub.

Suppose, for example, that you have an old tub on legs and you decide to put in a combination tub and shower. If you have enough space, here is all you need to do. Usually, the old tub was not closed in at all; therefore, you must provide walls on each end and waterproof the side wall. Moreover, since the existing pipes are out in the open, you want to enclose all the pipes in the wall you build at that end. Frame the wall at the plumbed end first.

Check to see if the new tub needs to have tub supports running around the three sides facing the walls. If so, put the supports in at the specified height. It is best to remove the plaster or tile from the outer wall so that you can nail the supports directly to the studs. Frame the wall at the other end as well.

Now you are ready to alter the pipes and add the pipe that goes up to the shower outlet. Use the existing hot and cold water pipes that are sticking up, and add whatever adapters, extensions, or offsets it takes to bring these two lines up to where they will connect to the tub/shower unit. Connect the pipe for the shower to the unit, providing at least one cross brace in the framing and using U clips to steady the shower riser. Notch a crosspiece to hold the faucet unit and its stub-outs. Next, alter the drain pipe to fit both the overflow and the drain openings of the new tub. Now you have a new rough-in tailored to your new tub.

You are ready to position the tub on its supports and fasten it down. Follow whatever method of securing the tub the manufacturer recommends. Of course, you must do whatever has to be done to the walls around all three sides to make them waterproof and to make them look as good as your new tub. You should be aware that there are prefabricated units of fiberglass that include the tub and three walls. These fiberglass units eliminate all the tiling and much of the caulking. They come in several colors and look great. There are even one-piece units that can never leak because there are no seams to be caulked. The rub is that the one-piece units cannot pass

105

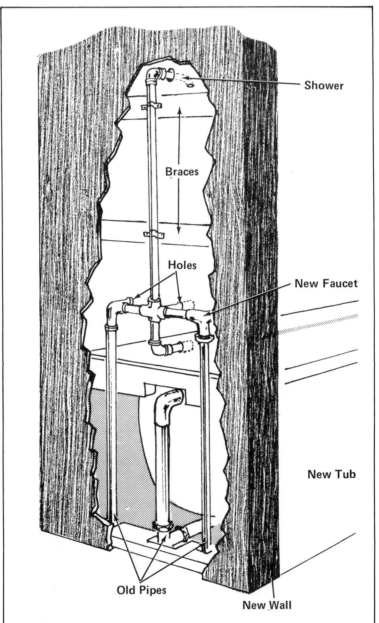

Shower

Braces

Holes

New Faucet

New Tub

Old Pipes

New Wall

You can use existing pipes for new tub/shower unit, but you must add pipe for shower and install cross brace for support.

through the average bathroom door; they are designed to be installed in a new home.

Before you complete the back side of the new wall at the head of the tub, give serious consideration to making an access panel that will allow you ready entry to the pipes. If you have a basement below or a crawl space, you may not need the access panel because you can get to the pipes from underneath. Otherwise, you would be very smart to install an access panel.

The final touch after the new walls are in is to add the handles, plates, spout, and shower head. Your installation is now complete.

A shower stall installation is handled about the same way as far as the plumbing hookup is concerned. Again, it is merely a matter of adapting the old plumbing to the new fixtures. Any seamless shower stall unit offers a big advantage over a tiled shower floor in that it does not require a pan underneath. It is, in effect, a shallow bathtub. There are also prefabricated units to take much of the work and worry out of the installation and use of your new shower stall.

Replacing Lavatories And Sinks

LAVATORIES COME in several different varieties. They may be hung on a wall, supported by legs (or a combination of both), held up by a cabinet, or rested on a pedestal. If the one you want to remove has a great deal of ugly plumbing underneath, you should consider the cabinet-type replacement which also offers some additional storage space.

Installation of all the units, other than the wall hung, is just a matter of hooking up the new fixture to the existing pipes. Chances are,

For a wall-hung lavatory, you must attach a wall bracket to a wooden crosspiece.

107

you need not even use any new adapters or fittings. If your ugly old plumbing will show, however, you should replace the unattractive parts with new chrome ones.

For a wall-hung unit, you must attach a wall bracket to a wooden crosspiece. The crosspiece must be nailed to at least two studs, and will probably look better if it is flush with the wall. The bracket and screws come with your new plumbing fixture. Use a level to position the bracket. When it is attached to the crosspiece at the prescribed height, the basin slips into place and hangs ready for the plumbing hookup.

Replacing a kitchen sink may necessitate replacing an entire drainboard because most replacements involve trading a single sink for a double. The cabinet work may also have to be changed, and this can become a major project. From the plumbing standpoint, however, replacing a kitchen sink is just as simple as any of the other replacements we have discussed. Chances are, moreover, that the new sink fixtures will be compatible with the old, using few if any adapters or additional fittings.

Connecting An Automatic Clothes Washer

YOU WILL need to have a hot and cold water supply handy to install an automatic washer. Your task is much easier if you have shut-off valves that are threaded, because you can use a threaded hose to bring the water into the washer. You should also have a drain to which you can connect a standpipe. If you have to do the plumbing yourself to bring the water supply to the unit, be sure to provide air chambers; an automatic washer turns the water off and on so often that if there were no air chambers, the water hammer might shake your house down.

Generally, there are hoses already attached to the washer, and all you need do is screw them on to the cutoffs. A rubber hose washer insures a tight connection. Just inside the entrance to the hose is a screen type filter; other filters are located at the water intake valves. All these filters must be kept clean of sediment. It is a good idea to use the cutoffs to relieve the water pressure against the less sturdy valves when the washing machine is not in use.

The standpipe should be higher than the highest level of the water in the machine. The washing machine drain hose need not be actually connected to the standpipe; if it is just pushed down into the pipe about six inches, it should be able to stay in place. Wedges cut from a section of an old tire are sometimes used to make the drain hose stay in position. The admission of air into the standpipe around the drain hose is a safety precaution to prevent a possible cross connection between waste water and the water supply lines.

108

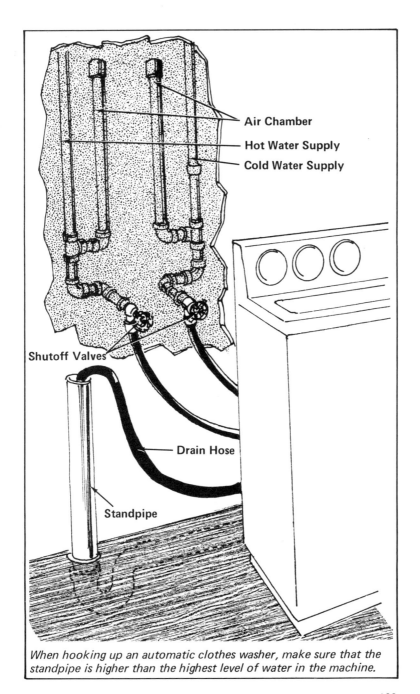

Air Chamber

Hot Water Supply

Cold Water Supply

Shutoff Valves

Drain Hose

Standpipe

When hooking up an automatic clothes washer, make sure that the standpipe is higher than the highest level of water in the machine.

109

A clothes washer hint that has absolutely nothing to do with plumbing can, nevertheless, give your washing machine longer life. When the unit is all hooked up, get out your level and make sure that the washer is level.

Automatic Dishwashers

MOST DISHWASHERS require only one water supply line, and that is the hot one. Right away you are ahead of the game, therefore, because you only have to worry about one connection. The dishwasher probably has a hose which attaches to a faucet type cutoff. This cutoff should be threaded to accept the hose.

If the unit drains directly into the drain lines, it needs a trap like any other plumbing fixture. Follow whatever procedure your plumbing situation dictates for connecting the necessary pipes and trap. Another type of dishwasher system drains through the kitchen sink drain pipe. For such an installation you need to purchase a dishwasher branch tailpiece to replace the regular tailpiece. The dishwasher branch tailpiece has male threads to which the drain hose from the dishwasher attaches. A rubber washer inside the hose connection makes it watertight. Since the dishwasher has a pump to remove water, the drain connection can be above the water level in the unit and still all the water will be drawn out. The drain connection then directs the waste water out through the sink trap.

Sometimes, the dishwasher hose is directed into the sink's garbage disposer. In order to be hooked up to the dishwasher, the disposer must have a short inlet pipe on the side, and most models do. To remove the knock-out plug from the inside of the disposer, just angle a screwdriver into the disposer, and position it against the knock-out plug. Then tap with a hammer until the plug comes loose. If you have such a connection, you must make sure that the disposer is kept free of clogs at all times to avoid a backup into the dishwasher.

Leaks from an automatic dishwasher usually do not occur at the plumbing connections. They more often result from door gaskets that are pulled loose or have become defective. If you do determine that there is a leak at a hose connection, however, be sure to trip the circuit breaker switch or remove the fuse before you reach in under the unit to tighten the connection. Otherwise, you might touch a live wire that could spell an end to your simple repair endeavors.

Remember: When making any replacements or additions in an effort to remodel or modernize your plumbing facilities, you must be sure that each fixture (except a toilet) is properly trapped. In addition, make sure that whatever you are doing falls within the bounds set by your local plumbing code.

110

Plumbing Troubleshooting Chart

PIPES

Problem: Leaking Pipe

Possible Causes	Repairs
1. Joints not watertight.	1. Tighten if possible. Remove and cover threaded joints with pipe dope. Remove and resolder sweat joints.
2. Hole in pipe.	2. Place clamp-type repair kit over hole. Replace bad section of pipe or reroute new tubing if bad pipe inaccessible.

Problem: Pipe drips water, but no leak

Possible Cause	Repair
1. Condensation.	1. Wrap pipes with no-drip material.

Problem: Noise in pipes — hot water only

Possible Cause	Repair
1. Steam causes rumbling in hot water pipes.	1. Turn down thermostat setting on hot water heater or replace faulty thermostat.

Problem: Water has sucking noise when draining

Possible Cause	Repair
1. Improper venting.	1. Clean vent on roof. Add antisyphon trap if no vent is there.

Problem: Hammering noise when water is shut off

Possible Causes	Repairs
1. Air chambers water logged.	1. Shut off and drain supply line to allow air to reenter.
2. No air chamber.	2. Install air chambers.

Problem: Banging noise while water running

Possible Cause	Repair
1. Loose pipe.	1. Track down which pipe is loose and brace, cushion, or strap it.

FAUCETS

Problem: Faucet Drips

Possible Causes	Repairs
1. Faulty washer.	1. Replace the washer. For single-handled faucets, install all parts in repair kit.
2. Improper seat.	2. Use reseating tool to grind seat even, or replace seat.

Problem: Drips around handle

Possible Causes

Repairs

1. Packing nut loose.
2. Packing not adequate.

1. Tighten the packing nut.
2. Replace the packing.

Problem: Leaks around spout

Possible Cause

Repair

1. Faulty O rings.

1. Replace the O ring.

Problem: Handle hard to turn; squeals when turned

Possible Cause

Repair

1. Spindle threads binding against threads in faucet.

1. Lubricate spindle threads with petroleum jelly, or replace spindle.

Problem: Hot water slows to trickle

Possible Cause

Repair

1. Washer expands when hot.

1. Replace with proper nonexpanding washer.

EMERGENCIES

Problem: Bad water leak

Possible Causes

Repairs

1. Burst pipe.

1. Shut off water at main cutoff. Repair leak. Avoid electrical shocks due to contact between appliances and water.

2. Hot water heater tank leaking.

2. Shut off water at hot water heater. Turn off heat source; repair the leak.

3. Appliance leaking.

3. Cut off water at the appliance. Cut off electrical current to the unit

113

Problem: Drains overflowing

Possible Cause	Repair
1. Clogged pipes.	1. Use plumber's friend or snake to remove blockage.

Problem: No water supply

Possible Cause	Repair
1. Frozen pipes.	1. Open taps. Start thawing at closest point to tap and work back.

TOILETS

Problem: Water in tank runs constantly

Possible Causes	Repairs
1. Float ball or rod catching.	1. Look to see if ball is touching back tank wall. Bend float rod gently to move ball or rod.
2. Float ball not rising high enough to shut off valve.	2. Gently bend rod down, but only a little.
3. Tank ball not seating.	3. Check lip of valve, and scrape away any corrosion. Replace tank ball if worn. Adjust lift wires and guide if ball cannot fall straight.
4. Ball cock valve does not shut off.	4. Washers need replacing, or entire unit needs replacing.

Problem: Nonflush or inadequate flush

Possible Causes	Repairs
1. Clogged drain.	1. Remove blockage.
2. Not enough water in tank.	2. Raise level of water by gently bending float rod up.
3. Tank ball falls back before enough water leaves tank.	3. Move guide up so that tank ball can rise higher.
4. Clogged ports around side of bowl.	4. Clean the ports.

114

Problem: Water on floor around toilet

Possible Causes	Repairs
1. Cracked tank or bowl.	1. Replace or try to patch.
2. Leak around base of bowl.	2. Replace wax ring.
3. Leak around water supply entry.	3. Tighten locknut. Replace faulty washer in bottom of tank.
4. Leak where tank joins bowl.	4. Tighten spud nuts or replace spud washer.
5. Condensation.	5. Install tank cover, drip catcher, or unit to bring hot water to tank.

Problem: Tank whines when filling

Possible Causes	Repairs
1. Ball cock valve not operating properly.	1. Replace washers or install new ball cock unit.
2. Water supply restricted.	2. Be sure cutoff is open all the way. Check for scale or corrosion at entry and on valve.

115

A Word About Plastics In Plumbing

IT IS A fact that some local codes do not allow the use of plastic pipes. Moreover, if you ask some plumbers about the new plastic replacement parts for inside a toilet tank, you get a very negative reply. Where, then, should you stand on plastics?

If the local plumbing code forbids the use of plastic pipe, do not use it. As far as the plumber's aversion to plastic, however, keep in mind that he makes more money selling you the more expensive brass parts, and this fact may taint his thinking.

Actually, plastic offers some big advantages over and above its low cost. It is incredibly easy to work with; it cannot rust or corrode; it resists acids; and it is very lightweight. Thus, while the plumber can cite some advantages for metal plumbing parts, he should not ignore the advantages of plastic. Neither should you. Make up your own mind. As long as what you do is accepted by your local code, you know that whatever decision you make is a good one.

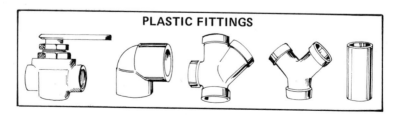

PLASTIC FITTINGS

Glossary Of Plumbing Terms

Adapter: A fitting used to connect pipes and/or fittings that are of different sizes or of different materials.

Air Chambers: Sections of supply pipes that contain air to cushion the shock waves created when rushing water is suddenly shut off.

Air Gap: The distance between the faucet and the highest level that water can reach in a basin.

Air Vent: See Vent.

Auger: A tool designed to be fed into pipes or fixtures to clean out blockage. Often called a "snake."

Backflow: The potentially dangerous introduction of water from another source into the supply lines.

Branch: Either water or waste offshoots of main pipes that connect to fixtures.

Calking or caulking: Material, including oakum and lead, used to seal cast-iron pipe joints.

Cap: A solid piece used to close off a pipe end.

Chase: A cutout made in the framing to allow for the installation of pipe.

Cleanout Plug: A threaded cast-iron cap that provides an opening into drains for easier access to clogged areas.

Closet: Toilet; often called a water closet.

Continuous Waste: A waste pipe from more than one fixture, but utilizing only a single trap.

Coupling: A fitting used to connect two pipes.

Developed Length: The total measured length of a run of pipe, including pipe and fittings. Measured along the center line of the pipe.

Diverter: A valve that changes the flow of water from one tap to another (as between a tub and shower).

Dope: Pipe joint compound.

Drain: Any pipe that carries away water and waste.

Ell: Short for elbow. A fitting used for making turns in pipe connections.

Escutcheon Plate: A metal plate used to enclose the point where a pipe or fixture enters the wall or floor.

Female Thread: The end of a fitting with internal threads.

Fittings: Any device used to join sections of pipe together.

Fixture Unit: A unit of measure describing the amount of waste load a particular fixture discharges. A unit is the equivalent of one cubic foot of water per minute.

FPT: Female Pipe Thread.

118

Frost Line: The depth to which soil freezes.

FSPS: Female Standard Pipe Size.

Gate Valve: A valve that regulates the flow of water through a gate-like disc inside.

Globe Valve: Valve with a spherical globe-like body.

Grade: The slope of a pipe.

Group Vent: Vent that functions for more than one trap.

Hanger: A hanging pipe support.

Horizontal Branch: Any offshoot drain coming off of the vertical stack.

Increaser: A fitting that has a larger opening at one end to allow it to be connected to a larger sized pipe.

Inspection Panel: A plate allowing access to pipes and traps that are inside a wall; used primarily for bath tubs.

Joint: Any connection between two pipes or parts of a plumbing system.

Joint Compound: A compound put on threaded connections to prevent leaks.

Main: The principal supply pipe to which branches may be connected.

Main House Drain: The pipe that collects waste from all the branches going to fixtures and delivers it to the main house sewer.

Main House Sewer: The pipe that connects your house to the sewer main or to a septic tank.

Main Sewer: See Sewer Main.

Male Threads: The end of a fitting pipe or fixture with external threads.

119

MPT: Male Pipe Threads.

MSPS: Male Standard Pipe Size.

Offset: A combination of pipe and elbows that move the run of pipe over to make it run parallel to the original pipe.

Pipe Strap: A metal strap used to hang or hold pipe in place on walls, supports, or ceilings.

Pipe Support: Any kind of brace used to hold up pipes.

Pitch: The degree of slope in a run of pipe.

Potable Water: That which is suitable to drink.

Putty: A soft sealer material; not to be confused with glazier's putty used in replacing window panes.

Reducer: A fitting with a smaller opening at one end to allow for connecting to a smaller size pipe.

Risers: The vertical supply pipes that carry water upward into various fixtures in the house.

Rough-In: The complete installation of all plumbing pipes (both supply and drain) along with vents, but not including any fixtures.

Septic Tank: A watertight receptacle that converts sewage to harmless liquid by a bacterial action; used when a community system is not available.

Sewer Main: The community sewage line that takes the waste from private property to the disposal system.

Soil Pipe: Pipes that carry away sewage from toilets.

Stack: All vertical mains that are part of the soil, waste, or vent system.

Tap: A faucet or hydrant for drawing water from a supply line; also, a tool used for cutting internal threads.

Tee: A T-shaped fitting with three openings to receive pipes, fittings, or fixtures.

120

Trap: A curved portion of a drain pipe designed to retain water that prevents backup of sewer gas without hindering the flow of waste water.

Union: A fitting used for joining pipes that allows for disconnecting without removal of the pipe.

Vent: A pipe that allows a supply of air into the drain system to help control syphoning and back pressure, aiding in the flow of water out of the drain.

Vent Stack: A vertical vent pipe.

Water Hammer: The noise that results when air chambers do not control the force of the rushing water as a tap is shut off.

Water Main: The supply pipe that brings water to your house main.

Wet Vent: A pipe that serves for both drainage and venting.

Simple Electrical Repairs

Many people avoid making electrical repairs because they fear getting shocked. As a result, they call in an electrician to do all kinds of things they could do for themselves. There is no reason to be fearful, however, once you understand the electrical system in your home and you know how to deal with it safely. Then you can not only repair broken electrical devices, but you can also harness the flow of current to add new convenience and beauty to your home.

How Your Home Is Wired

IN ALL EXCEPT the older houses in which the wiring has not been upgraded, home electricity is supplied by three incoming wires as 120/240 volts AC. By using three incoming wires, this system allows you to have 120 volts for lights and wall outlets — plus 240 volts for an electric range, dryer, hot water heater, air conditioner, and (in some homes) an electric furnace.

Electrical power enters your home from a transformer, either one that is underground, or one that is on a nearby pole. If you see three wires from the transformer to the place (called the service entrance) where the wiring enters your home, then your home is wired for 120/240 volts.

A heavy cable brings the electrical service through a meter, then into your home to a box called the load center; here is where the fuses or circuit breakers are located. In the load center, the electrical input is divided up into branch circuits capable of delivering various amperages as needed. The amperage each branch circuit can deliver is determined by the wire size and is limited by a fuse or circuit breaker. Wire size and circuit breaker (or fuse) are matched for current-carrying capability.

Most likely, you will find that the power in your home is distributed by a variety of wire called nonmetallic sheathed cable, type NM. Often referred to as Romex — although Romex is the trade name of only one of the many manufacturers of type NM cable — NM cable is used in various electrical boxes, clamps, and fittings.

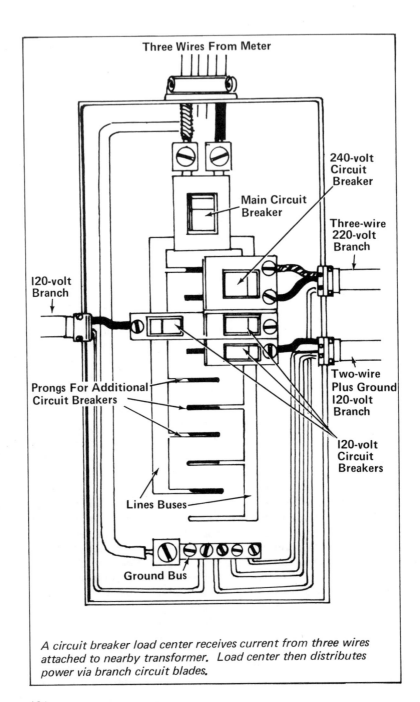

Three Wires From Meter

240-volt Circuit Breaker

Main Circuit Breaker

Three-wire 220-volt Branch

120-volt Branch

Two-wire Plus Ground 120-volt Branch

Prongs For Additional Circuit Breakers

120-volt Circuit Breakers

Lines Buses

Ground Bus

A circuit breaker load center receives current from three wires attached to nearby transformer. Load center then distributes power via branch circuit blades.

124

Type NM cable is available with two or more insulated conductors plus a bare conductor in the cable assembly. The bare wire is the grounding conductor. The insulated wires are color coded as follows:

2-wire cable: one white, one black, one bare.
3-wire cable: one white, one black, one red, one bare.
4-wire cable: one white, one black, one red, one blue, and one bare.

When we refer, for instance, to white wire, we mean a conductor covered by insulation that is colored white; the wire itself is copper and has the color of copper.

Where the cable enters an electrical box, it must be protected from chafing by a bushing, and it must be held firmly in place by a clamp. Usually, the bushing and clamp are combined into one piece. The cable must be continuous from box to box. As many of the illustrations in this book show, all wire joints are made in boxes.

Type NM cable is run alongside rafters and studs, or through holes drilled in rafters and studs. The runs are supported by suitable staples every three feet and at a distance of one foot from the hole where the wire comes through a stud or rafter to start a run. The runs in holes through studs and rafters are supported well enough and need no staples or clamps.

The cable runs are distributed through your home from a load center containing either fuses or circuit breakers. Three wires come into the load center. On one side, the wire connects to a bar (bus bar) going to a column of circuit breakers; the same connections exist on the other side. The central wire goes to an exposed bus bar. All the wires going to this bus are white, green, or bare; this is the ground bus. In most homes it is actually connected to the ground — to earth — by a wire that is clamped to the cold water pipe or to an underground bar or plate.

Circuits

FOR 120 VOLTS, a circuit branches out through a circuit breaker from one of the outer buses, and also from the ground bus. For 240 volts, only the outer two buses are used. For devices that operate on either 120 or 240 volts (like the electric range), all three wires are used. All three wires are also run to devices that operate at 240 volts but need the center wire for a ground.

The 120-volt branch circuits go through fuses or circuit breakers labeled either 15 amperes or 20 amperes. The 15-ampere branch

125

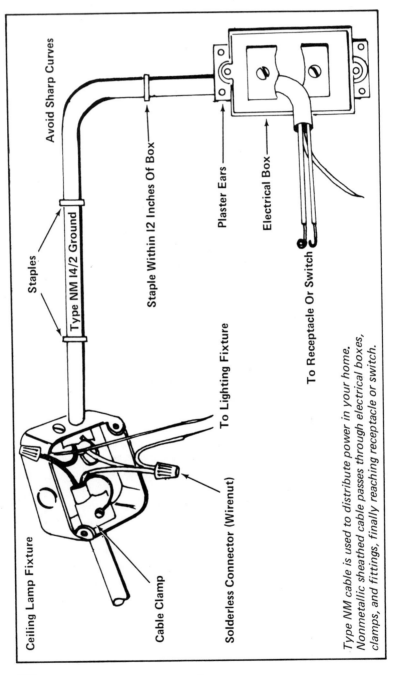

Avoid Sharp Curves

Staples

Type NM 14/2 Ground

Staple Within 12 Inches Of Box

Plaster Ears

Electrical Box

To Receptacle Or Switch

To Lighting Fixture

Ceiling Lamp Fixture

Cable Clamp

Solderless Connector (Wirenut)

Type NM cable is used to distribute power in your home. Nonmetallic sheathed cable passes through electrical boxes, clamps, and fittings, finally reaching receptacle or switch.

126

circuit uses Number 14 (or 14-gauge) wire; the 20-ampere circuit uses a larger size, Number 12 (or 12-gauge) wire. The larger 20-ampere branch circuit goes to receptacles in the kitchen, dining, and laundry areas; there should be at least two such 20-ampere circuits. The 20-ampere circuits go where heavy-duty appliances are used: washing machine, dryer, dishwasher, refrigerator, toaster. The 15-ampere branches go to ceiling lamps and to receptacles in rooms where less consuming appliances — mainly floor and table lamps — are used.

On the back of the load center door, you should have a listing of the branch circuits by number and the locations of the circuits connected to each fuse or circuit breaker. If, as sometimes happens, the list is incomplete or casually prepared, you may want to verify the list and perhaps make it complete.

The simplest procedure is to pull each fuse or to trip each circuit breaker to the off position; then see which circuits are thereby deenergized. It is easy to see when a ceiling light goes out. You can determine that an outlet is deenergized by plugging in a lamp; a small night light that is merely inserted in the outlet is an ideal indicator. Then, when you discover which outlets and fixtures are on a particular branch circuit, write that information down on the index card and attach the card to the inside of the load center door.

Fully loaded, a 15 ampere circuit can handle a total of 1800 watts, and a 20-ampere circuit can handle a total of 2400 watts. They should, however, never be fully loaded. The load on the 15-ampere circuit should be held down to no more than 1440 watts, and the 20-ampere circuit should never exceed 1920 watts. You can easily add up the wattages of the lamps and appliances used on each circuit to see how close the load comes to the maximum allowable.

When figuring the load on a branch circuit, keep in mind that many motor-driven appliances draw more current when the motor is just starting up than when it is running. If, for example, your refrigerator is run by a 1/4-horsepower motor, it might draw up to 15 amperes when starting, then settle down to around 4 amperes while running. Suppose that the refrigerator is plugged into a 20-ampere branch circuit outlet along with a 1000-watt electric toaster that draws a little more than 8 amperes, and suppose that while the toaster is operating the refrigerator starts. For a short period, the total current is nearly 25 amperes on a circuit intended to blow a fuse or trip a circuit breaker at anything over 20 amperes. This situation could provide an unhappy lesson in how your home is wired.

127

Electrical Wire

ONE TYPE OF wire cannot take care of all electrical wiring situations. The kind of wiring used inside walls is not flexible enough for electrical appliances; the kind of wiring used in lamps does not have the ruggedness required for larger appliances; heavy wire is not needed for small currents; and special insulation is needed to withstand the temperatures of heat-producing appliances. Due to all these differences, many types of wire are available.

Types of Wire

NM WIRE is used inside the walls of nearly all recently constructed homes. A tough outer sheath, usually plastic, covers two or more plastic-insulated solid copper conductors plus a bare copper wire. Of the various sizes available, you will not be likely to use any except the two- or three-wire (sizes #14 and #12) cables.

Very similar to the NM wire is type UF, a cable consisting of plastic-insulated conductors encased in a tough plastic sheath. You will find out how tough the plastic is when you have to remove it to bare the ends of the inner conductors. Since the plastic is resistant to every environmental condition, UF cable can be buried underground and it is not affected by hot or cold, wet or dry, light or shade. UF cable plays a prominent role in outside lighting.

Type SJ is the tough rubber- or plastic-coated wire used for heavy-duty appliances. You have seen it on washing machines,

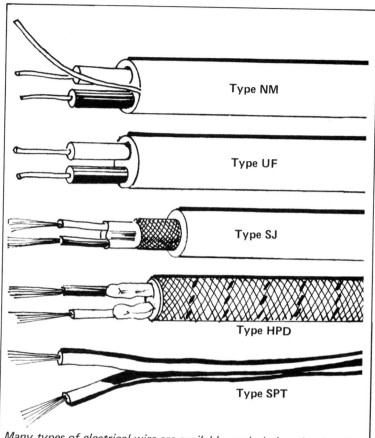

Type NM

Type UF

Type SJ

Type HPD

Type SPT

Many types of electrical wire are available, each designed to handle specific current, insulation, and installation requirements.

electric tools, refrigerators, and — in a small-diameter version — on vacuum cleaners. It is the workhorse cord for appliances that need a great deal of current but that do not produce heat.

For many years, cloth-covered type HPD was the only kind of heater cord used. It might be that you have HPD cord on your electric iron; a packing of asbestos around the inner conductors makes type HPD resistant to heat. With the development of temperature-resistant thermoplastics, however, type HPN — which looks like lamp cord — is replacing type HPD on many heat-producing appliances.

Type SPT (lamp cord) contains two conductors, each of many strands, to make the cord flexible. Each conductor bundle is covered with a plastic insulation. A molded groove between the two wires allows them to be split apart; SPT, therefore, is sometimes called rip cord. You will find this cord on lamps, radios and TV's, electric clocks, etc.

Wire Capacity

WIRE IS RATED according to its current-carrying capacity. For example, #14 type NM has an "allowable current carrying capacity" of 15 amperes. This does not mean that if the current were to exceed 15 amperes the wire would evaporate, disintegrate, or suffer some sort of immediate damage. What it does mean is that a wire of a particular size can carry a certain amount of current continuously — day in and day out — and that the insulation will not be damaged by the heat resulting from the current flow.

Wire that continuously carries excessive current suffers insulation deterioration. The insulation dries out, flakes, and cracks long before it has served its useful life. In a high-quality home or building, the wiring should last for the lifetime of the structure. Present-day wiring can do just that, but its allowable current-carrying capacity must not be exceeded.

Fuses and Circuit Breakers

SINCE THE TYPICAL homeowner probably does not know about current-carrying capacity, devices to prevent overcurrent — fuses and circuit breakers — are built into the electrical system. A 15-ampere fuse should "blow" when the current through it exceeds 15 amperes. A 20-ampere circuit breaker should "trip" when the current through it exceeds 20 amperes.

These are safety devices. When the fuse blows on high current it is operating properly. It tells you there is trouble: Either too many things are plugged into the outlet, or a faulty device — perhaps an appliance with an internal short — is in the circuit. A fuse blowing or a circuit breaker tripping is the signal to look for the trouble, not to put in a higher amperage fuse or to blame the circuit breaker for being defective.

If several appliances all are plugged into the same circuit — that is, into the various outlets all on the same line — you can figure the total current by adding together the individual current pulled by each appliance. You can usually find the appliance wattage by looking at the manufacturer's nameplate. In this way, you can determine how close the load approaches the full capacity of the line.

130

How To Work Safely With Electricity

AN ELECTRIC shock is always distressing, often hazardous, and frequently fatal. All electrical devices and electrical wiring methods are designed to insure the greatest measure of safety, but carelessness around things electrical can undo all the good in design and construction. An understanding of both the hazards and the precautions to take is essential when you work with electricity.

Electrical safety is based on the idea of avoiding physical contact with any live part of the circuit. Ordinarily, one wire in the system — the ground wire — is safe to touch without hazard. The problem is that often you cannot be certain as to which is the ground wire; sometimes, even the identifying markings are not totally reliable. Your best bet, therefore, is to avoid any situation which would bring you into contact with any part of the circuit.

Unplug, Pull or Trip

TWO SAFETY rules are obvious but warrant repeating. If you plan to work on a portable electrical device, unplug it; if you want to work with a household circuit, pull the fuse or trip the circuit breaker to the off position.

About the only thing you can safely do with a portable electrical device without first unplugging it is to change a light bulb. Do not ever attempt an appliance repair when the device is still plugged into a circuit. Do all electrical work with the appliance "cold," and

Stapling an extension cord to a wall surface (A) is a fire hazard. Always replace cords (B) that have brittle insulation. If you use an adapter to connect a ground plug to a two-prong receptacle (C), fasten the safety ground wire under the cover plate screw. When attaching wires to terminal screws (D), make sure that the insulation goes all the way up to the screw.

132

do not plug it in until all work is finished. If it then blows fuses, disconnect the device until you find the cause of trouble and make the appropriate repair.

When changing a receptacle or a switch — or doing any other work on the household circuit — always disconnect the power. If your house has fuses, pull the fuse in the circuit you are working on, remove it, and place it far away from the fuse box to diminish the possibility of someone replacing it while you are working on the circuit. If your house has circuit breakers, turn the breaker to off. To make sure that someone does not accidentally turn the circuit breaker back on while you are making electrical repairs, put a piece of tape over the switch. Better yet, make a sign that tells people that you are making electrical repairs, and fasten the sign to the fuse box or circuit breaker box.

If deenergizing the circuit plunges into darkness the area where you intend to work, use a flashlight or a trouble light with a long cord that is plugged into a still energized outlet.

Insulation

THE INSULATION on the conductors prevents the actual bare copper wires from touching each other and also allows you to handle attachment cords without danger. In working with electrical materials, do nothing to compromise the integrity of the insulation.

Do not staple an extension cord to a baseboard or a wall. The staple can cut through the insulation and create sparks that can cause a fire. Always discard any cord with brittle insulation, and replace it with a new one having good "live" insulation.

Make all wire joints inside an electrical box, preferably using the solderless connectors called, familiarly, "wirenuts." Never connect wires together in a behind-wall or in-ceiling location that is not accessible by opening an electrical box. When joining wires, or when fastening wires under terminal screws, do not allow the uninsulated bare length to extend beyond the connector. Fully insulated wires should go right up to the connector or terminal screw.

Ground Wire

THE GROUNDING arrangement in the wiring system is important to safety and must be kept intact. In all inside-the-wall type NM (Romex) wiring, white wire always connects to white wire. Most nonmetallic sheathed cable contains a bare wire that connects to the metal part of the electrical box by being fastened under a screw fitting of some sort in the box. The bare wire is supposed to carry

133

the connected-to-earth condition from box to box.

The bare wire also connects to the green screw on grounded receptacles — the kind that accepts a plug with two blades and one prong — in order to carry the connected-to-earth condition to the appliance plugged into the grounded receptacle. The prong carries the safety ground to the metal frame of any appliance that has a 3-wire plug and cord.

For safety's sake, do not remove the prong from a 3-wire plug to make it fit a two-blade receptacle. Instead, use one of the 3-wire to 2-wire adapters, and fasten the short wire on the adapter under the attachment screw of the receptacle's cover plate.

In many places throughout an electrical system, wires enter a metal box or pipe (conduit): where the cord enters a lamp or lamp socket; where the cord enters an appliance; and where in-wall cable enters an electrical box are a few examples. Surfaces at these points must be free of burrs in order not to chafe the wire or damage its insulation. Washers, grommets, and special fittings have been devised to protect the wire at the various points of entry. Get to know the kinds of fittings made for the boxes and conduits in your electrical system and use the fittings appropriately.

134

Repairing A Broken Doorbell

I F YOUR DOORBELL or door chimes do not ring, the fault could be in any part of the circuitry — from the push button to the bell or chime to the transformer. Doorbells and chimes operate at a low voltage supplied by the transformer, which steps the 120 volts down to around 15 volts. Since voltage this low will not give you a shock, you can work safely with everything in the doorbell circuit — except the transformer — without disconnecting the power.

Even if your doorbell is not broken, you may want to consider replacing the bell or chime with a new model. Some of the newer buttons have a small built-in light bulb that glows all the time. Such a light makes it easy for your guests to locate your doorbell after dark, and the bulb uses so little electricity that its operating cost will make no significant alteration in your utility bills.

How To Repair Your Doorbell

START BY removing the screws that hold the doorbell push button to your house; pull the button away from the building as far as the attached wires will allow. Loosen the terminal screws on the button, and remove the two attached wires.

Touch the bare ends of the two wires together. If the bell rings, that is a sign that the push button is defective. Install a new one by connecting the two wires under the terminal screws of the new button. If the bell does not ring when you touch the bare ends of the two wires together, the fault lies somewhere else in the circuit. Reconnect the button. As with most switches that have only two wires attached (single pole switches), the doorbell push button can be reconnected with either wire under either screw; it makes no difference.

If the problem was not in the push button, go to the bell or chime itself and remove the snap-on cover. Since there are several types of snap-on covers, you may have to try several different procedures to remove the one you have. Try lifting the cover upward slightly; then pull it outward. If that does not work, try pulling the cover straight out; be sure that you do not pull so hard, however, that you damage the case. Your snap-on cover may have prongs that hold it to the bell or chime assembly; if so, depress the prongs and pull on the cover to release it.

Once you get the cover off, you will see two, three, or more wires. If there are only two wires, detach them by loosening the

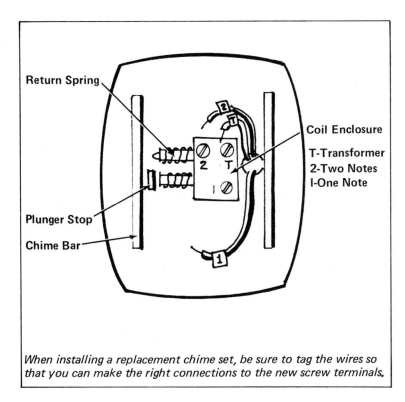

When installing a replacement chime set, be sure to tag the wires so that you can make the right connections to the new screw terminals.

136

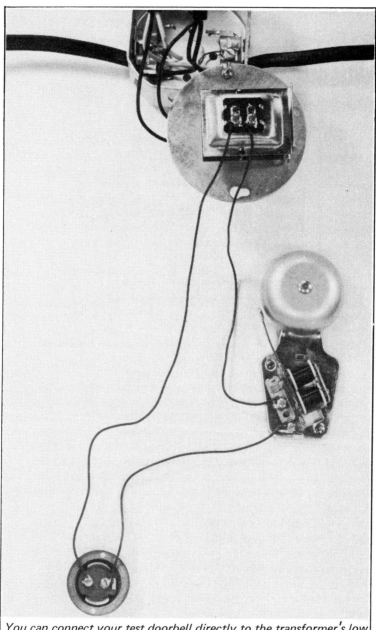

You can connect your test doorbell directly to the transformer's low voltage terminals. If the bell does not ring, replace transformer.

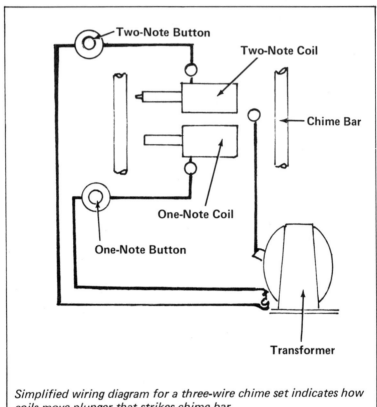

Simplified wiring diagram for a three-wire chime set indicates how coils move plunger that strikes chime bar.

terminal screws. Attach these circuit wires to the terminal screws on a substitute bell or chimes; for this purpose you can use (1) an inexpensive bell or buzzer, (2) a spare chime set, or (3) a 12-volt automobile lamp bulb in a socket with two wires. If the substitute bell rings when you push the doorbell button, it shows that the old bell or chimes are defective and must be replaced.

If your chime assembly contains three or more wires, tag them in the following manner: T (for transformer), 2 (for the two-note front door chime), and 1 (for the one-note rear door chime). Loosen the terminal screws, remove the wires, and connect the wires labeled T and 2 to the screw terminals on the substitute test bell. If the test bell rings when you push the front door button, it shows that your old chime set is faulty. To test this conclusion, connect

138

the wires labeled T and 1 to the screw terminals on the test bell. If the bell rings when you push the back door button, you are doubly certain that the chime set needs replacement.

You should have no difficulty in installing a new chime set; merely follow the mounting instructions on the package. Three-wire chimes have two magnet coils. Both coils do the same thing: They move a plunger that hits the chime bars. One plunger hits one bar, then springs back to hit the other (two tones for the front door). The only chime sets that operate differently are those like the Westminster type. The Westminster chimes contain a small motor — like the one in an electric clock — that goes on when someone pushes the door button. As it rotates, the motor opens and closes switches to energize the coils which operate the plungers for the various chimes. The motor shuts off automatically when the tone sequence is complete.

Transformer Troubles

IF YOU FIND that neither the push button nor the bell or chime set is at fault, you must test the transformer. The transformer is usually mounted on or near an electrical box. After you locate it, observe the transformer's connections to the power lines and to the bell or chime wiring. The 120-volt wires go into the box, and the bell wires are attached under terminal screws on the side of the transformer.

Connect the test bell directly to the transformer's low voltage terminals and push on the door button. If the bell does not ring, then you know that it is the transformer that is at fault.

Deenergize the branch circuit that supplies power to the transformer by removing the appropriate fuse or tripping the correct circuit breaker to the off position. If you do not know which fuse to pull or circuit breaker to trip, then throw the main circuit breaker to off and use a flashlight to work on the transformer.

Remove the defective transformer and install a replacement of the same voltage and wattage or VA (volt amps). The electrical information should be stamped on the transformer, and the installation instructions for the model you buy should be on the package. Use solderless connectors to attach the transformer wires to the line wires.

With the new transformer installed, connect the bell wires to the transformer. Turn the power back on by replacing the fuse, tripping the appropriate circuit breaker back to on, or throwing the main switch that controls all the electricity in your home. Push the door button, and you should hear the ring or tone of your new bell or chime.

Changing A Receptacle

IT IS RATHER obvious that an outlet — or, to use its electrical name, a duplex receptacle — will be damaged by improper use. Sticking a hairpin or paper clip in it is a sure way to shorten a receptacle's useful life. Although you may be careful to avoid sticking hairpins or paper clips in, you can do essentially the same damage if you plug in a short-circuited appliance. When so damaged, the receptacle should be replaced. Likewise, when it is so old and has been used so often that it is worn out — when it can no longer hold a plug securely and the cord drops out of its own weight — then it is time to install a new receptacle. If you want to be sure that the newly installed receptacle operates efficiently and safely, follow the correct installation procedures precisely.

The first thing to do is to deenergize the receptacle. Pull the fuse or trip the circuit breaker to off. Protect yourself from someone turning the circuit back on accidentally; put the fuse in your pocket, or place a piece of tape over the turned-off circuit breaker and write "Hands Off' with a felt-tipped pen on the tape. With the circuit dead, you might need a flashlight — or a trouble light with a cord long enough to reach the nearest live outlet — to see what you are doing.

How To Change The Receptacle

INSPECT THE outlet to see if you need a replacement that takes a

140

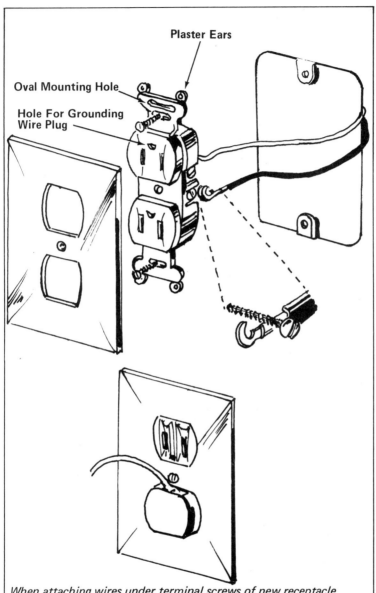

Plaster Ears

Oval Mounting Hole

Hole For Grounding
Wire Plug

When attaching wires under terminal screws of new receptacle
(top), loop the wire in a clockwise direction so that tightening the
screw draws the wire in tighter. Position a three-prong plug
receptacle correctly, not the way shown (bottom). Three-prong
plug should hang down from the receptacle with no loop.

141

plug with two flat blades and a round prong (the grounding type) or the type that accepts only two flat blades. Purchase the appropriate duplex receptacle.

Remove the center screw on the receptacle cover plate and remove the plate. The cover plate should fall off when you take the screw out. If the plate is "glued on" by many coats of paint, however, cut the paint all around the edge of the cover plate with a razor blade type tool so that pulling off the cover plate will not pull off flakes of paint, leaving an unsightly appearance around the outlet.

Remove the two screws holding the receptacle in the outlet box, and pull the receptacle out of the box as far as the attached wires will allow. Loosen the terminal screws on the receptacle and remove the wires. If the wiring is quite old, the insulating cloth and rubber coating may be brittle. Handle the wire with great care in order to prevent the insulation from coming off. In addition, slide electrical loom over the insulation.

Connect the wires to the new receptacle as follows: white wire under the silver screw, black wire under the brass-colored screw, green or bare wire under the screw with the dab of green color on it. Loop the wires under the terminal screws in a clockwise direction so that tightening the screw draws the wire in tighter. Connect wires in such a manner that all wire not under the screw head is covered with insulation. Clip off excess wire with electrician's diagonal cutters.

The slots in the receptacle are not identical; one has a longer opening than the other. This difference in shape tells you which slot connects to the black or "hot" wire and which one connects to the white or "neutral" wire. Just remember that the letter "W" stands for the wider slot that goes with the "W" for white wire. Some plugs have one wide and one narrow blade and, therefore, will plug into the receptacle one way only. This "polarized" plug can be used when you want to make sure that the "hot" and "neutral" wire identity is continued into an appliance.

Push the receptacle back into the box carefully, while nesting the wires into the space behind the receptacle. If the receptacle is for use with a three-prong plug — one in which the cord meets the plug at a right angle — position the receptacle so that the cord will hang down without a loop. There is no such thing as "right-side-up" for a two-prong outlet.

Tighten the receptacle's attaching screws, and replace the cover plate. Restore the fuse or trip the circuit breaker back on, and test the new receptacle with a table lamp. You should discover a marked improvement in the receptacle's performance.

142

Extending
A Receptacle

NDOUBTEDLY, there is a place in your home where you badly need another outlet. If your home was wired according to the National Electric Code, there should be no point along the wall more than six feet from an outlet. Nevertheless, you sometimes need another receptacle. Older homes, of course, were not constructed to have the required number of outlets, and you just might need an extra one. For safety's sake, do not ever think of installing an outlet in the bathroom wall. There is an unpleasant history of appliances plugged into the bathroom outlets that fall into an occupied tub with fatal results.

When you install a new receptacle, you must get into the walls to attach an electric box and to run wiring. Often, the simplest way to enjoy the advantages of another outlet is to extend wiring from an existing outlet nearby. You can do so safely if the circuit supplying the outlet is not already loaded to capacity. If the old outlet is handling only a light load and if your intended use of the new outlet does not add enough to overload the circuit, you will have no problem with extending from the existing outlet.

If, however, the circuit containing the nearest existing outlet is already loaded near to capacity, do not use it. Instead, run a totally new circuit from your power distribution panel. Moreover, you may find it advisable to install a new circuit breaker if there is not a vacant spare in your load center distribution box.

The job of extending a receptacle is relatively easy if you have a basement area under — or an attic space overhead — the present

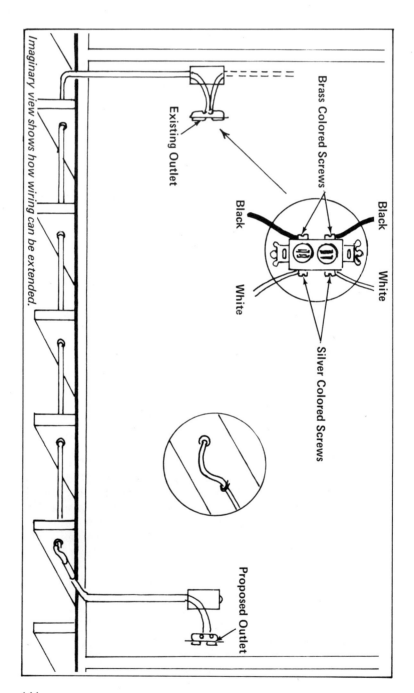

Imaginary view shows how wiring can be extended.

Existing Outlet

Brass Colored Screws

Black

Black

White

White

Silver Colored Screws

Proposed Outlet

144

and the planned outlets. People who live in multiple dwellings, with living units above and below, should probably turn the job over to a licensed electrician. Extensive carpentry and plastering are involved in such cases.

You will probably find it most convenient to use nonmetallic sheathed cable (type NM—Romex), either 12 gauge or 14 gauge, 2-conductor with a bare grounding wire. The type NM cable you buy for your new outlet should be the same wire size (gauge) as the wire in the existing outlet box.

Before beginning any work, make sure that the existing outlet is deenergized. Pull the fuse or trip the circuit breaker to off, and protect yourself from someone's turning the circuit back on while you are working on it: Remove the fuse and put it in your pocket; or, plaster a piece of tape over the turned-off circuit breaker and, with a felt-tipped pen, write "Hands Off' on the tape. With the circuit dead, you might need a flashlight — or a trouble light — to see what you are doing.

How To Extend a Receptacle

REMOVE THE cover plate from the existing receptacle. Loosen the mounting screws and pull the receptacle out as far as allowed by the length of the attached wires.

Determine the wire size by one of the following methods: (a) Examine the uncut length of nonmetallic shielded cable outer sheath to see if the wire size is imprinted on that part that is in the box; (b) Compare the cable with another length of known size; or, (c) Measure the diameter of the bare copper conductor with a micrometer or vernier caliper. No. 14 is approximately 1/16 of an inch thick; No. 12 is approximately 6/64 of an inch thick.

Determine the location of your new receptacle. Locate the new outlet, if possible, so that the side of the electrical box is against a wall stud to provide a post for secure attachment of the box. Locate the box at a height of about one foot up from the floor. If there are other outlets in the room at a different height, however, make the new outlet the same height as the others for a uniform appearance in the room.

Having determined the location of the new receptacle, place the electrical box — open end away from you — against the wall. Draw a line around it to outline the cut you will make in the wall. If the box has adjustable plaster ears, remove the ears before drawing the box outline. Next, with the box turned so that the open end faces you, refine the outline to include corner projections on the box.

At the corners of your outline drill 5/8-inch holes through the plastering into the hollow part of the wall. Drill the holes at places

145

such that the hole edges will take care of the projections on the electrical box. Then, starting at your drilled holes, use a keyhole saw carefully to cut away the plaster wall along the lines of your outline. Insert the electrical box in the hole in the wall to see how good the fit is, but do not attach the box to the wall yet. If necessary, use the saw to trim the hole for a suitable fit.

By careful measurement made below the floor, locate the point in the floor inside the wall directly below the outlet hole. If there is absolutely no way you can locate the point, try removing the baseboard and driving a thin nail through the floor down to the basement level. The nail gives you a point of reference, but be sure that the nail is in a location that will be covered over after you put the baseboard back in place.

From the basement level, drill a 5/8-inch hole up into the between-wall space. Feed one end of the cable through the hole into the wall space and up to where you can reach it in the hole you made for the electrical box. A slight bend in the cable allows you to hook it over the edge of the hole. Otherwise, the weight of the cable can pull it back down into the basement, and you will have to start feeding it back up into the wall all over again.

Use a screwdriver to pry out one of the knockout disks on the end of the electrical box. If the electrical box you have contains no internal clamps, but does have 1/2-inch size knockouts, use a cable clamp in the knockout to act as a protective bushing and to hold the

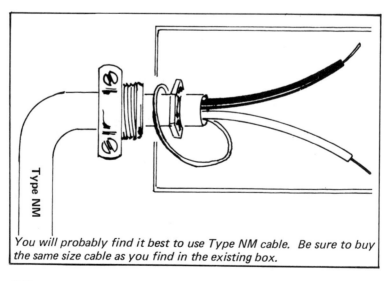

You will probably find it best to use Type NM cable. Be sure to buy the same size cable as you find in the existing box.

146

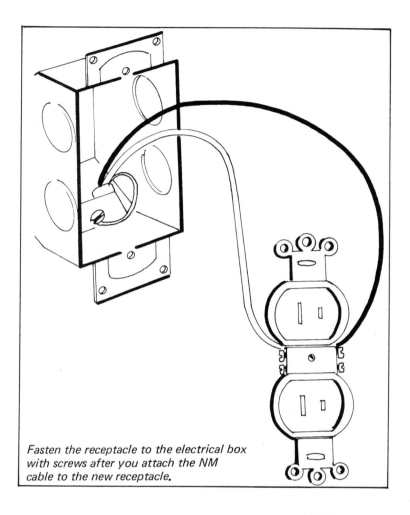

Fasten the receptacle to the electrical box with screws after you attach the NM cable to the new receptacle.

cable in the box. Feed about six inches of the cable through the knockout hole, and secure it in place by tightening the clamp screw.

With cable attached, push the electrical box into the wall opening — front edge flush with the wall — and fasten it against the wall stud. To fasten the box against the stud, use nails or screws through the holes in the side of the box. Or, if you have lath and plaster walls, put the adjustable ears back on the box and put screws through the holes in the ears into the laths.

Attach the new receptacle to the NM cable, and fasten the bare grounding wire under the clamp screw. The receptacle grounding

147

Drill 5/8-inch holes in rafters between existing and new outlets.

148

terminal is also connected to the bare wire. Fasten the receptacle to the electrical box with the screws provided, and attach the cover plate.

As you did before, locate a point in the floor below the existing outlet, and drill a 5/8-inch hole in the floor up into the inside wall space. Next, drill a 5/8-inch hole in each of the rafters between the existing outlet and the location of your new outlet. Your drilled holes can be at a slight angle, just so long as all are in a fairly straight path and each one is about two inches up from the bottom edge of the rafter.

Do the following things inside the electrical box for the existing outlet: Remove the screw from the lower cable clamp; remove the clamp; and, with a screwdriver, pry out whichever knockout disk is located in the best position for the entry of the new cable.

Thread the free end of the NM cable through the rafter holes and alongside the rafter as necessary to reach the hole you drilled in the floor. Then, feed the cable up the hole in the floor and through the knockout opening in the outlet box. Getting the cable into the outlet box, however, may not be easy to do. Try the following procedure if you have trouble: (1) Run a stiff wire (a bent-open wire coat hanger will do) through the floor hole up into the box; (2) Hook a strong cord to the wire, and pull out the wire leaving the cord in place; (3) Tie the cord to the end of the NM cable; and (4) Use the cord to help pull the cable up into the outlet box.

If you need to change the direction of cable run from through the rafters to alongside rafters, put a generous loop in the cable. A sharp right-angle bend might weaken the inner copper conductors and damage the insulation. Fasten the cable in place with a staple not more than 12 inches from the hole and then every three feet along the rafter.

Put the cable clamp back, and tighten it against the new cable. Remove the outer cover and bare the ends of the NM cable. Attach the conductors to the existing receptacle — white wire to white wire, black wire to black wire, bare wire under the cable clamp screw. All connections are made under terminal screws. Never try to get two conductors under the same screw head — it is considered an unsafe procedure. You will probably find two mounting screws on each side of the receptacle. The screws are side-by-side, both the same color, and both in the same metal strip; they are there to provide for just what you are doing — extending the cable without making any splices.

Put the receptacle back into its box, and attach it with the same screws you removed. Attach the cover plate, put back the fuse or trip the circuit breaker to on, and test your new receptacle with a table lamp.

149

Replacing A Wall Switch

WHEN IS THE time to replace a wall switch? There are four primary symptoms of switch failure: (1) When the switch loses its snap, the handle hangs loosely in any position, or when there is no clear feel between on and off; (2) When flipping the switch no longer turns the light on or off; (3) When flipping the switch causes the light to flicker, but not to stay on or off; and (4) When the switch works sometimes, but the handle must be jiggled back and forth several times to keep the light on.

Types of Wall Switches

DUE TO THE variety of switches available, you have a wide choice for a replacement. All work on the same general principle, and you can base your selection on the features you like best.

The conventional toggle switch is the most popular. The words "on" and "off" are embossed on the toggle lever. When the switch is mounted properly, these words are upright and the light goes on when the switch lever is flipped up.

The toggle switch is also available in a quiet version. One type of quiet switch contains a capsule of mercury that the toggle handle tilts in order to make contact. The totally quiet mercury switch is quite durable, but it costs more than the ordinary nonquiet type. It is especially important that you mount the quiet switch correctly; otherwise, the mercury capsule contacts cannot work properly.

The lever action switch, a variant of the toggle switch, offers

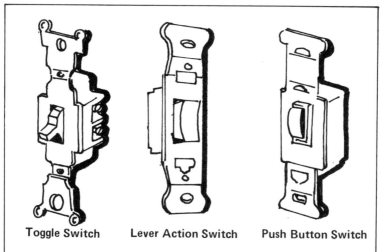

| Toggle Switch | Lever Action Switch | Push Button Switch |

A great variety of wall switches are available. All work on the same general principles, and you can install them easily.

as its main feature a styling that makes it almost totally flush with the wall. When the switch is mounted right-side-up, depressing the uppermost part of the button turns the circuit on.

The push button switch turns the light on when you press it; when you press it again, the light goes off. This kind of switch is available with a built-in neon lamp that glows when the switch is turned off. The glow is visible, particularly in the dark, through the translucent plastic push button. At night, the glow makes it easy to find the switch. You can install the glow lamp switch as a direct replacement for the regular toggle or for the push button switch.

Perhaps the most recent innovation in light switches is the switch that has no terminal screws for attachment of line wires. Instead, there are small holes on the back of the switch, only slightly larger than the bare copper conductor part of the wire. Remove the insulation from the wire for a distance of about 1/2-inch, and push the bare end into the hole. Locking tabs make the electrical connection and grip the wire so that it will not pull out. You can release the wire by inserting a narrow-bladed screwdriver in the slot next to the wire-grip holes. Two such wire-grip holes at either end of the switch make it possible to continue wiring from the switch to another electrical device.

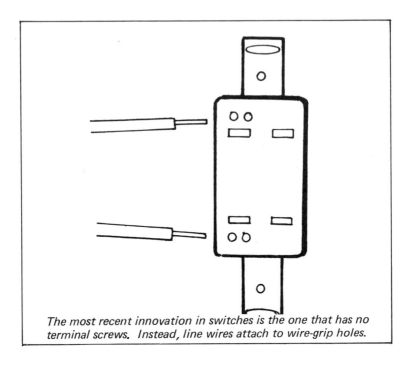

The most recent innovation in switches is the one that has no terminal screws. Instead, line wires attach to wire-grip holes.

How To Change The Switch

THE FIRST thing to do is to deenergize the switch. Pull the fuse or trip the circuit breaker to its off position. Protect yourself from someone's turning the circuit back on while you are working on it: Remove the fuse and put it in your pocket, or attach a piece of tape over the turned-off circuit breaker and write "Hands Off" with a felt-tipped pen on the tape. With the circuit dead, you might need a flashlight (or a trouble light with a cord long enough to reach the nearest live outlet) to see what you are doing.

Inspect the old switch to determine the type of replacement you need to buy, but remember that in most instances you can upgrade to a quiet or lighted switch. Remove the mounting screws on the switch cover plate and remove the plate. If the cover plate does not fall off when you remove the mounting screws, the plate may be "glued on" by many coats of paint. Carefully cut the paint all around the edge of the plate with a razor blade tool. Otherwise, when you pull off the cover plate you will pull off flakes of paint, leaving an unsightly appearance around the switch.

152

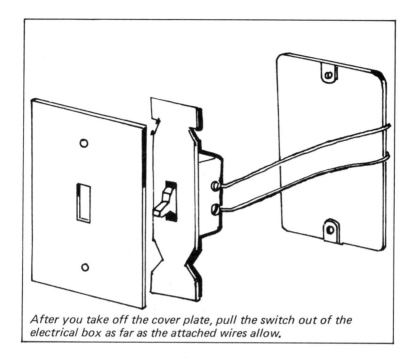

After you take off the cover plate, pull the switch out of the electrical box as far as the attached wires allow.

Remove the two screws holding the switch in the electric box, and pull the switch out of the box as far as the attached wires allow. Inspect the backside of the switch. A simple on-off switch has two screw locations for attachment of wires. If wires are attached to three screws, it is called a three-way switch. Three-way switches are used when a light is turned on or off in two different locations — such as by one switch at the top and another at the bottom of a stairway. There are no "on-off" markings on three-way switches. If the switch is the three-way type, do not disconnect any wires until you visually compare the old switch with the replacement switch. Notice the color of the screws — two one color, the third a different color.

Loosen each terminal screw — one at a time — on the old switch, remove the wire, and connect it under the corresponding terminal screw on the new switch until all wires have been attached to the new switch. Be especially careful with a three-way switch to verify your wiring by comparing it with the diagram on the box in which the new switch was packaged. If the wiring is quite old, moreover, the insulation may be brittle. Handle the

153

You can install a dimmer in the same box that held an on-off switch.

wires with care. For added protection, slide electrical loom over the insulation.

If you are using the wire-grip type of switch, cut away each bare wire end until only a 1/2-inch of straight length remains. Push one bared end into a wire-grip hole at each end of the switch body. You will find markings on the back of the switch body telling you where to insert the wire ends.

Push the switch into the electrical box carefully, with the connecting wires fitted neatly into the box behind the switch. Extending from the ends of the switch mounting bracket are small tabs called plaster ears. As their name implies, these ears fit against the wall outside the electrical box, assuring that the switch stays flush with wall even though the electrical box may be angled inside the wall. Oval holes in the bracket allow you to fasten the switch straight up and down even when the electrical box screw holes are tilted.

Screw the switch back in place, using the two mounting screws held onto the new switch by cardboard retainers. Attach the cover plate with the screws you took out when you removed the plate, and restore the fuse or trip the circuit breaker back to its on position. Now you should be able to enjoy the convenience of a switch that works properly and/or the new features — quiet operation or glowing lamp — that distinguish modern wall switches.

Dimmer Switches

YOU CAN replace your simple on-off wall switch in minutes with a dimmer that allows you to adjust the light in the room from high brilliance to total darkness. Before you rush out and buy a dimmer, however, there are some facts that you should consider.

The dimmer switch can be used only on incandescent lamps. Do not try to use one on fluorescent lights; you will be thoroughly disappointed with the results, and you can damage the dimmer in the process. The dimmer is at its best when it is used to control a ceiling lamp or a chandelier.

Do not exceed the dimmer switch rating. If it is labeled for 600 watts, use it for no more than six 100-watt bulbs or an equivalent amount. Never try to control the speed or the heat of an electrical appliance with a dimmer switch. Appliances which need to be controlled have their own built-in controllers.

The typical dimmer switch is built to fit in the same electrical box as a regular switch, but not all dimmers can replace a three-way switch. Be sure that you purchase the right model. Usually, when you replace an on-off switch with a dimmer you can use the same cover plate; the size of the knob hides the fact that a round

155

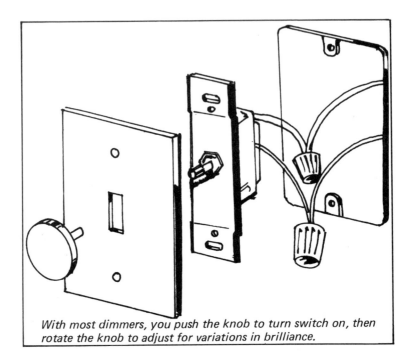

With most dimmers, you push the knob to turn switch on, then rotate the knob to adjust for variations in brilliance.

shaft is coming through a square hole.

Dimmer switches are an outgrowth of solid state electronics, but the electronic parts are kept as simple as possible to keep the cost reasonable. One effect of this economical design is that the lamp is considerably dimmer than when the same lamp is turned on by an ordinary switch. The reduced brilliance, however, is precisely the purpose behind installing the dimmer.

The most commonplace dimmer is operated by pushing the knob to turn the switch on, then rotating the knob for variations in brilliance. Pushing the knob again turns the switch off. Although most people prefer a dimmer that renders continuous brilliance changes, there is a type that has four click positions: off, low, medium, and high brilliance. Another style more closely resembles an ordinary on-off switch. When the switch handle is down all the way, the circuit is off. Slowly raising the handle gradually increases the brilliance. Highest brilliance occurs when the switch handle is all the way up. You can use such a dimmer as a simple on-off switch.

Some on-off dimmer switches have no terminal screws for the attachment of line wires. There are small holes on the back of the

156

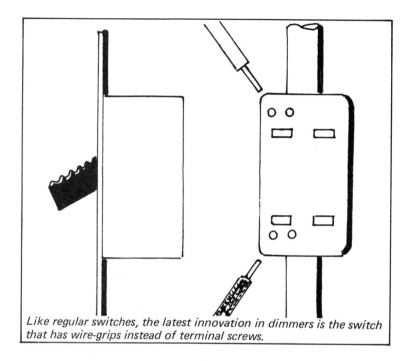

Like regular switches, the latest innovation in dimmers is the switch that has wire-grips instead of terminal screws.

dimmer switch that are only slightly larger than the bare copper part of the wire. For conductor attachment, you remove the insulation from the wire for a distance of about $1/2$-inch, and then push the bare end into the hole. Locking tabs make the electrical connection and also grip the wire so that it will not pull out. You can release the wire by inserting a narrow-bladed screwdriver into the slot next to the wire-grip holes.

How To Install A Dimmer Switch

BEFORE WORKING on the switch, be sure to deenergize the circuit. Pull the fuse or trip the circuit breaker to off. Put the fuse in your pocket or place a piece of tape over the turned-off circuit breaker and write "Hands Off" with a felt-tipped pen on the tape. With the circuit dead because you removed the fuse or tripped the circuit breaker, you might need a flashlight — or a trouble light with a cord long enough to reach the nearest live outlet — to see what you are doing.

Remove the mounting screws on the switch cover plate and re-

157

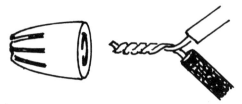

To make a good wirenut connection, twist the line wire and switch wire together tightly, and screw wirenut cone on securely.

move the plate. The cover plate should fall off when you take the screws out. If the plate is "glued on" by many coats of paint, however, cut the paint all around the plate's edge with a razor blade type tool so that pulling off the cover plate will not pull off flakes of paint, leaving an unsightly appearance around the switch.

Remove the two screws that hold the switch in the electric box, and pull the switch out as far as the attached wires will allow. Loosen the terminal screws on the switch far enough to allow you to take the line wires out from under the screw heads. If the switch is still in good condition, save it; you may want to use it somewhere else.

Use wire cutters to cut away the loop part of the wire ends. If necessary, remove enough insulation from each wire to give you about 3/4 of an inch of bare copper conductor. Twist together one electrical line wire end and the end of one of the dimmer switch wires. Screw a solderless connector onto the joint tightly. Repeat this procedure for the other line wire and the remaining dimmer switch wire.

A good wirenut connection is obtained when: (1) the two wires are twisted together tightly enough to stay together of their own accord, (2) the wirenut screws on so tightly that it can no longer be turned by hand, and (3) all the bare wire ends are within the wirenut cone. The insulation goes right up to the wirenut.

Push the line wire and attached wirenuts back into the electrical box carefully and in a manner so as to leave space for the dimmer switch. Position the dimmer switch in the remaining space, and affix the switch to the box with the screws provided in the dimmer switch package. Attach the cover plate with the same screws that held it formerly. Restore the fuse or trip the circuit breaker back to on, and — if you have followed the instructions carefully — you will be pleased with the operation of your new dimmer switch.

158

Simple Electrical Repairs

Installing A Three-Way Switch

IS THERE somewhere in your home where you would like to be able to switch a light on and off from more than one location? Perhaps there already is a switch at the top of the stairs and you would like one at the bottom. Or maybe you want a switch in the kitchen at the garage entry as well as by the door that goes out to the yard. How about at both ends of that long hallway?

To turn a light on from two separate locations requires a special kind of device called a three-way switch. Both switches must be the three-way type. Thus, if you want to add a second switch, not only must it be a three-way, but also you must convert the existing switch to the three-way type.

Two wires connect to the ordinary on-off switch. The three-way switch is so called because three wires go to it, and a three-wire cable is needed between the two switches.

Depending on how your present switch and the light it controls are wired together, you will find either of two types of connections. One type has the branch circuit go to the lamp fixture, then continue on to the switch. To switch the lamp from two places, you must install another switch box, run three-conductor cable between the two boxes, install a three-way switch in the new box, and change the existing on-off switch to a three-way switch.

Looking at the three-way switch, you will see that of the three screws, two are alike while the third is different in some way: color, shape, or location. For the time being, we will call the different ter-

159

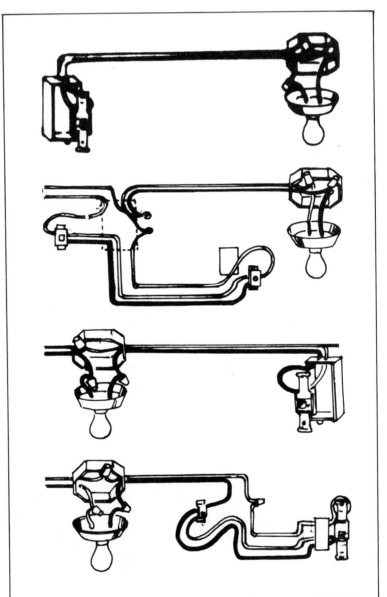

There are two types of connections between switches and the lights they control. One (top) has the branch circuit go to the lamp fixture, then continue on to the switch. The other (bottom) has the branch circuit go first to the switch and then on to the lamp fixture.

minal screw "A," the two similar ones "B" and "C." After you work with three-way switches and are familiar with the typical circuits, you will no longer need our "A," "B," and "C" designations. "BL" and "WH" refer, of course, to the black and white wires. We label the three-conductor cable "BL," "WH," and "R" because you will find a red wire in it.

The other type of switch/fixture connection has the branch go first to the switch, then to the lamp fixture. Again, we add an extension from the switch box to another switch, and put three-way switches in both places. These connections are a little more complicated.

Just what is going on in the three-way switch circuit? The outside terminal on each switch is the "different" one, the facing-in terminals are the similar ones. If the two similar wires got crossed, the switch would still work.

We cannot say it too often: Before starting the installation, deenergize the circuit. Pull the fuse or trip the circuit breaker to off. You will probably need a flashlight or trouble light.

How To Install A Three-Way Switch

DETERMINE THE location of the second switch. We assume for our example that the switch is to be located so that it can be fastened to a stud, either exposed or behind the wall, at the bottom of the stairs. Measure the length of cable run from the existing switch box to the location of the proposed new switch, including an extra length for inside each box. Use this measurement for purchasing the right amount of type NM three-wire cable. Buy the kind of cable that contains three No. 14 insulated conductors and one bare wire. The conductor size is marked on the cover of the cable.

At the existing switch, remove the cover plate; remove the switch mounting screws; and pull the switch out as far as the attached wires allow. Inspect the wiring in the box to determine whether the branch circuit goes first to the lamp fixture or first to the switch.

If the new three-way switch is to go inside a wall, follow these steps (the same as described in "Extending a Receptacle").

- Mark the outlet position.
- Saw the hole in the wall.
- Drill holes through the floor and rafters.
- Thread the wire through the holes.
- Clamp the cables in the box.
- Fasten the box to the stud.
- Run the cable from the new box into the existing box.

161

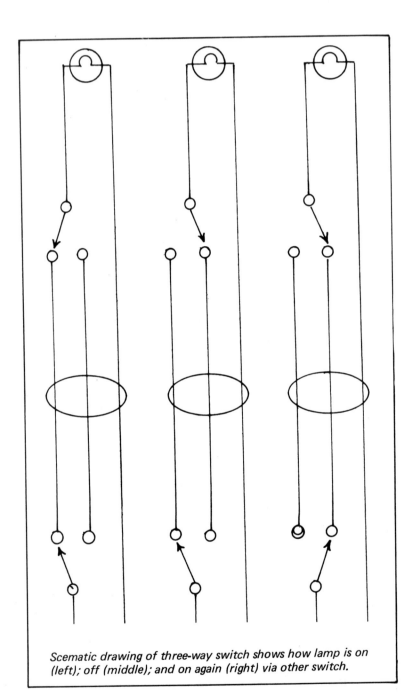

Scematic drawing of three-way switch shows how lamp is on (left); off (middle); and on again (right) via other switch.

162

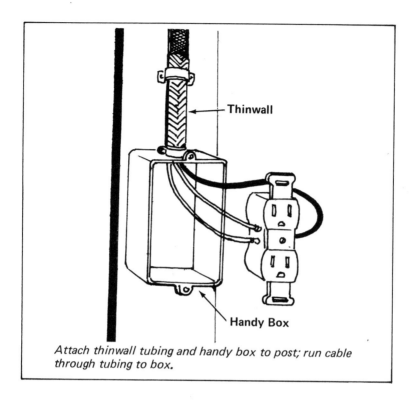

Thinwall

Handy Box

Attach thinwall tubing and handy box to post; run cable through tubing to box.

If the new three-way switch is to be attached to an open post at the bottom of the stairway, obtain the kind of switch box called a "handy" box. Attach to the box a suitable length of thinwall tubing, using a thinwall connector. The thinwall tubing protects the cable from damage. Attach tubing and box to the post; then, run the cable through the tubing into the box. If you have access to a tube bender, you can shape the tubing to fit against the post.

Attach the three-wire cable conductors to the three-way switch at the bottom of the stairway. You may have to loop the bare wire around the cable clamp under the locknut for a ground bond to the handy box.

At the existing switch box, disconnect and remove the on-off switch, and attach a three-way switch. Mount the switch in the box, and attach the cover plate. Follow the proper wiring connections to the switch, depending upon the type of connection that exists between your switch and the light it controls. Restore the power and test your new three-way switch.

163

Installing
A Pilot Light

WHERE IN YOUR home is there a light that burns unnoticed: in the garage, in the basement, in a closet? Many people like to have a reminder to turn off that unseen light, and there is a way to do so if the wiring between the light and the switch box is suitable. Right alongside the switch you can have a pilot light that shines as if to say, "You forgot to turn off the light."

Look into the electrical box; if the wiring in the box is two cables coming in, one wire from each going to the switch, and the white wires from each cable connected together with a solderless connector, you can easily install a pilot light switch. If the wiring in the box is just one cable with both wires connected to the switch, however, the best you can do (without getting into inside-the-wall wiring) is to settle for a switch that glows when the light is off.

Let us suppose that you found the kind of wiring that allows you to install a pilot light. Now, depending on how noticeable you want the warning light to be, you can either use the side-by-side switch and pilot light, or you can have the push-to-operate switch that turns on a small neon glow lamp behind the translucent push button. The installation procedures are nearly identical for both types of pilot lights. For our example, we will use the one with the bright pilot light.

Before starting to install the switch, deenergize the circuit. Pull the fuse or trip the circuit breaker to off. Protect yourself from someone's turning the circuit back on while you are working on it:

Bright pilot light can tell you when unseen light is burning.

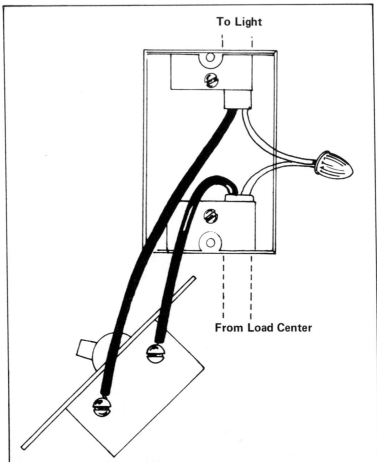

If wiring in box is two cables coming in; one wire from each going to switch; and white wires from each connected together, you can easily install a pilot light switch.

Remove the fuse and put it in your pocket; or, plaster a piece of tape over the turned-off circuit breaker, and with a felt-tipped pen write "Hands Off" on the tape.

With the circuit dead because you removed the fuse or tripped the circuit breaker, you might need a flashlight — or a trouble light with a cord long enough to reach the nearest live outlet — to see what you are doing.

166

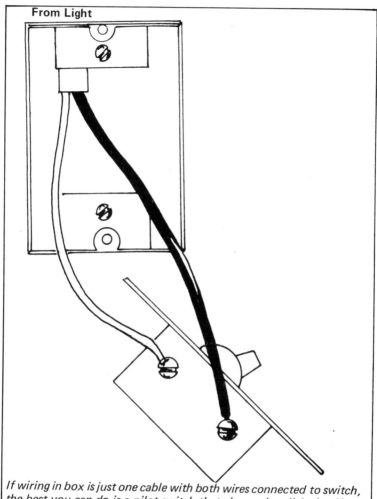

From Light

If wiring in box is just one cable with both wires connected to switch, the best you can do is a pilot switch that glows when light is off.

How To Install A Pilot Light Switch

REMOVE THE cover plate; remove the switch mounting screws; and disconnect the wires from the switch. Remove the solderless connector from the white wire pair, and separate the wires.

Fasten the white wires to the pilot light switch under the terminal screws marked "NEUT." If markings are not evident, attach the

167

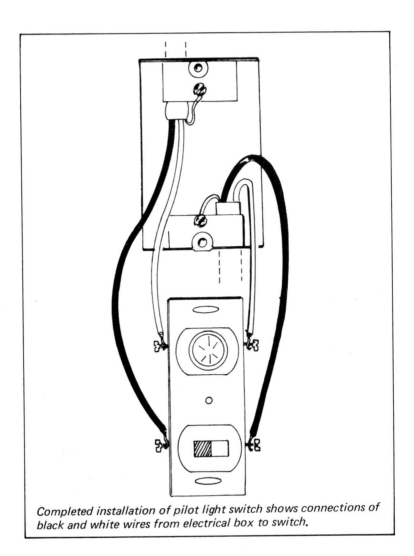

Completed installation of pilot light switch shows connections of black and white wires from electrical box to switch.

white wires under the terminal screws connecting to the screw-in part of the indicator lamp socket.

Fasten the black wire from the power source under the terminal screw marked "LINE," and fasten the black wire from the ceiling light under the terminal screw marked "LOAD." If you do not know which is the line and which is the ceiling light wire — and make the wrong connection — you will find that the switch will not turn off

168

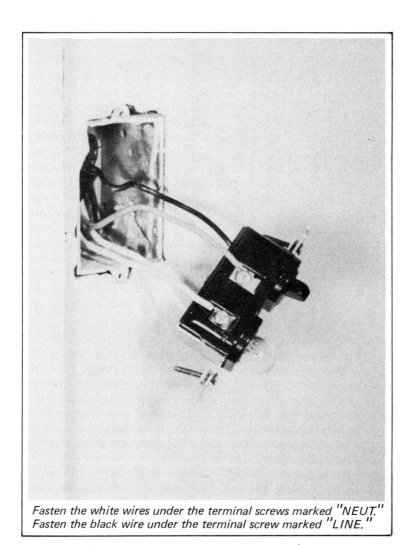

Fasten the white wires under the terminal screws marked "NEUT."
Fasten the black wire under the terminal screw marked "LINE."

the pilot lamp. To correct the wiring, interchange the connections.

Tuck the wires into the electrical box; push the pilot light switch into place; and fasten it to the electric box with the screws provided. Attach the cover plate; remove the pilot lamp snap cover; and screw in the indicator lamp. You now have a pilot light to remind you of the unseen light that could otherwise shine for many hours of unnecessary use.

169

Replacing A Lighting Fixture

I F YOURS is an older home that you want to modernize, you will of course want to replace those old-fashioned kitchen, bathroom, and dining room lighting fixtures with newer ones. Even though you might be fond of the old fixture, consider the possibility of one of the following having happened:

- The heat generated during continuous use may have caused the finish to get dingy, the sockets to become loose, and the metal contact parts to become corroded and electrically unsatisfactory.
- Heat and age may have taken their toll on the internal wiring which may now be dangerous due to brittle, cracked, and flaked-off insulation.
- Although you may have grown quite accustomed to it, many older lamp fixtures have less decorative appeal than the newer ones. If you have an old fixture of genuine antique value, that is a different matter. In that case, consider rewiring it for better performance and safety.
- An older fixture was not built to the more stringent electrical standards to which modern fixtures must adhere.

As far as the electrical work is concerned, replacing a light fixture is relatively simple. You may, however, run into a mechanical problem when you try to attach a new fixture to older electrical mounting hardware.

The first thing to do is deenergize the lamp fixture. If your house is properly wired — with switching done in the black wire — turning off the wall switch deenergizes the fixture. If you are at all uncertain about the wiring, however, then pull the fuse or trip the circuit breaker to off. Protect yourself from someone's turning the circuit back on while you are working on the fixture: Remove the fuse and put it in your pocket; or, plaster a piece of tape over the turned-off circuit breaker and with a felt-tipped pen write the words "Hands Off" on the tape.

With the circuit dead, you might need a flashlight — or a trouble light with a cord long enough to reach the nearest live outlet — to see what you are doing.

How To Replace Lighting Fixtures

PLUG IN YOUR trouble light and hang it in a location that will help you see what you are doing. Remove the outer globe from the old fixture and remove all bulbs.

Remove the screws holding the fixture against the ceiling. Some fixtures are mounted against the wall or ceiling with no visible mounting hardware. If you cannot find any bolts, look for a decorative feature — such as a knob at the bottom of the fixture — that doubles as a fastener. Remove the fixture.

Detach the lamp fixture lead wires from the branch circuit wires. If at the wire joint there is a clump of old insulating tape that is fused together beyond easy removal, you may find it simpler just to cut the wires close to the lump of insulation. Inspect the electrical box and your new fixture to determine which of the following methods you should use.

Standard Electrical Box

TO INSTALL a new fixture on a standard electrical box, proceed as follows. If necessary, remove enough insulation from each line wire to give you about 3/4 of an inch of bare copper conductor. Twist together one line wire end with the end of one of the light fixture wires. Screw a solderless connector tightly onto the joint. If the fixture is quite heavy, do not let it hang by its own weight on the electrical wires; hold on to it to support its weight until you attach the mounting screws.

If the fixture contains several sockets for bulbs, connect one wire from each of the sockets to one of the line wires; the second wire from each socket connects to the other line wire. In other words, connect all the sockets in parallel across the line. If you fasten three or four socket wires to a line wire, it may be necessary to use the

171

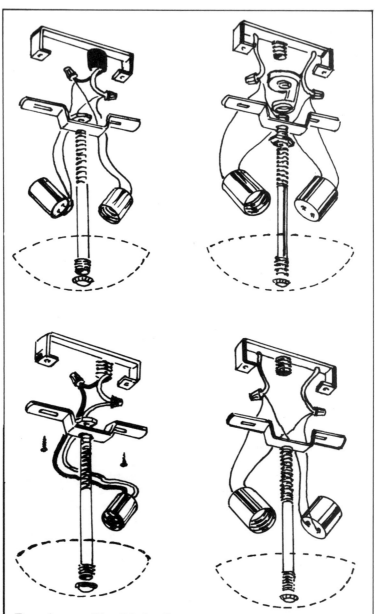

To replace a ceiling lighting fixture, remove the mounting screws, detach the old lamp, and install the new one according to the type of fixture and the type of electrical box you have.

172

next larger size solderless connector.

Start a long screw into each of the electrical box attachment screw holes, inserting it only far enough to hold it in place — just four or five turns. Usually, screws of the proper length are included in the box with your new lamp fixture; otherwise, size 8-32 (about 2 or $2^1/_2$ inches long) will take care of most fixtures.

Locate the fixture in place, allowing the mounting screw heads to pass through the keyhole slots in the fixture; then rotate the fixture slightly so that the screws are in the narrow parts of the keyhole slots. Tighten the screws sufficiently to hold the fixture firmly up against the ceiling, but do not tighten the screws too tight or you will distort the light fixture. The screws should be just tight enough to make sure the fixture is firmly in place.

Screw in the bulbs; attach the globe; restore the fuse or trip the circuit breaker on; and the job is done! Flip the wall switch and see your new fixture light up. If it does not, swallow your disappointment and try to find which connection you made incorrectly.

Electrical Box With No Threaded Ears

TO MOUNT YOUR fixture on an electrical box with no threaded ears, proceed as follows. Remove the old fixture as described for the standard electrical box. Fasten a fixture strap to the threaded stud inside the electrical box, using a locknut that fits the threads on the stud. It is not unusual for a suitable fixture strap to be included in the package with your new fixture. If you need to buy a strap, however, make sure that the screw holes are spaced apart the same distance as the new fixture's mounting holes. Start the mounting screws two or three turns in the threaded holes at the outer wings of the fixture strap.

Connect line wires to fixture wires; position the fixture in place; and attach it with mounting screws. Make sure that the wiring and the solderless connectors are tucked up into the vacant space between the fixture and the electrical box; they should not be squeezed between the fixture strap and the new fixture itself.

Screw in the bulbs, attach the globe, and restore the fuse or trip the circuit breaker on. Turn on the lights at the wall switch. The first thing you will notice is the enormous difference between that old fixture and the new one!

Pipe-Supported Fixtures In New Boxes

TO MOUNT a replacement fixture that has the globe held by a pipe running through its center on a new style electrical box, proceed as follows. Remove the old fixture. Fasten a fixture strap firmly to the electrical box. Quite often, the fixture manufacturer includes a fixture strap of exactly the right size. If you must buy one, however, ask for a strap with a center hole threaded to accept a 1/8-inch pipe thread.

Connect the line wires to the fixture wires. Thread a locknut on the long-thread end of the mounting tube. Holding the fixture ceiling flange up in its final mounting position, run the threaded tube through the hole in the fixture, and thread it into the fixture strap far enough to hold the fixture up in place firmly.

Screw a bulb in the fixture socket; restore the fuse or trip the circuit breaker on; and verify the operation of the newly installed fixture. Be sure not to exceed the maximum wattage for a bulb; this information is generally provided on the fixture itself or on the fixture's packaging.

Attach the globe, using the threaded cap supplied with the fixture. If the globe does not fit properly, try tightening or loosening the tube a few turns from the fixture hanger, while adjusting the position of the locknut to keep the fixture secure against the ceiling. Do this until just the right length of tube hangs down for the globe and its mounting knob.

Pipe-Supported Fixtures In Old Boxes

TO INSTALL a pipe-supported fixture in an older style electrical box, proceed as follows. Remove the old fixture. Install in the electrical box a hickey that fits the stud in the box and which has a 1/8-inch pipe thread on the other end. The remainder of the installation is the same as that described for mounting a pipe-supported fixture in a new style electrical box.

174

Installing A New Lighting Fixture

IN THIS PROJECT, we assume that you want to put a light in the ceiling of a room and install a wall switch to control the light. We also assume that you want the power for the lamp to come from the circuit breaker or fuse box, and that you will use type NM nonmetallic sheathed cable (Romex) for the installation. The new lamp's wiring will route through both attic space (for the light) and the basement space (to the fuse box). Just to show how the job is done, we assume that you want more than one ceiling lamp fixture controlled by the switch.

When you install a light and switch, you must get into the walls for the wiring as well as cut openings for the electrical boxes. Naturally, if the fixture is to go into a newly constructed room, installing the cable and electrical boxes before the walls are covered is much simpler than trying to do the job after the plaster or drywall is up.

The last part of our project involves connecting the cable to the fuse box. Therefore, no part of the circuit will be energized while you are working on it.

You probably have some ideas regarding where you want the light fixture to go, but do you know the best place to locate the switch? Here are some points to consider. Normally, when entering a darkened room, you automatically reach to the right to find a switch. Thus, plan to locate the switch to the right and at a height of about 4½ feet above the floor. Avoid locating the switch where it will be covered by the door when the door is fully opened. The

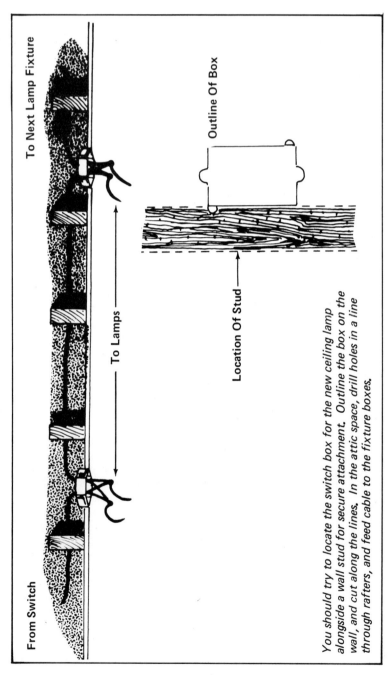

To Next Lamp Fixture

From Switch

To Lamps

Outline Of Box

Location Of Stud

You should try to locate the switch box for the new ceiling lamp alongside a wall stud for secure attachment. Outline the box on the wall, and cut along the lines. In the attic space, drill holes in a line through rafters, and feed cable to the fixture boxes.

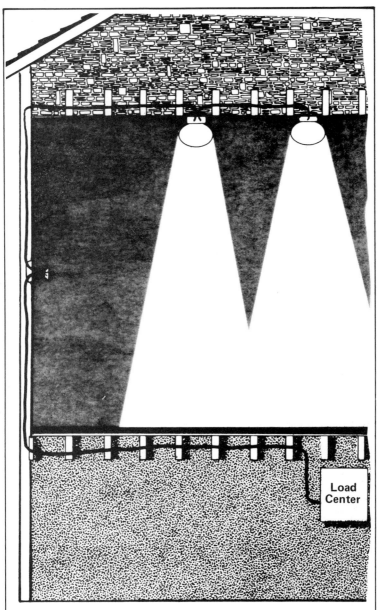

Ceiling lamp installation shows how Type NM cable is run from load center in basement, to wall switch, and on through attic space to two new ceiling lamps.

switch box is best located alongside a stud for secure attachment, unless you are going to use the kind of switch box that has a flare clamp to hold it against wallboard.

Locating the lamp fixture in the exact center of the ceiling provides the most uniform light distribution, but you might want it somewhere other than in the center; you may for instance, want it over a table for the most useful lighting. You should try to locate the lamp fixture box centrally between ceiling beams. On the other hand consider the possibility that a permanently mounted wall fixture might fit your decorating scheme better than a ceiling fixture.

How to Install A New Ceiling Lamp

MEASURE THE length of the cable run, including a six- to eight-inch length for inside each box. Use this measurement when purchasing type NM cable. Buy the kind of cable that contains two Number 14 insulated conductors and one bare conductor. The conductor size is stamped on the cable.

Having determined the ceiling location for your new lamp fixture and the wall location for the switch, place an electrical box, open end forward, in each location. With the box against the wall, draw a line around it to outline the cut you will make in the wall. Your drawn outline should not include the plaster ears. Turn the box so the open end faces you, and refine your outline to include corner projections on the box.

At the corners of your outline, drill 3/8-inch holes through the plastering into the hollow part of the wall. Drill the holes at places such that the hole edges will take care of the corner projection space.

Starting at your drilled holes, use a keyhole saw carefully to cut away the plaster wall (or drywall) along the lines of your penciled outline. At the same time, cut the holes for the switch and for as many ceiling fixtures as you plan to install.

Using a hanger bracket, mount the lamp fixture box in the hole you have made in the ceiling. You will find that there are several types of box hangers. Select one that works well in your chosen location. You will be working in the attic space while mounting the box and its hanger. Do not mount the switch box yet.

By careful measurements made below the floor and above the ceiling, locate the points directly below and above the switch box position. From the attic space and basement, drill 5/8-inch holes through the floor and ceiling into the space inside the wall. From the top hole, drop a weighted cord — an 8 or 10 penny nail on the end of a length of venetian blind cord works quite well. Retrieve the

178

cord at the switch box hole.

Since you will need help for the next few steps, have someone at the other end of the cord. Attach type NM cable to the cord. To do so, bare the wire ends and bend in a loop. Tie on the cord and wrap the joint with tape to make it smooth enough to go through the hole without snagging. Feed the cord up into the hollow wall space, through the hole you drilled, and into the attic space. Use the cord to assist in feeding the cable up the wall space and through the drilled hole, but depend mainly on pushing the cable. Pulling too firmly on the cord can separate it from the cable.

Pull through enough cable to reach the ceiling fixture, plus some extra for inside the electrical box. Once the cable is through the wall and out the hole, remove the cord and work with the cable.

Cut the cable where it enters the wall at the switch box location, allowing some extra for inside the electrical box. Do not install the switch box yet. From the switch position, drop the weighted cord inside the wall down through the hole to the basement. If you cannot hit the hole, try pushing a stiff wire up from the basement location through the hole to where you can reach it through the switch box hole. In the basement area, attach the remaining cable to the cord. Feed the cable up into the wall space and out the switch hole for a distance of six to eight inches. Push on the cable instead of pulling on the wire or cord in order to relieve the strain where the cable connects to the pull wire or cord.

Remove one knockout from each end of the switch box. Feed the two cable ends into the ends of the switch box, and fasten with the clamps in the box. Push the box into its prepared hole, and fasten it to the wall stud with the front edge of the box flush with the front surface of the wall. Holes in the side of the box allow you to nail or screw the box to a wall stud. In addition, you can use the plaster ears to attach the box to a lath-and-plaster wall.

With a knife, slit the outer cover along the exposed end of the cable. Peel off and cut away the outer cover. Then, remove the insulation for about one inch from the end of the white and black wires. A good way to remove the insulation without nicking the wire is to clamp it tightly between the handles — not the jaws — of a pliers right up at the hinge. This crushes the insulation against the conductor, causing it to break away in two strips you can cut off easily.

Twist the white wires together firmly, and attach a solderless connector. Loop the black wires, one under each of the two screws on the switch. Tighten the screws. Remember: The black wires, not the white, go to the switch. Switching is always done in the "hot" wire, not in the "neutral" wire. Mount the switch in the box and attach the cover plate.

In the attic space, drill holes in a line through the rafters from

179

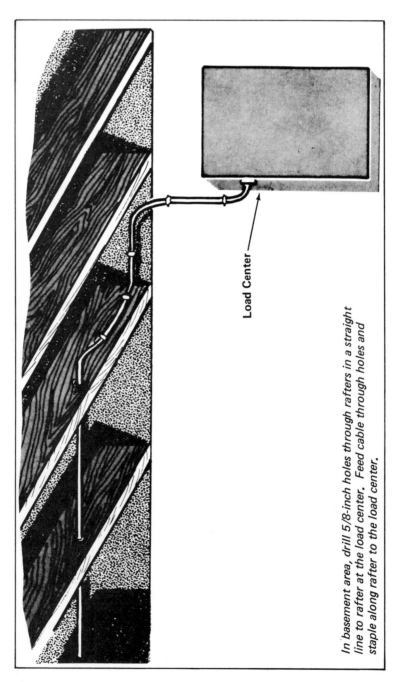

Load Center

In basement area, drill 5/8-inch holes through rafters in a straight line to rafter at the load center. Feed cable through holes and staple along rafter to the load center.

180

wnere the cable enters to the rafters holding the ceiling fixture. Drill the holes in the center of the rafters to keep the wires down far enough to prevent anything from hitting them.

Feed the cable through the drilled holes and along the rafters to the ceiling fixture box. Make a loop, not a sharp bend, where the run starts along the rafter. Staple the cable to the rafter every three or four feet and within 12 inches of the ends of the run.

Remove a knockout from the ceiling box, and feed the cable through it. Tighten the cable clamp in the box. If you measured correctly, you should have enough wire to extend into the box with a six- or eight-inch length remaining.

Attach the lamp fixture as described in "Replacing a Wall or Ceiling Fixture." If you want more than one lamp fixture controlled by the switch, repeat the wiring procedures to each of the added fixtures. All lamps are wired in parallel — black to black, white to white.

In the basement area, drill ⅝-inch holes in a straight line through the rafters to the rafter at the load center. Feed the cable through the drilled holes and along the rafter to the load center.

Turn the top circuit breaker in the load center to off — or remove the top two fuses — to disconnect all load center circuits from the incoming lines. Now you will need your flashlight because all circuits in your house are dead.

Remove the cover from the load center box, but be careful! There are wires at the top still energized. Remove the knockout disk most conveniently located near where your cable run ends. Use a general-purpose tapered punch to hammer against the side of the knockout to start its removal. Then, use a pliers to break it out of the box wall.

Fasten a cable clamp in the knockout hole, run the cable through, and tighten the clamp. Strip off the outer cable cover, and remove the insulation for a distance of about ¾ of an inch.

If you can, find a spare circuit in the load center box. If there are no spares, select the most lightly loaded circuit. Alongside each fuse or circuit breaker is a terminal screw. Loosen the screw a few turns, insert under it the bared end of the black wire, and tighten the screw. Fasten the white wire and the bare wire under available screws on the ground bus.

Put the cover back on the load center box. Trip the main circuit breaker or line fuses back to on. You are now ready to place the light bulbs in the lamp fixtures and to test your installation by flipping the on-off switch.

181

Rewiring A Lamp

THERE ARE many good reasons for wanting to put new wiring in a desk lamp or floor lamp: an antique lamp or one with a great heirloom value may have a cord in unsafe condition; a cord may be too short to reach the outlet; a lamp may not function properly because the socket is bad or the wires in the cord are broken. Whatever the reason, you can replace the cord easily and inexpensively.

The cord, plug, and socket are the parts most likely to become defective and need replacement. You can get replacements for all of these parts at any well-stocked hardware store; you need not go to a supplier specializing in electrical parts.

Plugs have a way of becoming misshappen, broken, or of failing to make a satisfactory connection when plugged in an outlet. The quick-clamp type of plug lets you add a new plug in seconds without worrying about fastening wires under terminal screws.

You can get a replacement socket in brass color, nickel color, or a plastic one in black or brown. Choose a color to match the tones of the remainder of the lamp. If you are going to replace the socket, consider buying a three-way socket. Wiring a three-way socket is as simple and easy as wiring a regular on-off socket.

Most lamps contain a tube or pipe that the cord goes through. When exposed to view, the tube is usually brightly plated or decorated; if not visible because it is inside a metal or ceramic base, the tubing may be plain iron pipe, threaded at the ends for attachment of socket and assembly hardware. In addition to protecting the cord, the pipe sometimes acts as a long hollow bolt to hold the lamp together. Because it is the most rugged part of the lamp, the tube seldom needs replacing.

If you are going to replace the cord, be sure to use the correct wiring. Lamp cord is known as type SPT; but if you ask for "rip cord" at your hardware dealer, you will probably get the right kind. Choose the color — black, brown, white, and transparent are the most common — that best fits the lamp tones. The customary length is six feet, but there is no reason why you cannot install a longer cord.

It is far better for the lamp to have a cord long enough to reach the nearest receptacle than for you to add an extension cord; not only does it look nicer, but also it is electrically preferable. Before you buy the cord, measure the length of the lamp and the distance from lamp to receptacle. Add on another foot for the attachments to socket and plug, and for a bit of slack.

How To Rewire A Lamp

REMOVE THE lamp shade and unscrew the bulb. Naturally, you must make sure that the lamp is unplugged before you go any further. Do not do any electrical work while the circuit is "hot."

Squeeze the socket shell at the switch, allowing the shell to be pulled away from the socket cap. Do not pry the socket apart with a screwdriver if you plan to reuse the socket. Pull the socket out of the shell as far as the attached wire will allow. If you cannot get the socket to come out far enough to work with, you might have to push some of the cord up from the bottom of the lamp for more slack.

Loosen the socket terminal screws, and remove the cord wires from under the screws. Tie a substantial string to the bare wire ends, and cover the tie with tape. You do not need electrical tape for this step; cellophane tape will do.

Pull the old electrical cord out while feeding the string through the lamp. Remove the string from the old cord, and tie it to the new one. The string makes it easy to pull the new cord through a lamp that has a great many turns in the wire's path. If the lamp is a short one with no turns, you probably can skip the string and merely feed the new cord through by itself.

Pull the string back through the lamp carefully, while feeding the new cord in behind it. Do not pull too hard on the string; instead, push on the cord. If the cord and string should come apart in the center of the lamp, you will have great difficulty in your rewiring work. When the cord is all the way through the lamp, remove the string.

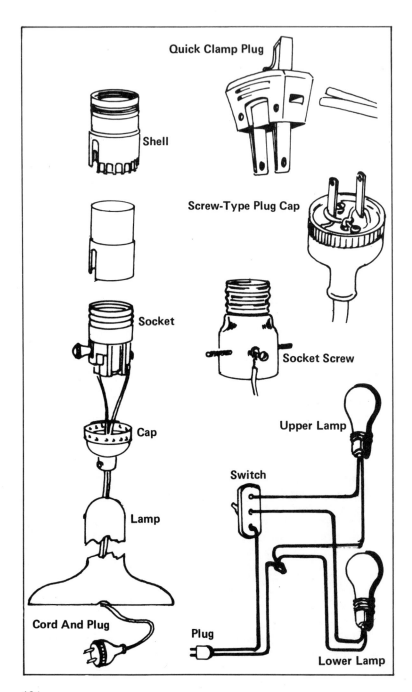

Quick Clamp Plug

Shell

Screw-Type Plug Cap

Socket

Socket Screw

Cap

Upper Lamp

Switch

Lamp

Cord And Plug

Plug

Lower Lamp

Rip the two wires apart for a distance of about three inches, and tie a single loop in the cord to take up the strain and to keep the wires from loosening from under the socket screws. Remove the insulation from about one inch of the wire's end, and twist the strands together. If you use a knife to remove the insulation, be careful not to nick the wires. You can buy a tool that is designed to remove insulation without damaging the wire. If you want to go to the trouble, you can use a soldering iron to melt some solder onto the wire strands in order to make a stiff end with which to work.

Loop one bare wire end under one of the socket screws and tighten the screw; loop the other bare wire end under the other socket screw and tighten in a similar fashion. Be sure to loop the wires in a clockwise direction so that tightening the screw will pull the wire tighter under the screw head. If you loop the wire the other way, it will squeeze out from under the screw head while you tighten the screw. Use a wire cutter (the kind of pliers called "diagonals") to clip off any excess wire, and be sure that almost all of the uninsulated wire is under the screw head.

Slip the shell over the socket, push the socket down into the shell, and snap the shell into the cap. Attach a plug cap — the part with the prongs on it — down at the other end of the wire. Try to obtain a quick clamp cap, because with this kind of plug you do not need to do anything to the cord. You stick the end of the cord into a slot on the side of the cap and push down the lever on the cap's top. Metal prongs in the cap bite through the cord's insulation to where the wires are and make the electrical connection.

If you use the screw-type plug cap, prepare the wire ends as you did to install the wire in the lamp. Loop each wire around a prong before tightening the bare end under the screw head. This keeps the wires apart and also gives some strain support, making it more difficult to loosen the wires by pulling on the cord. Of course, you should never disconnect a lamp (or any other appliance) by yanking the cord out of the wall socket.

Did you do everything right? There is an easy way to find out. Screw a bulb in the socket, plug in the cord, and turn on the switch. You should discover that your antique lamp with an unsafe cord, your cord that was too short to reach the outlet, or your lamp that did not function properly because the wires in the cord were broken is no longer a problem. Instead, you should find that for very little effort and expense you have made your lamp functional once again.

Simple Electrical Repairs

Installing And Repairing Fluorescent Lamps

IN THE FIRST part of this article, we will consider rewiring an ordinary incandescent lamp fixture and replacing it with a fluorescent lamp fixture. In the latter part, we will treat repairing a fluorescent lamp that is defective or inoperative.

The kind of fluorescent lights normally found in the home contain three electrical parts: the fluorescent tube, the ballast, and the starter. The starter is usually an automatic switch, but some fluorescent fixtures have a manual switch. If you are installing the fluorescent lamp in a circuit turned on by a wall switch, you will want the kind of fixture with a starter. The ballast is a magnetic coil that adjusts the current through the bulb.

The fluorescent lamp parts are wired together inside the lamp fixture as follows: Beginning where the line comes in at the top, the circuit goes through the ballast, through one end of the lamp, through the starter, through the other end of the lamp, and out to the A.C. line. The current heats the two small elements in the ends of the fluorescent tube; then the starter opens, and current flows through the lamp.

The ballast does two things: It makes a surge of current "jump" through the lamp when the starter opens, and then it keeps the current flowing through the lamp at the right value while the lamp is glowing. The starter, sensing that the lamp is glowing, stays open. It will close when the lamp is turned off at the wall switch.

As mentioned, some fluorescent lamp fixtures do not have an automatic starter. In its place are two push button switches. Push one

186

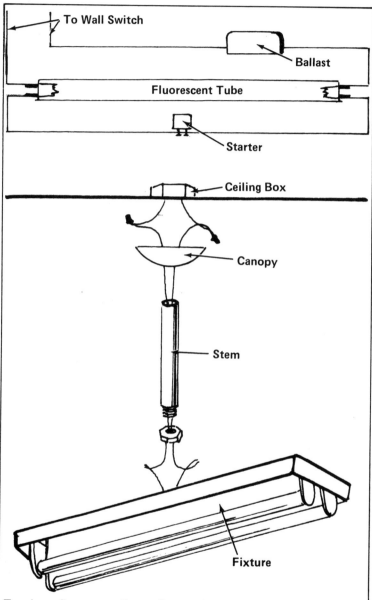

To Wall Switch

Ballast

Fluorescent Tube

Starter

Ceiling Box

Canopy

Stem

Fixture

Two-lamp fluorescent fixture (bottom) can be installed easily as either a new lamp or as a replacement for an existing incandescent lamp. Current flows (top) from branch circuit through ballast, through one end of lamp, through starter, and through other end of lamp.

button and then release it; the lamp turns on. Push the other button to disconnect the entire lamp circuit; the lamp turns off. This kind of arrangement is used in many fluorescent desk lamps where you turn the lamp on and off at the fixture, but it is the wrong kind to have if you plan to turn the lamp on and off with a wall switch.

In order to provide more light, many fluorescent fixtures contain not one but two lamps. In such cases, each lamp must have its own starter and its own ballast. You might run across a fixture that seems to have two lamps working off one ballast, but actually it is two ballasts built into one box. Similarly, four-lamp fixtures have four starters and four ballasts.

For the purpose of an example, let us consider the procedure for installing a two-lamp fixture. The lamp may either be a replacement for an existing incandescent lamp fixture, or may be installed as a new fixture. We will describe the procedure for a replacement. If yours is to be a new fixture, follow the procedure described in "Installing a New Ceiling Fixture."

Before beginning any work, deenergize the lamp fixture. If your home is properly wired, with switching done in the black wire, turning off the wall switch will deenergize the fixture. If you are uncertain about the wiring, however, then pull the fuse or trip the circuit breaker. With the circuit dead, you might need a flashlight — or a trouble light with a cord long enough to reach the nearest live outlet — to see what you are doing.

How To Install A Fluorescent Lamp

REMOVE THE hardware that holds the existing lamp fixture in place, and disconnect the lamp fixture wires from the A.C. line wires. If your fluorescent fixture requires them, attach a canopy and stem.

Disassemble the fluorescent fixture as far as necessary for access to the fixture wires. Run a length of lamp cord through the stem, and connect its end to the fixture wires and to the A.C. line wires with solderless connectors. Try to maintain the wire color continuity: white wire to white wire, black wire to black wire.

Place the fixture into the ceiling position, and fasten it to the ceiling box with the screws provided in the new fluorescent fixture. You may find it necessary to reassemble the fluorescent fixture either before or after affixing it to the ceiling box, depending on the style of the fixture. Restore the power, and turn on your newly installed fluorescent lamp.

Repairing Fluorescent Lamps

AS CAN BE expected fluorescent lamps get dimmer with age, and

188

they may even begin to flicker or flash on and off. The best way to avoid an extensive repair is to replace the lamp as soon as it becomes noticeably dim. Otherwise, the worn-out lamp can be hard on the other parts. Repeated flashing wears out the starter, and it can eventually cause insulation failure in the starter.

Any of the fluorescent lamp fixture parts — lamp, starter switch, or ballast — can be electrically tested to determine if it is good or bad, but testing is not necessary. The fixture can be serviced quite simply by the substitution method. If you suspect a part to be defective, install a new one in its place to restore operation. The results of the substitution immediately show you if your diagnosis is correct.

Start with the fluorescent tube. You can either put in a new one or try the lamp in another fixture (if you have one). Doing both procedures gives you double verification. Throw away the defective tube, but do so with care, Perhaps you are aware of the possible hazard in throwing away fluorescent bulbs. Yougsters have been injured by glass cuts and the effects of the chemicals inside the bulb when removing discarded bulbs from trash containers. Therefore, either hide the bulb at the bottom of the trash container or destroy the bulb. To destroy it safely, wrap the bulb in heavy paper (grocery bags are good), break it with a hammer, and stuff the still-wrapped broken glass in another bag.

If the problem is not in the bulb, make a substitution for the starter. Since starters are rated according to lamp wattage, be sure to use the correct replacement.

That leaves the ballast until last, and rightly so. The ballast is the least likely part to fail, and it is the most difficult to replace. If, however, neither bulb nor starter proves to be defective, the problem must be the ballast. To replace the ballast, deenergize the circuit, and disassemble the fixture in the reverse of procedures given for installing a fluorescent lamp. Observe that since the ballast also is rated according to lamp wattage, a correct wattage replacement should be obtained. In replacing the ballast, transfer wires one at a time from the old ballast to the new ballast to avoid an incorrect connection. Finally, reassemble the fixture exactly as you would were you installing a new fluorescent lamp.

189

Installing A Clock Receptacle

ACLOCK ON a table, dresser, or night stand is fine, but there are probably a few places in your home where you would like to hang a clock on the wall. Almost invariably, the nearest outlet is in the wrong place. You can try to solve the problem either by letting the cord drape unattractively from the clock to the outlet or by putting the clock near an outlet where you really do not want it.

The ideal solution is to put an electric box right in the wall where you want the clock to go, install a clock receptacle in the box, and hang the clock over the outlet to hide the connection altogether. Pretty neat! The clock operates with no cord visible at all.

Here is the way it works: The clock outlet has a recessed receptacle deep enough to hold the entire plug cap. You cut the clock attachment cord down to a short length — no more than a few inches — and hang the clock on either a hanger-type cover plate or on some other hanger of your choice. Place the clock so that it covers both the outlet and its own short cord.

There are several ways of wiring a clock receptacle. You can extend the wiring from a nearby existing receptacle, up into the attic space, through rafters, and down into the wall to the clock outlet. If that is what you want to do, follow the instructions given in "Extending A Receptacle." If you want to run cable down inside the wall to the basement area and across to the circuit breaker or fuse box, follow the procedures outlined in "Installing a New Ceiling Lamp." The last installation is somewhat different from those in

190

Inset picture shows how much better clock looks when it is plugged into a receptacle immediately behind it, instead of trailing wire down wall to meet baseboard receptacle.

191

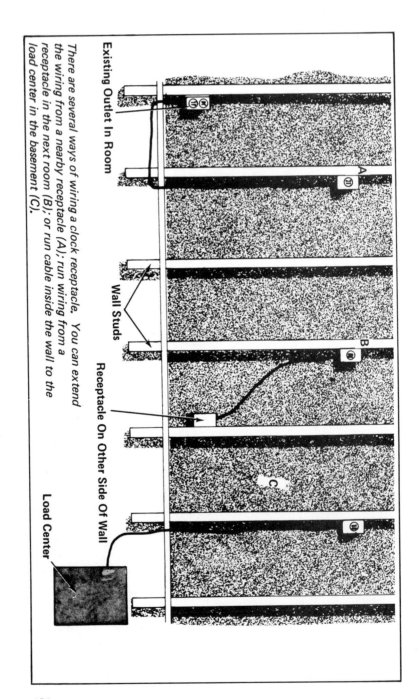

Existing Outlet In Room

Wall Studs

Receptacle On Other Side Of Wall

Load Center

There are several ways of wiring a clock receptacle. You can extend the wiring from a nearby receptacle (A); run wiring from a receptacle in the next room (B); or run cable inside the wall to the load center in the basement (C).

192

other sections. This situation is when there is a receptacle in the next room on the other side of the wall. Wiring is run from it up to the clock outlet.

Electric clock motors use very little electrical power — typically two to five watts! Extending from an existing receptacle to provide power for a clock outlet, therefore, adds practically nothing to the branch circuit. Do not forget that when working with household circuits you must observe basic electrical safety principles. Before starting to install the receptacle for the clock, deenergize the circuit. Pull the fuse or trip the circuit breaker to off. With the circuit dead because you removed the fuse or tripped the circuit breaker, you might need a flashlight or a trouble light with a cord long enough to reach the nearest live outlet in order to light the place where you are working.

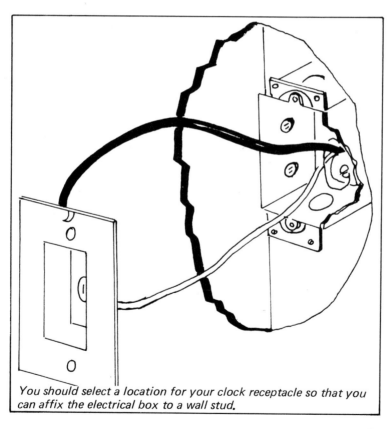

You should select a location for your clock receptacle so that you can affix the electrical box to a wall stud.

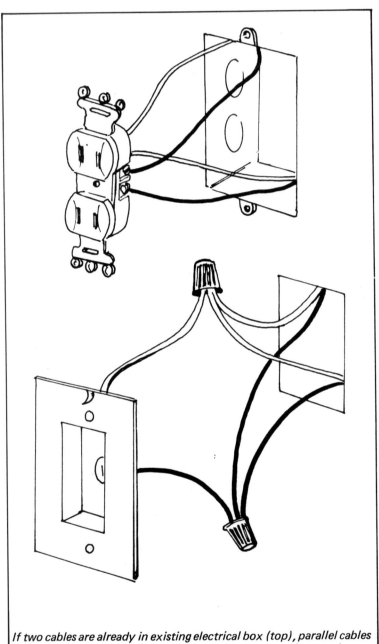

If two cables are already in existing electrical box (top), parallel cables by using short wire lengths and solderless connectors (bottom).

How to Install A Clock Receptacle

MEASURE THE distance from the new clock outlet location to the existing receptacle. Use this information to obtain the correct length of type NM cable. You might compare the per-foot cost of NM cable with the price of a full box — 50 feet, 100 feet, or 250 feet. If you know you will be doing more wiring later, you might find the full-carton economy to be worthwhile.

Outline on the wall the cut you plan to make to install the box for the clock outlet. Select a location alongside a stud (studs in the walls are 16 inches apart) so that the box can be affixed to it. Stay between the same two studs as the existing receptacle on the other side of the wall. If you are going to run cable from an outlet in the same room, refer to the discussion in "Extending a Receptacle." If you are going to run cable from the load center, refer to the discussion in "Installing a New Ceiling Lamp." Cut the hole for the outlet as described in "Extending a Receptacle."

Now, go to the outlet on the other side of the wall. Remove the cover plate, loosen the receptacle mounting screws, and pull the receptacle out as far as the attached screws allow.

Loosen the cable clamp, and remove a knockout in the box location most consistent to the cable from the clock outlet. Feed a suitable length of cable from the existing box to the hole you cut for the outlet. Or, you may find it handier to feed the cable from the hole into the existing box. Use the technique described in "Extending a Receptacle."

Attach the cable to the existing receptacle. If there already are two cables in the box, such that the spare mounting screws on the receptacle are already occupied, use short wire lengths and solderless connectors to allow attaching (paralleling) three cables.

Now, go to the clock outlet end. Loosen the clamp, and remove a knockout from the switch box. Run the cable through the knockout, and fasten the clamp. Place the box in the wall opening, and fasten it to the stud. If you find that the short space available makes it too awkward to affix a switch box to a stud, you can obtain the kind of switch box that is equipped with a flare type support bracket (Appleton 892, or the equivalent) that holds the box in the hole by gripping the backside of the wallboard or plaster wall.

Strip off the cable's outer cover, bare the wire ends, attach the cable to the clock receptacle, and fasten the bare wire under the clamp screw. Install the clock receptacle with the two screws provided. Restore the power by replacing the fuse or turning the circuit breaker to on.

Before altering the clock attachment cord, inspect the backside of the clock. Some clocks have a space for coiling up the excess cord

195

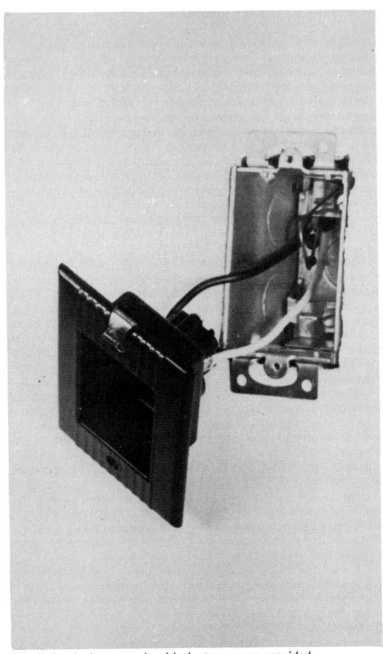

Install the clock receptacle with the two screws provided.

196

Trim excess cord or wrap it inside before hanging clock over outlet.

when the clock is to be plugged into a recessed outlet. If your clock does not have such a space, then the cord must be shortened.

Determine how much — or how little — cord it takes to let you plug the clock in while holding it close to its wall mount. Add three inches to the cord length to include the space you will need to set the clock, and cut the cord. Attach a new plug cap, set the clock, plug it in, and hang it up. The result: you have a no-cord-showing clock on the wall just where you want it.

197

Adding A Permanent Timer Device

DO YOU FEEL that a home security system is a must? If so, perhaps you know that one of the most effective security measures is to give the appearance that someone is at home when no one is. A good way to render the someone-at-home effect is by having lights burning and the TV turned on or a radio playing. Moreover, the effect can be even more realistic if, at a reasonable hour of the night, the lights go out and the radio goes off.

You can equip your home for the someone-at-home effect by installing a 24-hour timer switch that can turn the lights and radio on and off. Here are some of the ways you can employ the various kinds of timers:

- You can get a portable timer. The timer plugs into a receptacle, and the lamp and radio are plugged into an outlet on the timer.
- You can install a permanent timer switch in one of your outlets in place of the duplex receptacle. Such timers possess both time-controlled and continuous-on receptacles.
- You can install a heavy-duty timer. A circuit can be run from the load center through the timer to as many receptacles as you want to be governed by the timer.

Most people who need a timer because they are frequently away from their homes should install a permanent on-off device.

The timer is, basically, an on-off switch that is tripped by an electric clock motor. Equipped with a dial marked off for 24 hours, the timer can be set for the turn-on hour and for the turn-off hour. If, for example, you set the timer to switch the lights and radio on at 8:00 p.m. and off at midnight, it will do so repeatedly day after day until you return. Most timers are somewhat difficult to set closer than about five minutes to a selected time, but that should be close enough for your purposes.

Before starting to install a permanent timer, deenergize the circuit to the receptacle where the timer will go. Pull the fuse or trip the circuit breaker to off. With the circuit dead because you removed the fuse or tripped the circuit breaker, you might need a flashlight — or a trouble light with a cord long enough to reach the nearest live outlet — to see what you are doing.

How To Install A Timer Switch

REMOVE THE cover plate from the receptacle, and loosen the receptacle mounting screws. Pull out the receptacle, and disconnect the line wires from under the receptacle terminal screws.

If the timer switch has a mounting plate, attach the mounting plate to the outlet box with the screws provided. You might find

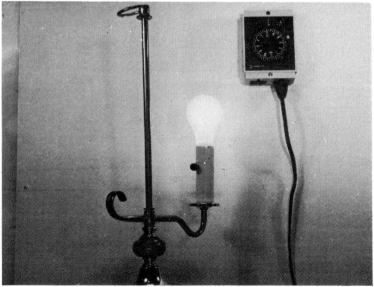

You can install a permanent timer switch in place of a receptacle.

199

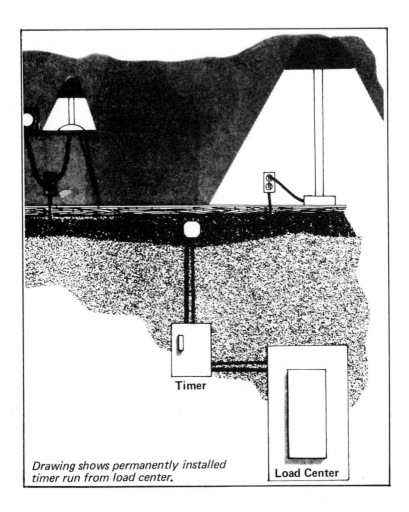

Timer

Drawing shows permanently installed
timer run from load center.

Load Center

that the manufacturer has attached the mounting plate to the timer, just to keep all the parts together. Detach the plate from the timer and fasten it to the outlet box.

Using solderless connectors, attach the timer wires to the circuit wires — black to black, white to white, green to ground. Solderless connectors are sized according to the quantity of various gauge wires the connector will attach safely. For this task you may need the "two #14" size.

Fasten the timer to the mounting plate, restore the power, and put the timer switch to use. Consult the instruction sheet supplied with your new timer switch for information on setting the turn-on and turn-off times.

Installing A Heavy-Duty Timer

NEXT, CONSIDER installing a heavy-duty timer switch. Well-known models include Paragon and Tork. Get the general-purpose type of timer with a single-pole single-throw (SPST) switch.

Since this kind of timer will switch at least 10 amperes, it can handle several security outlets. Prepare a sketch of the circuit to be controlled by your timer switch. It is a good idea to plan at least two outlets — one in the kitchen, one in the bedroom — or perhaps in three locations if yours is a large home. From the sketch, prepare a shopping list of the materials and supplies you will need. Your list will probably look something like this:

One general-purpose timer
Length of type NM cable
Several four-inch octagonal outlet boxes
Several 2x3 switch boxes
Several duplex receptacles
Solderless connectors, staples

If you plan your work such that the last task is connecting the timer-controlled network to the load center, you will be working with deenergized circuits until you get into the circuit breaker or fuse box. You may find it convenient to locate the timer near to the load center.

Mount the timer box, using expansion screw anchors or a similar fastener if you must attach the timer to a concrete or masonry wall. You will find it necessary to remove the screws holding the timer mechanism in its box; take out the mechanism to gain access to the mounting holes in the back panel of the box. Leave the timer mechanism out of the box until later.

Outline and cut the wall positions for the security outlets. Use the procedure described in "Extending A Receptacle." Drill holes in the inside wall floor and through the rafter joists, and pull the cable through the drilled holes to the wall outlet locations. Use the procedures discussed in "Installing a New Ceiling Fixture."

Mount the boxes, install the receptacles, and attach the cover plates as discussed in "Extending a Receptacle." Remove the knockouts from the timer box in the most favorable locations for incoming and outgoing cables. Install cable clamps in the knockouts. Run cable from the receptacles into the timer box, and fasten the clamps.

201

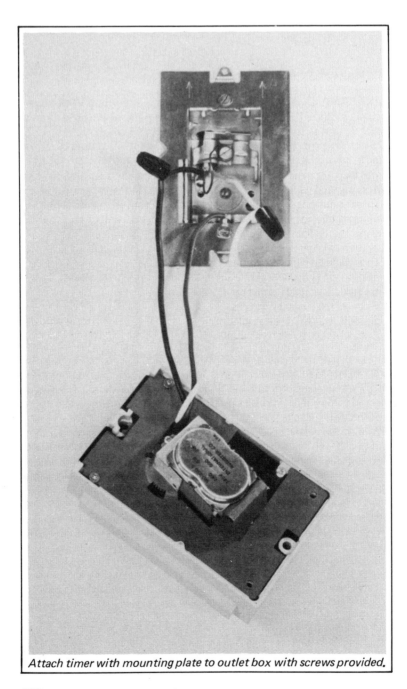

Attach timer with mounting plate to outlet box with screws provided.

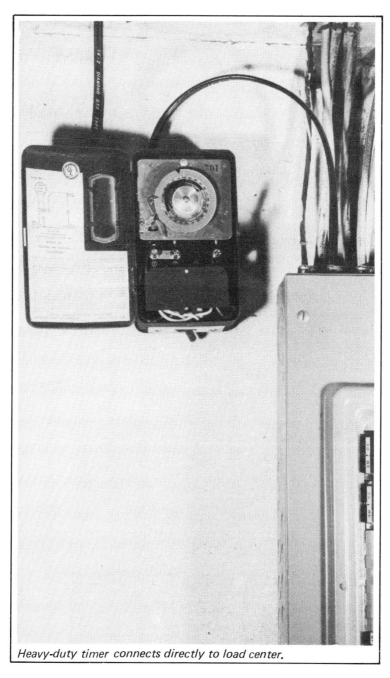

Heavy-duty timer connects directly to load center.

203

Open the load center door and turn the main switch to off. Your load center should contain the warning: "All circuit breaker handles must be in the off position to disconnect electrical service completely." Remove the cover from the load center.

Remove a knockout from the load center box in the location most convenient for a cable coming from the timer switch, and install a cable clamp. The cable with the loop is the short run from timer switch to load center. Run a cable from inside the timer switch box to inside the load center.

In the timer box, remove the outer cover and bare the ends of the conductors in the cable. Using solderless connectors, connect incoming and outgoing white wires. Attach the black wires to the timer terminals as shown by the diagram affixed to the inside of the door. Mount the timer in the box.

In the load center box, remove the outer cover and bare the cable ends. Attach white and bare wires to the ground bus. Attach the black wire under the terminal screw of the spare fuse or spare circuit breaker. Put the load center cover back on, and trip the main switch or circuit breakers to on.

Set the timer to the desired turn-on and turn-off hours. Test each timer-controlled receptacle with a lamp. The fact that the lamp actually does turn on and off at the preset times is proof that you installed your heavy-duty timer correctly.

Creating Outdoor Lighting Effects

OF ALL THE kinds of electrical wiring chores, installing outside lights probably gives you the best opportunity to exercise imagination and ingenuity in creative lighting. The results — a pool of light in the surrounding darkness — often exceeds even your fondest expectations. Lighting a walk, outlining a driveway, spotlighting an attractive garden spot, floodlighting an unusual tree, — these are but a few of the many things you can do with outside lighting. As you will see, outside wiring poses no new electrical problem; it is just that the materials and methods are different from indoor wiring.

For outdoor wiring you need a special type of nonmetallic sheathed cable — type UF, designed for direct burial in the ground. Its outer sheath of tough plastic is unaffected by being in the earth. For the purpose of an example, let us assume that you want an "escort" light alongside a sidewalk. The specific steps required illustrate the general principles for installing virtually any kind of outside wiring.

From the load center (we assume it is the basement), wiring goes through the wall outside, where you locate a weatherproof electrical box and a switch. From the switch, you put type UF cable down into the ground to a depth of not less than 18 inches, then through a trench over to a fixture. The cable runs up into the fixture, and back out to a second — or more — fixture(s).

Notice that you put no boxes underground where they would be totally inaccessible. To protect the wire and to support the fixture upright, rigid conduit is used where the cable enters and leaves the

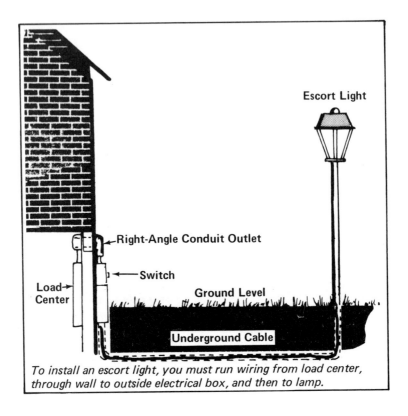

Escort Light

Right-Angle Conduit Outlet

Switch

Load Center

Ground Level

Underground Cable

To install an escort light, you must run wiring from load center, through wall to outside electrical box, and then to lamp.

ground. You must use the galvanized iron type conduit to forestall corrosion.

In the following steps, you do all the outside wiring first, leaving until last the connection to the load center. In that way, you will be working with circuits that are not energized until you have nearly completed the installation.

How To Install Outdoor Wiring

MEASURE THE length of the cable run from the interior of your home to the lamp socket in the outdoor fixture (or fixtures if you have decided on more than one). For the smaller fixtures that take no larger than a 100-watt bulb, you probably will use the 14-2 size cable ("w/g" means "with (bare) ground wire"). When measuring the distance from the fixture, add on enough to allow for the fact that your wiring never goes along the identical "shortest-distance"

206

path that your measuring tape followed. A length of cable that "just barely makes it," leaving you a short piece in the electrical box is — at best — exasperating; sometimes, it is virtually impossible to work with.

In the steps that follow, several of the procedures overlap. Therefore, be sure to read all the steps before starting the job to avoid unnecessary "backtracking" when making the underground installation.

The next step is to drill the hole for running cable from inside your home to the outside. Put a length of conduit in the hole; attach the boxes to the ends of the conduit; and run the cable inside the conduit. If you are using size 14-2 w/g cable, a length of 1/2-inch conduit will do. Preferably, it should be Electrical Rigid Conduit. Rigid conduit is the same size as the pipe used for plumbing, but it is made of a softer steel and can, if necessary, be bent to go around corners. In the short piece you need, no bending is required.

Drill a 7/8-inch hole for the conduit from the inside to the outside of your house. Often the best location for the hole is through, or immediately above, the wood plate at the top of the foundation. If, at your chosen location, there is masonry (bricks, concrete, stucco, or concrete blocks), you must use a suitable masonry drill to make the hole.

Dig a narrow trench, at least 18 inches deep, from the location of the yard light to a position immediately below your hole in the wall. Lay the cable in the trench, but do not bury it yet. You will have to maneuver the cable some before you are through.

Install the following electrical pieces at the point in the wall where you drilled the hole: the 18-inch length of conduit, the weatherproof box, the close nipple, the right-angle conduit outlet, and a length of conduit equal to the distance through the hole in the wall plus its threaded ends. The opening on the conduit outlet should face the same way as the open end of box. Feed the end of the type UF cable from the trench up through the hole in the wall and the 18-inch conduit into the weatherproof box, leaving a six-inch length in the box. Locate the assembly in place with the other conduit run through the hole in the wall and the 18-inch conduit down in the trench. Avoid a sharp bend where the cable leaves the conduit to run through the trench.

Inside the house, affix a four-inch octagonal box or conduit outlet to the end of the through-the-hole conduit. If you use an octagonal box, remove the 1/2-inch knockout in the bottom of the box, thread a 1/2-inch locknut in all the way on the threaded end of the conduit, put the box on through its knockout, and tighten another 1/2-inch locknut on the conduit inside the box. You may need to put some kind of spacer (a piece of plywood, perhaps) behind the octagonal

207

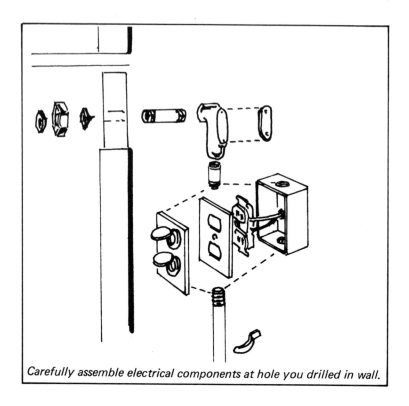

Carefully assemble electrical components at hole you drilled in wall.

box to allow you to fasten the box to the wall with screws or whatever you need to use.

Outside the house, affix the electrical parts firmly to the wall with conduit clamps. Locate one clamp right below the weather-proof box. Screw an 18-inch piece of conduit on the yard fixture. You might want one longer than 18 inches. Add 18 inches to the distance you want the fixture to be above ground, and get a piece that length. Or, you might want a still longer piece so that you can put the underground part deeper than 18 inches to be sure that it will be solid in the ground when you put the dirt back in the trench.

Next, disassemble the yard fixture far enough so that you can get to the terminal screws on the lamp socket. Run the end of the UF cable up through the conduit into the lamp fixture, allowing sufficient cable length in the fixture for baring the wires and attaching them to the socket terminal screws. If you want more than one fixture, run a cable up into the fixture and run another down to the next fixture.

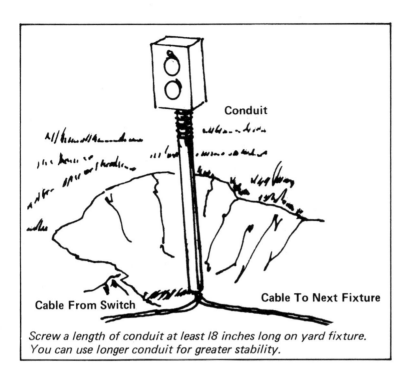

Conduit

Cable From Switch

Cable To Next Fixture

Screw a length of conduit at least 18 inches long on yard fixture. You can use longer conduit for greater stability.

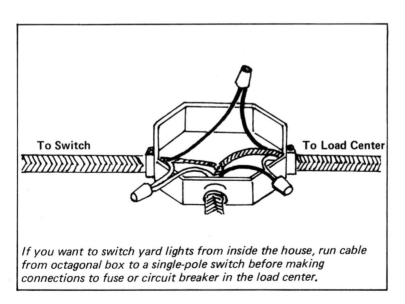

To Switch

To Load Center

If you want to switch yard lights from inside the house, run cable from octagonal box to a single-pole switch before making connections to fuse or circuit breaker in the load center.

209

Use wirenuts to join the wires; do not try to put two wire ends under one screw.

Place the fixture in its intended location with the end of the conduit at the bottom of the trench, being careful not to put a sharp bend in the cable. Fill in the trench. At the yard fixture socket, bare the cable ends and attach the conductors under the socket terminal screws. Reassemble the fixture — complete with bulb, globe, and deflector.

Back at the house, remove the cover plate from the right-angle conduit outlet. Run a suitable length of UF cable from inside the house through the conduit in the wall and down into the weatherproof box. The open side of the conduit outlet allows you to handle the cable in going around a corner and down to the weatherproof box. Replace the conduit outlet cover plate.

Bare the ends of the two cables at the weatherproof box. Join white wire to white wire with a solderless connector, and wrap the joint with plastic electrical tape. Connect the two black wires to a single-pole switch. Actually, the switch does not have to be located at this spot; you can have the switch inside the house. If you want the switch inside, omit the weatherproof box and fasten the conduit directly to the right-angle conduit outlet.

From octagonal box, run a length of NM cable (of the same size as the underground UF cable) to the load center, and attach the cable to a fuse or circuit breaker. Be certain, of course, that you first deenergize the load center by opening the load center door and turning the main switch to off.

If you want to switch the yard lights from inside the house, run a length of NM cable (of the same size as the underground UF cable) from the octagonal box to a single pole switch, before you run the cable to the load center. Make the connections inside the box; then connect the cable to the fuse or circuit breaker in the load center.

Finally, put a blank cover plate on the octagonal box, and turn the power back on. Installing outdoor wiring may seem like a great deal of trouble, but you will be so pleased with your new lighting effects that the work will certainly be worthwhile.

Installing A 240-Volt Receptacle

YOU BUY a new electric dryer (or range or window air conditioner), and when it arrives you discover that it operates not on 120 but on 240 volts. "You can't plug it into a 120-volt outlet; you need 240 for it," you are told. You find that you need a cable run from the load center to a location close enough to the appliance in order that you can plug in the thick cord that carries the 240 volts.

The range, the dryer, the air conditioner — these appliances draw a great deal of power. That is why they operate on 240 volts; that is why they are equipped with what are obviously heavy cables for heavy currents. For the same reason, the receptacle and the cable leading to it are of the heavy-duty type. Here is what you will find:

- Receptacles and cord sets for ranges are rated at 50 amperes; the cord set contains two No. 6 and one No. 8 conductors.
- Receptacles and cord sets for dryers are rated at 30 amperes; the cord set contains three No. 10 conductors.
- Receptacles and cord sets for window air conditioners are rated at 10 to 20 amperes; the cord set contains three No. 12 conductors.

The first thing to do is examine the end of the plug cap on the appliance cord. The prong and blade configuration is your guide to obtaining the correct receptacle, which must have mating holes for the prongs and blades. Since there are several varieties, and you prob-

211

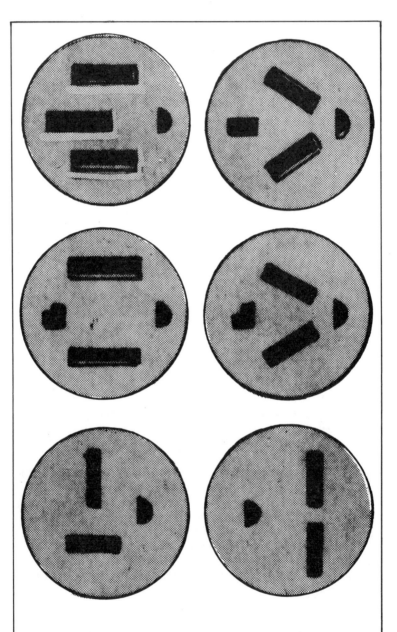

Since there are so many prong patterns, be sure that the one on your new 240-volt receptacle matches the plug cap on the appliance.

212

ably do not want to take the cord off the appliance just to carry it along when you buy the receptacle, make sure of the contact configuration.

Next, make some measurements and draw up a sketch showing where your wiring is to go — from outlet location to load center. From your sketch, calculate the length of NM cable you will need. Add to the distance the length going to the receptacle, plus that going to the load center.

To prevent the possibility of mechanical damage, that portion of the NM cable going from the outlet up to the ceiling is run through thinwall tubing. "Thinwall" is trade jargon for electrical metallic tubing — EMT — a steel tube that is somewhat thinner than plumbing-type pipe and is especially made for electrical work. EMT is sold in 10-foot sections, and cut to the required length. It should be cut with a tubing cutter, but with care it can be cut with a hacksaw. The cut end must be carefully reamed to remove all sharp edges in order that there is nothing to scrape or damage the cable which is run through the tubing.

A thinwall fitting is required to attach the length of EMT to the receptacle box. Two types are available: one kind is fastened to the tubing with an indenter tool that impresses a ring of dimples on the fitting to affix it to the tubing; the other type of fitting is attached by tightening a nut on the fitting, thereby compressing it on the tubing. Because no special tool is needed, you will probably favor using the compression type fitting.

At the knockout location on the receptacle box, there are two concentric circular indentations. Removing the center knockout disk leaves an opening for a 3/4-inch thinwall fitting; removing the ring as well increases the knockout opening to the size for a one-inch conduit fitting. Both box and tubing are fastened to the wall by conduit clamps.

From the 240-volt receptacle, you run cable to the load center. If you leave the attachment in the load center until last, you need not turn off the power until you are well into the installation.

How To Install A 240-Volt Receptacle

DETERMINE THE location of the receptacle so that it will be convenient to your appliance requirements. Measure the distance from the ceiling down to the top of the receptacle, and cut a piece of thinwall to that length. Be sure that the cut end is thoroughly reamed to remove the sharp inner rim. Remove the knockout from the receptacle box and connect the thinwall to the receptacle.

Fasten the thinwall and receptacle to the wall, using wood

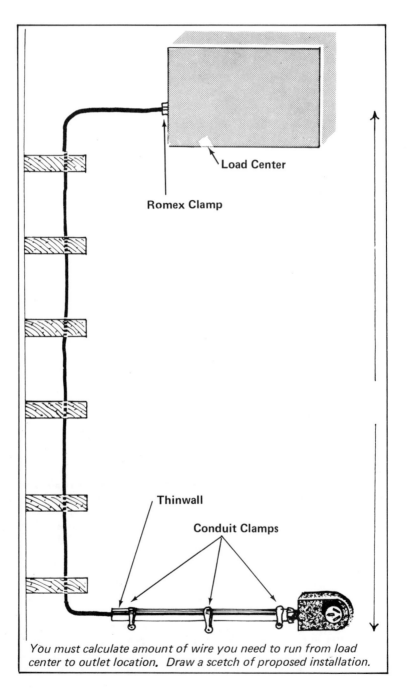

Load Center

Romex Clamp

Thinwall

Conduit Clamps

You must calculate amount of wire you need to run from load center to outlet location. Draw a scetch of proposed installation.

214

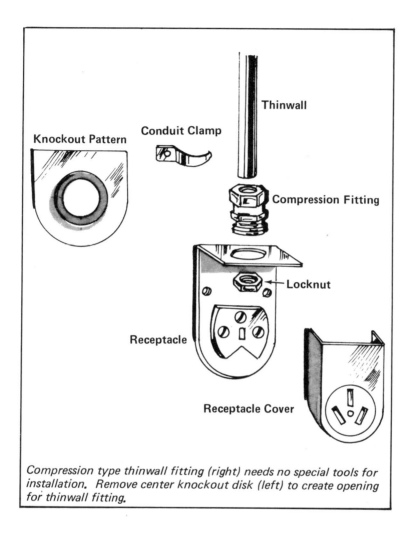

Knockout Pattern

Conduit Clamp

Thinwall

Compression Fitting

Locknut

Receptacle

Receptacle Cover

Compression type thinwall fitting (right) needs no special tools for installation. Remove center knockout disk (left) to create opening for thinwall fitting.

screws to affix to a wooden wall or expansion anchors to affix to a concrete or masonry wall. Install a conduit clamp at the top, another at the bottom, and clamps at intervals of three feet between top and bottom.

From the top of the thinwall, feed the NM cable down through the thinwall into the outlet box. Secure the NM cable with a staple at the point of entry to the thinwall. Since the thinwall-to-outlet box connector contains no gripping arrangement, the cable is held in

215

position by the nearest staple, and the one where the thinwall starts is the nearest staple.

Bare the cable ends and attach the wires under the receptacle terminal screws. Most likely, you will find printing adjacent to the screws to show you where to attach the red, black, and white wires. Drill holes in the rafters to run the cable from the receptacle to the load center. Deenergize the load center by opening the load center door and turning the main switch to off.

Install the cable in the load center. Remove the outer cable cover and bare the cable ends. Attach the white and bare wires to the ground bus, and attach the black wire under the terminal screw of the spare fuse or spare circuit breaker. Since you are wiring a 240-volt circuit, you connect wires in the circuit breaker type load center to a double-pole circuit breaker — the kind with two switches tied together such that both are tripped simultaneously. Red and black wires go under the two screws on the double-pole circuit breaker. Use either a spare circuit breaker or install a new double-pole unit.

Put the load center cover back on, and trip the main switch circuit breakers to on. You now have a 240-volt receptacle ready to supply power to your new appliance.

Adding
A Circuit Breaker

IN SEVERAL of the projects in this book, it has been suggested that, in running cable back to the load center, you tie into an empty spare circuit. But suppose there is no spare? Then one must be added. Look in the load center in your home to see if it has spaces where front panel metal segments are prepunched to allow knockout removal. These spaces on the panel are there to allow you to add new branch circuits. Many homes have electrical service that allows more branch circuits to be added as needed. Provision is made in the load center for installation of additional fuses or circuit breakers — mainly circuit breakers since that type of load center has, for many years, been the favorite of building contractors.

There are, of course, many makes of load centers; however, the principles to be outlined here for installing a new circuit are quite typical for virtually all load centers. The steps involved are essentially the same, and the parts involved look quite similar.

Any time you are working inside the load center panel box, of course, you face an electrical hazard. The first thing to consider, therefore, is caution. Since the load center is often in such a location that you — standing in a position to work on it — could possibly be grounded, it is advisable to place a sheet of dry plywood on the floor and be sure to remain on the plywood all the time you are working on the load center.

The wires entering the load center from the meter connect to buses — metal strips to which the circuit breakers are connected. If

217

Knockout Removed For New Circuit Breaker

Load centers often have spaces on the panel to allow you to add new branch circuits. Look for prepunched metal segments.

You can install a new circuit breaker yourself, but your must stay away from the "hot" buses in the load center.

219

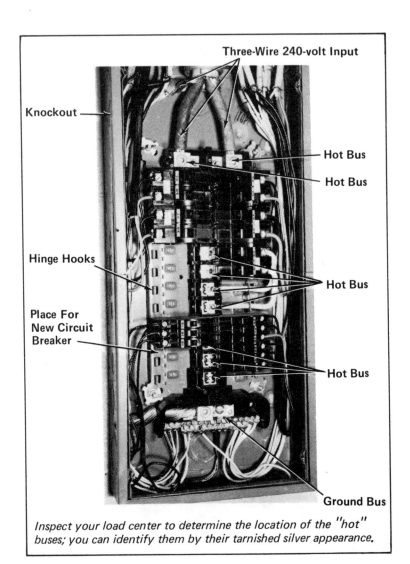

Three-Wire 240-volt Input

Knockout

Hot Bus

Hot Bus

Hinge Hooks

Hot Bus

Place For
New Circuit
Breaker

Hot Bus

Ground Bus

Inspect your load center to determine the location of the "hot" buses; you can identify them by their tarnished silver appearance.

your load center does not have a main switch (the one in our example does not), these buses must remain deenergized while you are adding the new circuit breaker. Inspect your load center; you can usually identify the buses as the metal pieces that look like tarnished silver. Never touch the buses!

A new circuit breaker can be installed in the load center without

220

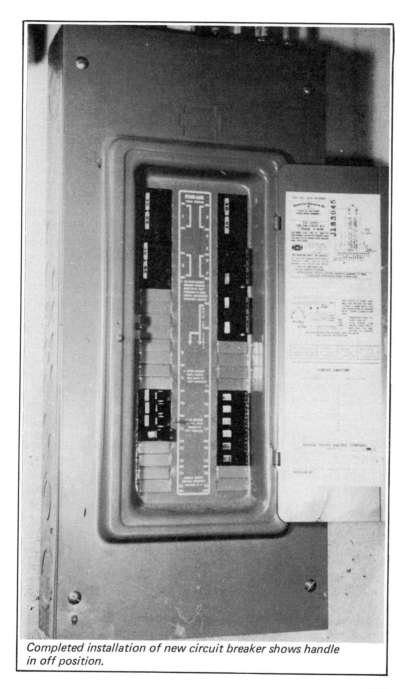

Completed installation of new circuit breaker shows handle in off position.

221

your touching anything in the box other than the plastic circuit breaker housing. Working cautiously, you can — you must — avoid ever touching an energized spot.

How To Add A Circuit Breaker

DETERMINE how many devices and appliances you wish to place on the new circuit, and add up the total wattage that would be drawn were all turned on at the same time. The wattage total determines the size wire you will need. For our example, we will assume that you have a total load on your new circuit of less than 1440 watts, and that you are adding a 15-ampere circuit breaker using 14-2 w/g, type NM cable.

There is a label inside the door of your load center that provides information for your use. From the information on the inside of the load center door, determine the kind and size of circuit breaker you need. Remove the front panel from your load center and lay it aside. Exercise great caution throughout the following procedures, and adhere closely to the directions you are given for electrical safety. Determine which parts are "hot" and must not, under any circumstances, be touched.

Inspect your new circuit breaker. Notice that one end is shaped to latch into a metal hinge in the box, and that the other end is a copper or silvery conductor clip that hooks into the "hot" bus bar. Before putting it in, be sure you understand just how your circuit breaker snaps into place. Remember, some parts in the panel are "hot"; you must be able to visualize exactly how you will clip in the circuit breaker safely before doing it.

Holding only the outer part near the switch handle, fasten the new circuit breaker into position; it takes only a moment to latch it into the hinge and snap the conductor tab into the bus bar. Make sure that the new circuit breaker is in the off position.

Remove the panel knockout that will allow the circuit breaker handle to extend through. You are now ready to run the cable from a branch circuit to the new circuit breaker.

Remove a knockout from the top, side, or bottom of the load center box. Install a cable clamp in the knockout hole, run the cable into the load center box, and tighten the clamp.

Remove the outer cover from the cable, and bare the wire ends for a distance of about 3/4 of an inch. Loosen the circuit breaker terminal screw a few turns, insert the black wire end under the screw, and tighten the screw. Fasten the white and bare wires under vacant spare screws on the ground bus, put the load center cover back on, and trip the circuit breaker to on. You now have another circuit breaker in your load center.

222

Electrical Troubleshooting Chart

LAMPS

Problem: Lamp blows fuses or trips circuit breaker.

Possible Causes

1. Overloaded circuit.

2. Short circuit in socket, in cord, or in lamp wiring.

Repairs

1. Check the total load on the circuit. If the circuit is overloaded, transfer some appliances to a different circuit.
2. Replace socket and cord. Rewire carefully to make sure that no bare wires touch each other or any metal parts of the lamp.

Problem: Lamp flickers when moved or touched.

Possible Causes

1. Lamp bulb loose in socket.

Repairs

1. Tighten bulb.

223

Possible Causes

2. A loose connection, usually where the line cord wires are fastened under the terminal screws on the lamp socket.

3. Defective contacts or faulty switch in socket.

4. Defective switch (if switch is separate from socket).

Repairs

2. First make sure that the lamp is unplugged; then take the socket apart and inspect the wire connections under the screws. Tighten or, if so indicated, cut off a short length of cord and reattach wire ends.

3. After you make sure that the cord is unplugged, remove the socket and replace with a new one.

4. Remove the switch and replace with a new one.

Problem: Lamp will not go on at all.

Possible Causes

1. Defective bulb or faulty receptacle.

2. Socket has defective contacts or a faulty switch.

3. Defective switch (if switch is separate from socket).

4. Defective lamp cord.

Repairs

1. Put in a new bulb; then plug lamp into a different outlet. Make sure that you are changing to a good bulb, as shown by its satisfactory operation in a different lamp.

2. Remove socket and replace with a new one.

3. Remove switch and replace with a new one.

4. Replace cord. Rewire carefully to make sure no bare wires touch each other or any metal parts of the lamp.

FLUORESCENT LAMPS

Problem: Lamp will not light.

Possible Causes

1. "Burned out" lamp.

Repairs

1. Replace with a new fluorescent lamp of correct dimensions and wattage.

224

Possible Causes	Repairs
2. Defective starter.	2. Replace starter with one of appropriate wattage.
3. Defective ballast, usually accompanied by the odor of burning insulation.	3. Consider the cost of a new ballast in comparison to the value of the lamp fixture before replacing the ballast.

Problem: Lamp glows dimly.

Possible Causes	Repairs
1. Defective lamp.	1. Replace lamp. If lamp has been flashing on and off repeatedly, for an extended period, the starter also should be replaced.
2. Defective starter.	2. Replace starter with one of correct wattage.

Problem: Lamp flashes on and off repeatedly.

Possible Causes	Repairs
1. Defective lamp.	1. Replace lamp and starter.
2. Defective starter.	2. Replace starter with one of correct wattage.

DOORBELLS OR CHIMES

Problem: Bell or chimes do not ring.

Possible Causes	Repairs
1. Defective button.	1. Test by removing button and touching wires together. If bell rings, it proves that the button is defective and must be replaced.

225

Possible Causes	Repairs
2. Defective bell or chimes.	2. Detach wires from bell or chimes and connect them to a spare bell, buzzer, or chime. If substitute bell rings when doorbell button is depressed, it proves that your present bell is defective and must be replaced.
3. Defective transformer.	3. Connect test bell to transformer and press door button. If bell does not ring, it proves that the transformer is defective and must be replaced.

Simple Household Repairs

Whether you live in an apartment or a house, you are constantly confronted with needed repairs. What about those three big holes in the wall you made when you were trying to hang the picture in the living room? What about that bedroom door that sticks, or the one that does not latch properly? You can make these repairs quickly and easily, and save yourself money in the process.

Replacing Broken Windows

IF YOU live in a neighborhood that has a budding Hank Aaron or a potential Joe Namath, then you are probably all too familiar with broken window panes. Replacing these broken panes is a fairly easy job, and if you follow our directions and suggestions, it will be an almost painless one.

Removing The Broken Glass

THE FIRST step toward replacement is removal of the old glass. And how do you do that? Very carefully! It is always a good idea to wear gloves while removing the slivers. Wiggle the pieces back and forth until they come out. If some pieces are stubborn, do not force them out. Instead, use a hammer and tap them toward the outside until they fall out. Your cleanup chores will be easier if you have a large box outside to catch the pieces. You can pick up little slivers of glass by dabbing at them with wet facial tissue.

After you remove the glass, scrape away all the putty that is left. Putty that is all dried out is difficult to remove. Since heat will soften it, play the flame from a propane torch over the putty; but be careful not to leave the flame on any one spot long enough to char the frame or start a fire. Another heat source you can use is a hot soldering iron held against the putty. If you do not have a propane torch or a soldering iron, you can brush linseed oil over the surface to help soften the putty.

Glass cutting (top) is not difficult, but it does take time and practice to learn to do it proficiently. After the pane and points are set in the frame, create a triangular seal of putty with a putty knife (bottom). Make the seal match the other windows.

If the broken window is in a wooden frame, you will find some small metal triangles hidden in the putty. These are called glazier's points. Save them. If the window frame is metal, save the spring clips you will find when you remove the putty.

Remove the last traces of the old putty with coarse sandpaper or a wire brush. The wire brush wheel attachment for a power drill is especially good on metal frames. With a wooden frame,

229

painting over the newly exposed wood with linseed oil seals the wood and prevents it from drinking the oil out of the putty.

Getting The New Glass

NOW COMES a very crucial step — measuring the opening for the new pane. Measure the inside of the frame both vertically and horizontally, and subtract about 1/8 of an inch from each measurement (with a very narrow frame, subtract a little less). The reason for the subtraction is so that the pane will be a bit smaller than the frame in which it is to be set. The glass should be a bit smaller to allow for any expansion due to temperature changes which could otherwise crack the glass. It also compensates for the fact that many frames are not perfect rectangles. Right before you leave to buy the new pane, measure the opening one more time — just to be sure.

While the hardware dealer is cutting the pane to size, go pick up a can of glazier's putty or glazier's compound. You will find that the compound is a little easier to work with, and it is less likely to harden and crack in the future.

If you are just replacing one or two panes, have them cut to size at the hardware store; but if you have a great many windows to replace, you can save money by purchasing larger sheets of glass and cutting your own window panes. Glass cutting is not difficult, but it does require a little practice to become proficient enough to cut right every time.

Actually, a glass cutting tool does not cut the glass. It merely scores a line. Then you snap the glass so that it breaks cleanly along the line.

Start with clean glass. Dirt of any kind can cause the cutter wheel to skip, and you cannot get a good break without an evenly scored line. Make sure that the cutter wheel is clean and sharp. When the wheel starts to dull, invest the small amount a new glass cutter costs. Dip the wheel in a lubricant; machine oil or kerosene is good. In addition, dip a rag into the lubricant and rub it over the glass along the line you plan to cut.

Place the sheet of glass on a flat surface that is covered with several layers of newspapers for cushioning. You need a straightedge — a wooden yardstick is good — along the line to be cut. Hold the straightedge down tight so that it cannot slip as you move the cutter tool along. You should always wear safety goggles, and some people like to wear lightweight gloves as well.

Draw the tool across the glass with a steady, even pressure. One pass is all you get. The only way to know what the right

230

pressure to use is to practice on the edge of what will become the scrap glass. The scored line does not have to be deep, but it must be straight and even. Too much muscle will produce a chipped line, while too little will not score all the way across the glass. Hold the glass cutter at a slight angle, and make sure that the wheel is parallel with the straightedge.

Once you master the touch, score the actual line. Start with the wheel not quite at the edge furthest from you. Make your pass, and let the wheel come right on off the edge of the glass closest to you.

Now you are ready for the break. Here you really should wear the gloves. Place the glass on a table with the line running along the edge. Press down on the glass on the table, and hold it firmly in place. Grab the edge of the scrap piece, and bend it downward. It should snap off along the line.

Another way to make the break is to place a yardstick under the glass along the scored line. Press down on both sides of the line with palms flat, and the glass will separate. Some glaziers merely place a pencil under the scored line, hold the pane steady, press down sharply at the edges, and the glass breaks all the way up to the other end. Always make your break of each line immediately after scoring it. If you wait, the glass will not break as cleanly.

Unless you practice your cutting technique, the money you save in buying a big pane of glass will be splintered away in broken pieces. Proficiency is the only answer.

Setting the Pane

TO SET the pane, first dig out a blob of the putty and roll it between your hands until it becomes a long string about as big around as a pencil. Press the putty against the frame all the way around where the glass is to fit. Now you are ready to press the window pane in place.

Panes of glass are not completely flat. If you sight along the edge, you can see that the pane possesses a slight curve. The side that bows out should face the outside. If it is a small piece of glass, you may not be able to detect the curve; but if you can spot it, put the glass in right.

Working from the outside of the frame, press the pane in place, Push it firmly against the bed of putty you applied to the frame. Putty will squeeze out of the frame on the inside of the glass; forget about it for now. Make sure that the glass is solidly against the putty all the way around the frame. If you spot any air pockets, push a little harder at these points.

231

Speaking of points, remember those glazier's points you saved? Now is the time to install them or the spring clips (for metal frames) to hold the glass in the frame. The clips are inserted into slots in the frame, while the points have to be pushed into the frame. Points should go in every four to six inches all the way around the frame. Use your putty knife to push them in place; they need not go in very far. If you have to tap them in with a hammer, be extremely careful not to break the new pane.

To finish off the outside, apply small blobs of putty all around against the glass and the frame. Press them in place, and then use your putty knife to create a smooth triangular seal that comes up flush with the outer edge of the molding and down to cover the inner frame that you can see through the glass. Look at the other panes around you, and try to make your putty seal match the others. Rake away the excess putty as you go around the outside of the frame, and put it back in the can. Now you can go inside and rake away the putty you squeezed out when you first put the glass in the frame.

After the putty has set for several days, you can paint it. Make sure that your paint goes all the way up to the frame and down to completely cover the putty, with just a hair of paint over onto the glass. The paint will seal the putty and prevent it from drying out.

Plexiglas

FOR LARGER windows in storm doors and in other areas where people may push against the glass, consider replacing the glass with an acrylic plastic sheet such as Plexiglas. The plastic is easy to work with and offers a safety factor that ordinary glass cannot match.

To glaze with Plexiglas, measure the opening and subtract the following thermal factors to compensate for expansion.

If long dimension measures: (in inches)	Subtract from both length and width
12 to 36	1/16 inch
37 to 48	1/8 inch
49 to 60	3/16 inch

Since Plexiglas comes in standard sheets, you will have to purchase a large enough sheet, and then cut it to size.

Cutting is easy. You can use a circular saw or a saber saw, but be sure to leave the backing paper on the Plexiglas. With a circular saw, use a plywood blade that has six teeth per inch. Set the

232

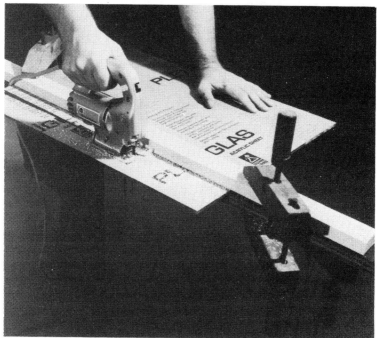

Since Plexiglas comes in standard sheets, you must cut it yourself. Use a circular or saber saw, and you will find that cutting is easy.

blade to stick up about 1/4 of an inch over the thickness of the plastic. When using a saber saw, use a blade with 24 to 32 teeth per inch for Plexiglas thicknesses up to 1/8 inch, and 14 to 24 teeth per inch for the thicker window material.

There are also scriber tools on the market that allow you to scribe a line on the sheet right through the backing paper, and then break the sheet at the line. It is recommended that you make from 5 to 10 passes along the line, depending on the sheet's thickness. Then, place the sheet over a 3/4-inch dowel that is positioned under the line. Holding the sheet steady with one hand, apply downward pressure on the short side with the other hand; the sheet should break at the line.

You can use regular glazing compound or any nonhardening sealant (such as silicon seal) to set Plexiglas in place. Remove the protective paper just before you press the pane against the compound. With this type replacement, you need not worry should even Hank Aaron himself hit a homer your way.

233

Silencing Squeaky Floors

IF YOU are embarrassed by a squeaking floor — always loudest when you are trying to sneak to the refrigerator for a midnight snack — maybe you can cure it. All floors that squeak do so as the result of movement, usually two boards rubbing against each other. The first thing you must do is locate the squeak.

If the flooring is hardwood, there are several tricks you can try to eliminate the squeak. One is to dust talcum powder into the cracks. Sweep it back and forth to get as much powder as possible between the boards. Powder can stop the squeaks, but the floors must be repowdered every so often as the powder sifts on down or is sucked up by the vacuum cleaner. Powdered graphite, you will discover, lasts longer than talcum powder. Another trick is to pour liquid floor wax or all-purpose glue between the cracks. Either of these liquids lasts longer than any of the powders.

Another method is to place a block of wood over newspapers on the floor and tap sharply with a hammer. Move all over the squeak and beyond to an area about two feet on all sides of the squeak. The pounding can often reseat loose nails that allow the boards to move.

These tricks are all easy to do, but sometimes more permanent repairs are needed. If the floor is exposed underneath (as in a crawl space or basement), go downstairs and look up while an accomplice steps on the squeaky spot. You can usually see movement in the sub-flooring. If you cannot see precisely where the movement oc-

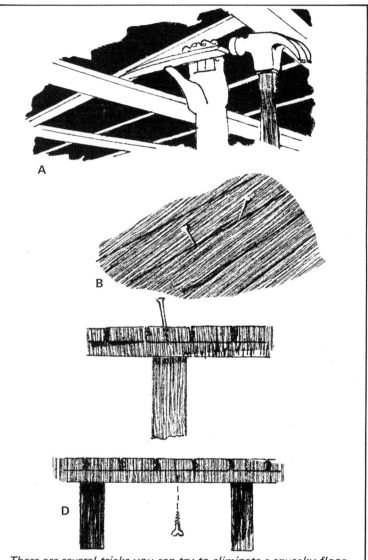

There are several tricks you can try to eliminate a squeaky floor. You can drive a wedge between the joist and the sub-floor boards (A). Or, you can drive 6d finishing nails in the crack between the moving boards (B). Sometimes, driving a 10d finishing nail through both layers of flooring and through the joist does the job (C). You can also try inserting a wood screw through the sub-flooring and on to the hardwood boards above (D).

curs, a magnet held right above the squeak and a compass below it will help you locate the trouble spot.

Once you know where the squeak is, you can sometimes drive a wedge between the joist and the moving sub-floor boards; the wedge pushes the boards up tight and stops any movement. If driving a wedge is not possible or does not silence the squeak, try inserting a wood screw through the sub-flooring and on up into the hardwood boards above. The screw should draw the two together. Make sure, however, that the screw is not so long as to go all the way through both layers, or else you will create a new problem. Drill a pilot hole for the screw.

If you cannot get underneath your hardwood floors, there are ways to attack from the top. If you ascertain that the squeak is caused by the hardwood boards rubbing each other, drive 6d finishing nails in the crack between the squeakers. A pair of nails 5 to 10 inches apart and at slight angles may silence the squeak; if not, try another pair in each adjoining crack. Drill pilot holes and use a nail set when you near the floor's surface. Then, countersink and cover with wood filler.

If the squeak is between the joist and sub-flooring — or between the two layers of flooring — and if there is no way to attack from the underside, use longer nails that can go through both layers and into the joist if possible. Try to locate the joist by sound. Put your ear to the ground and tap along the floor; you should be able to detect the hollow sound between joists. Toe nail 10d finishing nails, using the same procedure of pilot holes, nail set, and countersinking mentioned above.

If your squeak comes from under carpeting, vinyl tiles, or some other covering over sub-flooring — and there is no way to attack from underneath — you either have to remove the top covering or learn to live with the squeak. If you take the covering off, you can use nails or screws to pull the sub-flooring tight against the joists.

236

Simple Household Repairs

Patching
And Replacing
Window Screens

THE IDEA behind having screens over doors and windows is to keep bugs out while letting fresh air in. If there are holes or slits in the screen, however, the enterprising insect will find the hole and tell all his relatives. Besides, if it starts out as a tiny hole, it somehow enlarges each day, and soon every insect in the neighborhood can come in through the screen. Fortunately, screens are easy to patch, and although replacement is not so easy, it is a feasible do-it-yourself project.

Patching

MANY TIMES, a hole in a screen is the result of an object being poked through the screen. If the actual strands of wire are not broken, you can make the screen look like new. Simply use a sharp object, like an ice pick, to move the strands back toward the center of the hole.

If there are broken strands, but the hole is still very small, work the wires back with the ice pick, and then dab at the hole with clear fingernail polish or shellac. When one side dries, dab the other side. The polish or shellac closes the hole, prevents it from enlarging, and yet does not show.

You can repair larger holes by cutting a patch from a piece of the same type of screening material and fastening it over the hole. Cut the patch in a rectangular shape, and then peel away strands

237

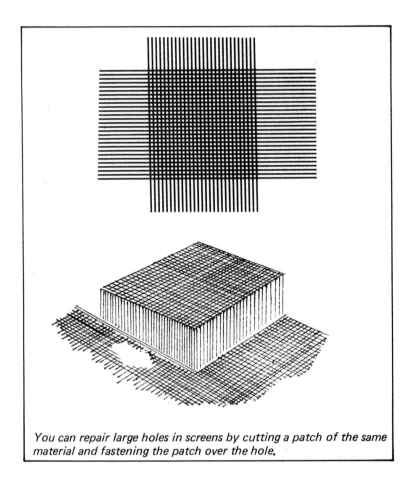

You can repair large holes in screens by cutting a patch of the same material and fastening the patch over the hole.

along all four sides to give you wire fingers about a quarter of an inch long. Bend the fingers over at right angles to the patch, and insert these into the openings in the screen all around the hole. Once all the fingers are through, and the patch is firmly against the screen, bend the fingers over underneath, and your patch is locked in place.

At first, the patch will stick out like a sore thumb, but as the new piece weathers, it will blend with the old screen. Patches are sold in packages at your hardware store. These factory-made patches have the additional advantage of providing finger ends that are already bent into hooks. As such, the patches are much easier to snap into place.

238

Another method of attaching a patch is to sew it in place with strands of wire unravelled from a scrap piece of screening. With the patch in place over the hole, you can weave the strand of wire in and out to attach the patch. Try to get the stitches as close as possible. Some people even use a needle and thread to sew on such patches.

When patching a plastic netting type of screen, you can glue the patch in place with plastic cement.

Replacement

WHEN THE hole poked through the screen grows so large that you can put your arm through it, you are usually faced with replacing the entire screen. If it is in a wooden frame, you must remove the old screen, taking extreme care to remove the flimsy molding without breaking it. Prying the molding off with a wide putty knife is the best way to go. You may find that the molding was put on with an automatic stapler; if so, clip off the ends of the staples rather than trying to drive them out. If small nails were used, you can usually tap them out.

Before you start putting the new screen on, examine the frame to see if it has any loose joints, and check it to be sure that the corners are square. If anything is wrong structurally, fix it. "L"-shaped metal mending plates are excellent for strengthening loose joints and also for keeping them on the square.

When putting the replacement screen in place, your biggest problem is in getting the material taut. If you just try to pull it tight, you will probably be unhappy with the effort. The best way is to bend the frame slightly. You can use a weight to cause the frame to bow down in the middle, but there are all sorts of ways to rig the frame to accomplish the same thing.

Once the frame is set up, attach the new screen material to one end of the frame. The best and easiest way to attach screening is with a staple gun. Now, pull the other end tight and staple it down. Remove the weight, and the frame will straighten out, leaving the screen very taut.

The rest of the job will go better on a solid surface; move the frame to the floor if you lack a work table big enough to accommodate it. Staple down the sides, starting at the center and working toward each end. Pull the screen tight as you go. If there is a center rail, staple the screen there after both sides are attached completely.

Trim off the excess screen using either tin snips or a utility knife, and replace the molding with small nails or brads. Countersink the brads and cover their heads with putty. Repaint the frame

239

if needed, rehang the screen, and hope that whatever caused the first hole will not attack this screen.

Aluminum Frames

ALUMINUM FRAMES are a different story, in which the screen is usually held in a channel in the frame by a flexible plastic spline. Sometimes, the spline gets out of the groove, and the screen pulls loose from the frame. Usually, you can pull the screen back tight, and force the spline back into the groove with a screwdriver, but there is a better way.

There is a special tool that makes it a snap to put the spline back in the groove. The tool has wheels that turn; one wheel has a goove, and the other is rounded. If you intend to replace screens in aluminum frames, this tool is a must.

There are some splines that are rigid plastic and fit into a larger square groove. You can put these back in the track easily by positioning a wood block over the spline and tapping it back in place with a hammer.

When replacing an entire screen, cut a screen at least as big as the overall frame. Place the frame on the floor or on another sort of flat surface, and use the lines of the wire in the screen as a guide to make sure that you have the screen on straight. Start pushing the spline in on one of the long sides. Pull the spline tight, but do not stretch it as you go along. Work all the way around the frame with one continuous piece of spline, or do the two long sides first with two pieces of spline. As you push the spline into the goove, the spline itself will pull the screen tight. Trim off the little excess screen that remains; tin snips or a utility knife will do the job.

You can buy replacement rolls of spline at most hardware stores, and purchase a splining tool there as well. All the materials you need to patch or replace screens are relatively inexpensive. The best time to work on screens, of course, is in the winter — when you do not need them. If you spot a hole that is letting bugs in, however, do not hesitate to patch.

Hanging Things On Walls

THERE IS nothing more exasperating than to hang a picture over the sofa and, as you step back to view the breathtaking effect, the picture crashes to the floor. Of course, not all wall hangings come down that quickly. Some wait until you have company, or they may come down in the middle of the night to scare the whole family. Yet, these disasters need not happen. There is a correct way to hang almost anything on any wall and to be fairly sure that it will stay there.

Inside Walls

MOST OF the walls today are hollow and of dry wall construction; the wall is made of something like gypsumboard or sheetrock, nailed to studs that form the framework of the wall. The wallboard may be textured over or covered over with a wall covering. If you just drive a nail into this material, the wallboard will crumble, and the weight of the hanging will gradually pull the nail out.

For fairly lightweight hangings — such as pictures and other items with wires or hooks on the back — you can use the picture hangers that work on the principle that a nail driven in at an angle with a flat piece on the outside helps spread the weight. There are two popular types. The first consists of just one piece. When using this type, put the point against the wall where you want the hanging to go and set the plate parallel with the wall. The other type consists of two pieces; the flat part of the hanger must line up with the

241

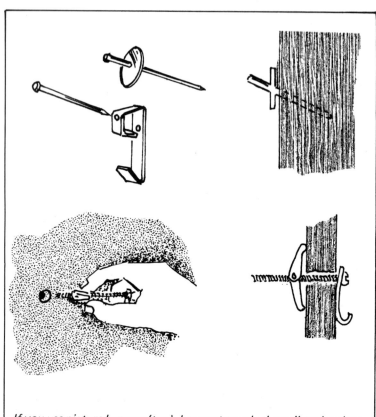

If you use picture hangers (top), be sure to angle the nail so the plate lies flat against the wall. Toggle bolts (bottom) are recommended for heavier hangings. Once the flange is inside the wall, tighten the bolt to make flange flare out against the inside of the wall.

wall so that it rests against the wall when driven in.

These hangers can hold from five to one hundred pounds, depending on their size. It is a good idea, however, any time that you drive any kind of nail into a gypsumboard wall to put a small piece of tape over the spot where the nail is to go. The tape helps prevent the wallboard from crumbling.

Finding The Studs

OF COURSE, if you can hit the studs when you drive a nail or screw into the wall, the nail or screw will be in very solid. There are ways

242

to locate the studs. One is to look for nails in the base molding. The nails are usually countersunk, but often a close look reveals where the nails are, which, in turn, indicates where the studs are. You will not find evidence like this on the quarter round molding because the nails are often driven into the floor or the base molding.

Another way to locate the studs is to tap along the wall. The space between studs has a hollow sound, while the wall directly over the studs sounds very solid. There are also magnetic stud finders that locate and point to the nails that hold the wallboard to the studs. Normally, the distance between the center of one stud and the one adjacent to it is sixteen inches. That is a good rough guide, but you cannot depend on it to be one hundred percent true. You are better off trying to locate each stud individually.

When you finally do locate the studs, they usually are never situated just where you want them to be to hang the picture. As a result, you wind up putting in some sort of wall anchor at the right spot on the wall. The most popular wall anchor is the expansion bolt, commonly called the Molly. To install a Molly, you must first drill a hole in the wall the size of which is indicated on the package that the Molly comes in. The hole must be a shade smaller than the barrel of the Molly. Then, you tap the Molly into the hole, and turn the slotted bolt in the end of the Molly with a screwdriver to draw the end of the Molly toward you. This causes the fluted sleeve to flare out until it is flat against the inside of the wall. Now, the bolt can be withdrawn and used to hold whatever you wish to hang. Molly fixtures can support weights up to five hundred pounds, and several of them together are used frequently to hold up something like a shelf or wall cabinet.

Other Anchor Devices

DRAPERY RODS and other lightweight items can be held secure with plastic anchors. Once you tap the anchor into a predrilled hole, insert the screw. The screw pushes out against the anchor, expanding the toothed barrel. The teeth bite into the surface of the hole, and the screw can then hold quite a bit of weight.

For heavier installations — like book shelves — the toggle bolt is recommended. A toggle bolt can support up to eighteen hundred pounds, depending on the size of the bolt. Drill a hole in the wall, and insert the toggle bolt. Once the flange is inside the wall, it has a spring that makes it flare out. Then tighten the bolt to bring the object being held up flat against the wall. Be sure that you have the bolt through the object or its bracket before you insert the flange. Once the flange flares, there is no way to get it back out; and if you have to remove the bolt, the flange will fall between the walls.

243

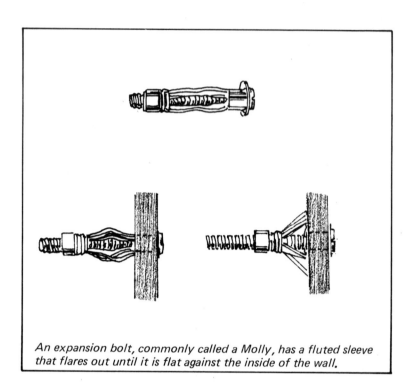

An expansion bolt, commonly called a Molly, has a fluted sleeve that flares out until it is flat against the inside of the wall.

Masonry

MASONRY WALLS present a different challenge. There are several anchors that will hold several tons of weight, but the problem here is in drilling the holes for the anchors. A star drill is the slow way to go. You tap the end of the drill with a hammer, turning the drill with your hand after each tap. Eventually you get a hole, but a better way is to use a masonry bit in your electric drill.

There are many types of anchors: fiber plugs with a lead core, lead anchors with hinged jaws, and even lead anchors with various sized threads inside to take different sizes of screws. With all, the idea is that when you put the screw in, expansion occurs that presses the sides of the anchor against the hole, making it impossible for the anchor to come out. Many people coat such anchors with epoxy adhesive to give the anchor even more holding power.

With all these variations of anchors and bolts to choose from, you should be able to select the right one for any hang up you might have.

244

Simple Household Repairs

Patching Wall Cracks

SINCE MOST homes have some walls that are made of either plaster or wallboard, most homes develop some ugly cracks from time to time. In addition to the cracks that develop naturally from the house settling, more cracks result when people put up pictures and mirrors, and then decide that these things would look better on another wall. Cracks and holes need not remain there to haunt you, however, because they can be repaired easily.

Cracks

WHETHER IT be a plaster wall or wallboard, you repair cracks in just about the same manner. The most popular patching material is spackling compound. It comes in dry form for you to mix, or as spackling paste which is ready to be applied. If you elect to use the dry, you just add water and stir until the spackling reaches a batter like consistency. When you are fixing just a few small cracks, the ready mixed paste is probably the better one to choose.

For the hairline cracks, you need only brush along the crack to remove any loose particles and to clean out the dust. Use a stiff bristled brush. Now, dip a finger into the spackle mix and rub your finger along the crack, pressing the mix into the crack. By following the application with a damp towel or sponge, you can remove the excess surface paste. Be gentle; the last thing you want to do

245

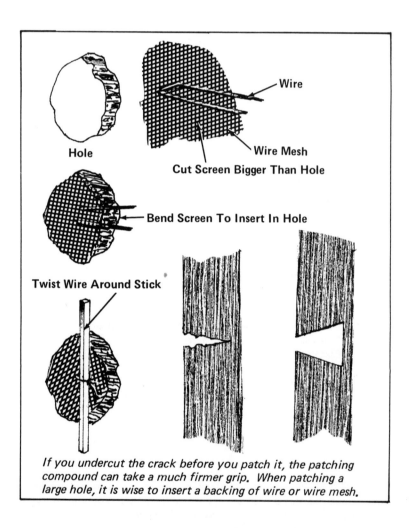

Hole

Wire

Wire Mesh

Cut Screen Bigger Than Hole

Bend Screen To Insert In Hole

Twist Wire Around Stick

If you undercut the crack before you patch it, the patching compound can take a much firmer grip. When patching a large hole, it is wise to insert a backing of wire or wire mesh.

is dig any of the patch out of the crack.

There are also sticks of patch material that look like big white crayons. The sticks do a fair job on hairline cracks, but while they are easier and neater than spackling compound, they do not do as good a job.

Larger cracks require a bit more work. For a stronger patch, you should undercut the crack. Undercutting means making the crack wider underneath, which allows the patching compound to get a firmer grip. One of the best tools for undercutting is an old punch type beer can opener. In undercutting you may widen the crack, which probably seems like going backwards, but it is in the interest of a firmer patch. After you finish, brush away all the loose dust. Now, dampen all of the surface inside the crack that will come in contact with the patching paste. If the crack is big enough, you can use a paint brush to get the water inside. If not, use a squeeze bottle and squirt the water on.

The spackling paste can be spread on with a putty knife. Work it into the crack, and make sure that the paste fills the crack completely. A damp towel or sponge removes the excess from the surface. A large crack can show some shrinkage by the time the patch is dry. If so, moisten the patch and apply more paste to make it level.

Some cracks come back after a few months, which is pretty disheartening. For such cases, get the kit that includes a fiberglass tape (which looks like surgical guaze) and a special fiberglass adhesive. You apply the adhesive, and then press the tape — which you have cut to cover the crack — into the adhesive. When this sets, you apply another coat of the adhesive to cover the mesh of the tape. Since the tape is flexible, it allows the crack to move underneath without showing on the surface. The kit — called "KrackKote" — is sold at most hardware and paint stores, but you can also buy the tape and adhesive separately.

Some people use plaster of paris to patch walls. It works fine, and you can apply it the same way you would spackling paste. You should know, however, that plaster of paris sets up very quickly; therefore, do not mix very much at one time. If it seems to be drying faster than you can use it, try mixing a little vinegar with the next batch. The correct amount of vinegar to add is a teaspoon to a quart of water.

Some cracks are the result of bad workmanship at corners or where cabinets and wallboard meet. Use caulking compound in a gun for these situations. If you find cracks around tubs or sinks, use the caulk specifically designed for tub and sinks.

If the walls around the crack are textured, you will want the patch to have the same texture. This takes some doing, however. You may have to add sand to give the patch the proper texture. Sometimes you can achieve the right effect with a paint brush by drawing the brush over the wet patching compound to give it a swirl effect. Or, you can dab the brush against the wall for a stipple effect; dabbing a sponge gives a different stipple treatment. If you place a wet trowel flat against the wet compound and then lift it straight away, you will cause some of the plaster patch to rise. The best thing to do is to apply some of the patching mate-

247

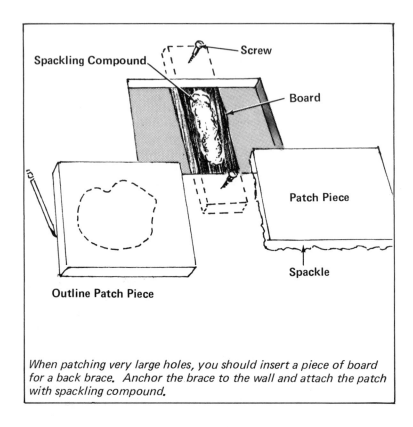

Spackling Compound

Screw

Board

Patch Piece

Spackle

Outline Patch Piece

When patching very large holes, you should insert a piece of board for a back brace. Anchor the brace to the wall and attach the patch with spackling compound.

rial to a scrap of sheetrock, and then try all these treatments until you find the best match to the texture on the wall.

After the patch material on the wall dries completely, you are ready to paint. Many people put a sealer coat of thinned shellac over new patches to prevent the patch from drinking too much paint. When the shellac dries, apply the finish coat.

Holes

IF YOUR walls are of the wallboard type, you probably have already discovered that there is no backing behind the surface. Since a big patch needs something to support it, some patchers provide a backing, and then use spackling compound to cover the hole. Others use a plug cut from a scrap of wallboard and piece it into the hole.

If you want to provide backing, screen wire or wire mesh

248

(called hardware cloth) is good. Cut the backing a little larger than the hole; you can curl it to fit into the hole. Before you put the backing in the hole, however, loop a short piece of wire through the screen. Use the wire to hold the screen in place until you can place a scrap of wood across the hole. Now, twist the wire around the wood scrap to hold the screen tight against the inside of the wall.

Wet down the edges where the patching material will go, and apply a first coat of patch that completely covers the screen and the edges of the hole. This means that the patch will be sunken in the middle. When the first coat hardens, untwist the wire and clip it off right next to the patch. Apply a second coat of patch, and fill the hole up until it is level with the surrounding surface. You may have to add a third coat if there is shrinkage, but two coats are usually sufficient.

Another backing piece you can use is the lid from a large tin can. Punch holes with a nail for the wire. Since the tin can lid must be bigger than the hole, and since the lid is not flexible, what can you do? Just cut a slit from the hole and slide the lid in edgewise. Then, use all the same techniques described for a wire mesh backing.

For a hole that is fairly large, first cut a patch from a scrap of wallboard; then you just have the cracks to fill with patching compound. Make sure that the scrap patch is big enough to completely cover the hole; rectangular shapes are best. Place the scrap over the hole, and then trace around it with a pencil. Now, enlarge the hole to fit the lines you drew exactly. A keyhole saw will do the job quickly.

The scrap patch needs backing too, but it needs a more rigid backing than screen. The best way to back brace is to cut a board about four or five inches longer than the width of the hole; slip it into the hole in the wall; and hold it flat against the inside of the wall. While holding it with one hand, run flat-head screws through the wallboard and the wood to anchor the back brace in place. If the hole includes a stud behind the wall, you will naturally use it as backing; in fact, you should nail the scrap piece of wallboard to the stud.

Now you can mix up your patching compound. Butter the back brace, and then the edges of the scrap patch. Ease the patch into place, and hold it there until the patching compound starts to set up. Finally, fill in the crack all the way around and cover over the screws.

For plaster walls, there is a little different procedure because such walls have lath behind the plaster. You first need to undercut

249

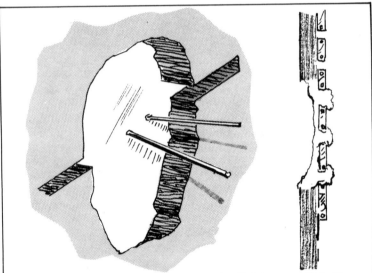

If you use a lid from a tin can for backing (left), cut a slit in the wall and slide can in edgewise. You can hold lid in position with a piece of wire run through punched holes. When patching plaster walls, press compound firmly so that some oozes between lath strips (right) to form keys.

the hole, and clean away all the loose particles and dust. Dampen the exposed edges, and mix up your patching compound. Spread on the first layer, and as you work against the lath, press the putty knife firmly to force some of the mix to go between the lath strips. This will ooze out behind and form "keys" that lock the patch to the lath. When the first coat hardens, finish it off with a second coat. For really big areas, a three-coat patch is even better. All the finishing, texturing, and sealing for plaster walls are the same as for wallboard.

Little nail holes in any kind of wall are not worth all the trouble of mixing up the compound and applying it. If you do not have the ready mix, make a little paste from a few drops of paint and some talcum powder. When the paste takes on a putty consistency, dab it into the holes. If the paint you use is the same color as the wall, you will not even be able to see the patch after it dries. A sneaky way to hide nail holes on white walls is with toothpaste. Once it dries, it is just about as good as patching compound, and it can even be painted over later on.

250

Simple Household Repairs

Fixing Shades, Drapes, And Blinds

WHETHER YOU use shades, drapes, or blinds for your privacy, there are a few fix-it facts you should know about. Most people never even think about how a shade works, for example. They pull it down, and it goes down. When they get it to where they want it, it stays. When they want it to go up, a slight tug takes it up. Actually, inside that simple looking wooden roller there is a fairly ingenious mechanism. Yet, the solution to your shade problems is probably a very simple one.

Shades

THE TWO brackets that hold a window shade are not alike. One has a hole for a round pin to fit into, while the other has a slot for a flat pin. The flat pin is connected to a ratchet. When you pull the shade down, a pair of pawls — called "dogs" — slide past the teeth on the ratchet. At the same time, a coil spring inside the long roller is tightened. When you stop pulling downward, the dogs fall in place and catch the teeth on the ratchet. The shade stays right there. When you want the shade to go up, you pull down slightly, and the dogs let go of the teeth. The tightened spring then takes over, and the shade goes back up. When the shade gets to the top, the spring tension has decreased.

If the shade does not go back up — or if it is very slow in going up — it obviously means that the spring inside has not got enough tension to lift the shade. All you have to do to give the spring the

251

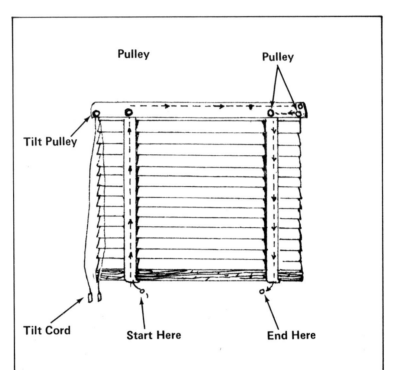

Pulley

Pulley

Tilt Pulley

Tilt Cord

Start Here

End Here

Follow arrows for correct procedure to install a new lift cord in venetian blinds, but make your own sketch so that you can be sure to replace cord properly.

extra tension it needs is to: (1) Pull the shade down about half way; (2) remove the ratchet end from the bracket; (3) roll the shade back up by hand; and (4) put the shade back in the bracket and test it.

This process will add tension, but if there is still not enough, repeat until the shade bounces back just right. If the shade snaps back up with enough force to rattle the window panes, it needs to be tranquilized. The procedure here is to: (1) Remove the ratchet end from its bracket; (2) unroll it by hand about half way; and (3) replace the shade in the bracket and test it. If it still has too much snap, repeat the tranquilizing process.

The next most common shade failing results from the brackets not being properly placed. If they are a fraction too far apart, the whole shade unit may fall out from time to time. Naturally, you just need to move them closer together. If they are mounted inside the

252

casing, however, the brackets cannot be moved. In that case, you need to put shims behind the brackets to move them toward each other. Usually, a piece of shirtboard behind each bracket is enough.

Brackets can be too close together, causing the shade roller to bind. If they can be moved, separate the brackets and you will solve the problem. Often, you can tap the brackets with a hammer and flatten them enough to stop the binding. If they are mounted inside the casing, file a tiny bit off of the round pin, thus making it a fraction shorter.

Sometimes the shade does not go up or down properly, and yet the tension seems to be all right. Check to see if the round pin has rust or corrosion on it. If so, clean the pin with steel wool or sandpaper. Also, check the round pin to see if it is bent. A bent pin can cause difficult or wobbly movement, but you can straighten the pin easily with a pair of pliers.

If the shade does not stay where you want it when you pull it down, the ratchet is not being held by the dogs. Sometimes a piece of grit behind the dogs stops their movement. Remove the metal dust cap that fits over the flat end pin, and check to see if any dirt or lint is interfering with the dogs. Spray a little lubricant to restore free movement; graphite powder or silicon spray will usually put the life back in the dogs.

If the shade itself comes loose from the roller, staple it back in place. Make sure that you have it on straight, however, or the shade will roll up at an angle. The same applies if you decide to change the old shade for a new fabric to match the decor. Use the old shade as a pattern, and staple the new piece in place. If the new fabric weighs more than the old shade, you may have to adjust the tension as if you had a shade that would not go back up properly.

Should you have to tailor the width of the roller to fit an odd sized window, always cut from the round pin side. Remove the metal cap over the end, pull the pin out, and then use a hacksaw and a miter box to get a straight cut. Reinstall the pin and its cap.

If you find that the spring is shot and will not rewind, or if you discover that the ratchet or dogs have lost their teeth, you have to buy a new roller unit. You can still use the old shade, however. Merely staple it to the new roller.

Drapery Rods

IF YOU PULL on a cord to open the drapes, you have what is called a "traverse rod." There are several different types of traverse systems, but they all work on a similar basic principle. By learning how such a system works, you will be better able to spot any problems should they occur.

253

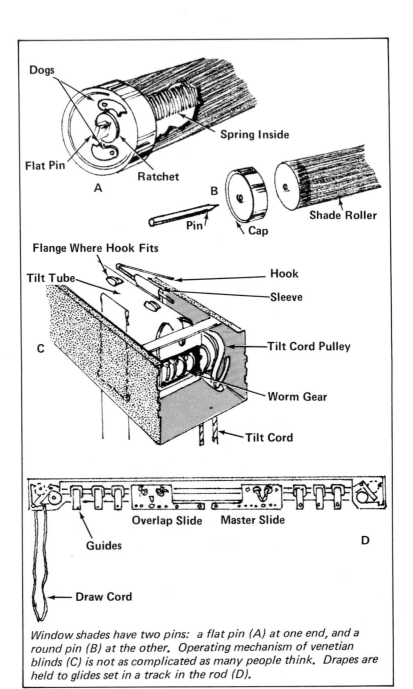

Dogs

Flat Pin

Ratchet

A

Spring Inside

B

Pin

Cap

Shade Roller

Flange Where Hook Fits

Tilt Tube

Hook

Sleeve

C

Tilt Cord Pulley

Worm Gear

Tilt Cord

Overlap Slide   Master Slide

Guides

D

Draw Cord

Window shades have two pins: a flat pin (A) at one end, and a round pin (B) at the other. Operating mechanism of venetian blinds (C) is not as complicated as many people think. Drapes are held to glides set in a track in the rod (D).

254

The drapes are held to glides set in a track in the rod. Hooks in the drapes are inserted in holes in the glides, and the leading edge of the drape is hooked into a hole in carriers or slides. The carriers are connected to the cords, and when pulled, the cords react by going one way or the other in the track, thus opening or closing the drapes. A look at the method by which the cord is threaded will show you how the tension pulls on opposite sides of the opposing slides.

Cord Adjustment and Replacement

SOMETIMES, THE cords can become detached. Either a knot coming loose in the overlap slide, or the loop on the master slide comes unhooked. To get the drapes back in drawing shape, pull them open as far as they will go. Hold onto the cord to keep it taut, and then unhook the loop in the master slide and push both slides back as far as the glides will let them go. Rehook the loop, and the drapes should draw back evenly.

A worn or broken cord should be replaced. Here are the steps to follow:

1. Remove the drapes for better visibility and accessibility.
2. Look at the way the old cord is threaded around the pulleys and through the track to make sure that you know the exact path it follows. Make a sketch if you have any doubts, and then remove the old cord.
3. Start the new cord by knotting it in place on the center side of the carrier slide.
4. Run it down the track to the pulley on the master slide side, and then back through the holes in the master slide.
5. Run the cord on through the track down to and around the pulleys on the pull side. Run it down through the tension pulley wheel, if there is one. If there is no tension pulley wheel, leave a loop for the pulls, and run the loose end up through the pulleys and tie it into the other hole in the carrier slide.
6. If your drapes have the tension pulley system, pull the cord tight before you tie it at the carrier slide. Snip off the excess cord before you knot it. If you do not have the tension pulley system, you can leave the loop in the draw cord or snip off the ends and add pulls.

Bracket Problems

OFTEN A drape does not work properly because a bracket is loose

255

or unevenly adjusted. Check first to see if any of the fasteners holding the brackets to the wall are loose. If so, tighten the screws or replace the nails with screws. Next, check the brackets to see if they are out of adjustment. Most brackets can be set at a certain distance from the wall, but the set screws holding the brackets in the right position can work loose. Measure the distance from the wall on each bracket, and then reset any that are off; make sure, of course, that the set screws are turned down tight.

Venetian Blinds

THERE ARE some people who cannot even operate venetian blinds; to them, the thought of repairing blinds is completely out of sight. True, blinds are much more complicated than window shades, but some blind problems are fairly easy to solve.

The cloth webbing that holds the slats in even alignment is called ladder tape. Tapes can become worn, frayed, and broken. They can also get dirty. Replacing them is not the complicated puzzle it might appear to be. The first thing you must do is purchase a replacement tape that can accommodate the same width slats and that has the same number of ladders.

Here is the procedure for replacing the ladder tape. Remove the blind from the window and place it on the floor or any flat surface big enough to accommodate it. If the blinds have a metal bottom bar, remove the clamp that fits over the tape as it goes around the bar. If the bottom bar is wooden, the tape will probably be stapled to the bottom of the bar. Take the staples out.

Now, you can get at the knots on the cords that run from the top all the way through the slats and through the bottom bar. Untie the knots and pull the cords up through the slots in the blinds all the way to the top. Unhook the tapes at the top. They are held by a wire hook that fits through tiny sleeves in the top of the tape and snaps into brackets in the top bar (which is called the tilt tube). Replace the old with the new, and fasten the tape at the top with the hook.

Put the slats in their ladders, and run the cords back through the slots in the slats, making sure that the cord goes between the staggered ladders. Tie knots in the bottom of the cords, and replace the clamps or staple the tapes in place. Rehang the blinds.

While you have the tape off, it is a good time to clean the slats. Inspect them to see if they might need painting as well. If there is any doubt about the cords, now is a good time to replace them too.

Cords

THERE ARE two cord systems in a venetian blind unit. The lift cords

256

raise or lower the blinds. The tilt cord opens and closes the blinds by tilting the slats. Normally, the cord problem is in the lift cord.

Look at the old cord to see for sure the way it is threaded over the pulleys. Make your own sketch so that you can make the replacement properly. Remove the old cord. Start running the new cord through the slats by beginning at the bottom bar on the opposite side from where the pull cords hang down. Run the cord through the slats and over the pulley at the top. Bring it all the way along the top until you get to the pulleys on the other side. Thread around the pulleys according to the sketch you made.

Pull the cord all the way through until the other end reaches the starting point. Tie a knot there. Start feeding the original end back through the pulleys over to the pulley at the top of the second tape and then down through the slats. When you get it down through the bottom bar, knot it. Install the equalizer and adjust.

The tilt cord is replaced by running the new cord over the pulley and back down. The pulls are held on by knots. If anything is wrong with the tilting process, check the worm gear that is operated by the tilt cords. Sometimes dirt gets into the gear, and sometimes it just needs some lubrication. A silicon spray lube or graphite will do the job without getting the tape oily.

Replacing Locksets In Doors

LOCKS AND latches can suffer from many problems. In addition to the bolt mechanism, there are the door knobs, the locks, and all the parts on the inside to get out of whack. Without trying to make you into a locksmith, here are some simple explanations of how different types of locks work and how to fix them.

There are three basic types of locks: the mortise lock, the rim lock, and the cylindrical lock. All three have cylinders, but the cylindrical lock has its key-way in the knob. After seeing the three styles, you will recognize that the cylindrical lock is the one most widely used. You will also note that most of the units on the doors inside your house are similar, but lack the key-ways. They are called tubular locks.

From a security standpoint, the most important part of the lock is the bolt. There are two basic kinds, the spring catch and the deadbolt. The spring catch bolt is so named because it locks when you shut the door. The face of the bolt is angled so that as it hits the striker plate, it is pushed back into the door. Then, when the bolt gets to the opening in the striker plate, a spring inside makes it jump back in place, and the door is locked. The spring catch bolt allows you to lock the door without digging out your keys or even turning the knob.

The bad part about a spring catch bolt is that your neighborhood burglar can usually reach in with any thin, flexible, but stiff object, and press against the angled end of the bolt until it recedes

258

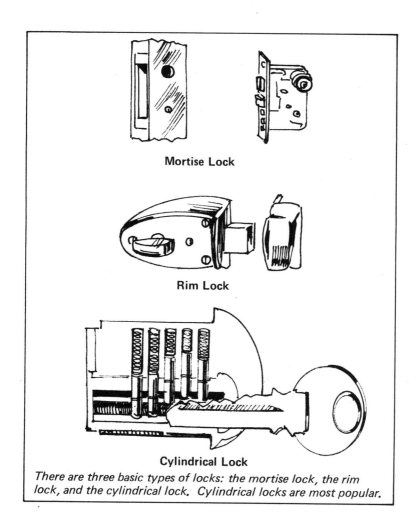

Mortise Lock

Rim Lock

Cylindrical Lock

There are three basic types of locks: the mortise lock, the rim lock, and the cylindrical lock. Cylindrical locks are most popular.

enough to clear the hole in the striker plate. Even a novice burglar can use a wire, credit card, or piece of celluloid to open your door quicker than you can fish around for the key.

If your outside doors are equipped with spring catch latches, you would be wise to switch over to deadbolts. Deadbolts are squared off, and they must be turned into the plate with either a key or a thumb bolt. Although there is practically no way to keep an intruder out if he is determined to get in, the harder you make it for him to enter, the better. Most burglars will follow the path of

259

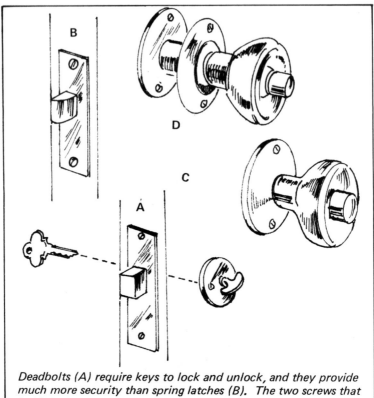

Deadbolts (A) require keys to lock and unlock, and they provide much more security than spring latches (B). The two screws that hold the knob can be located on the escutcheon plate (C), or hidden on the clamp plate under the rose (D).

least resistance, going to a door where the lock is easier.

Changing The Lock

IF YOU DECIDE to change locks, your first step is the removal of the old lockset. Working from the inside, look for the two screws that hold the two knobs together. The screws are located on the escutcheon plate — also called a knob rose — or on the clamp plate under the rose, depending on the type of lockset.

If the screws are exposed, both door knobs will slide out when you remove the screws. The latch assembly comes out when you remove the screws holding it to the edge of the door. The kind of

260

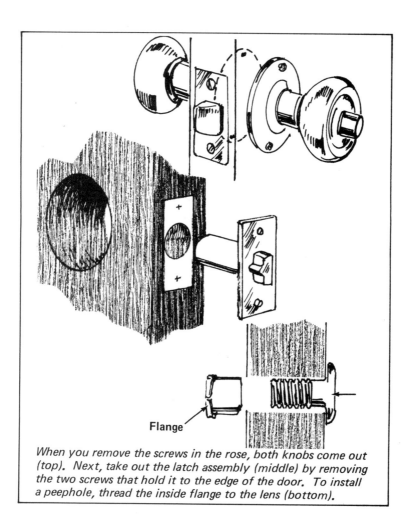

Flange

When you remove the screws in the rose, both knobs come out (top). Next, take out the latch assembly (middle) by removing the two screws that hold it to the edge of the door. To install a peephole, thread the inside flange to the lens (bottom).

lockset in which the rose conceals the screws also has a pin or button that holds the knob. Depress the pin or button and the knob comes off. You may find that a small nail will fit into the hole to help you release the knob.

Take the entire lockset with you when you buy a replacement. Chances are, you can purchase one that will fit back into the existing holes. If not, look for a replacement that can cover the holes from the old unit; and if you are still out of luck, look for a larger escutcheon plate that can hide the holes. A larger strike plate or

261

latch plate is no problem because you can enlarge the mortice for each.

Peepholes

ANOTHER POPULAR addition to the front door is a viewer that lets you see who is out there before you open the door. The best kind has a wide-angle lens that lets you see a full ninety degrees in all directions. All you have to do is figure out where you want the viewer, and then drill the appropriate sized hole. Position the viewer at eye level for the shortest person who will be at home alone. Even if you have to bend over to use the peephole, it is better to have the viewer located so that your children can use it too. Position the outside lens in place in the hole, and thread the inside flange to secure the unit.

Mail Slots

DECORATIVE MAIL slots can enhance the appearance of many front doors, and they are very easy to install. Position the unit, and draw a line around the opening. Drill holes at all four corners of your outline, and cut the slot with a keyhole saw. Attach the plates inside and out, and you are all set for the bills to start pouring in through the door.

262

Fixing Doors That Stick

DOORS ARE designed to close, open, latch, and lock. If they fail to do any of these functions — or if they do them unwillingly or noisily — they need some help. As we talk about how to fix each of these ills, we will explain how the door works. You can think of it as sort of a swinging story.

Hard to Open

THE STUCK door is the most common door problem. Once you do get it open, you find you cannot close it. The first thing most people do is get a plane and take a little wood off the top of the door. While that may be the right answer at times, usually it is the wrong way to go. The first step in solving the sticking door is to spot exactly where the problem is. Then you can take the proper action to correct it.

Here is how to find the problem. Check the door and frame for evidence of just where the door is sticking. Generally, you can spot the places where the paint is worn down. Close the door, if possible, and check the edge opposite to the sticking surface. If you see a large gap on the opposite edge, there is a good possibility that the problem is in the hinges. If there is little space all the way around, and the sticking place is fairly large, it probably indicates that moisture has swollen the wood, making the door too big to fit properly in the frame. Check the frame with a square; it may be out of kilter. If so, the house has settled and has forced the

263

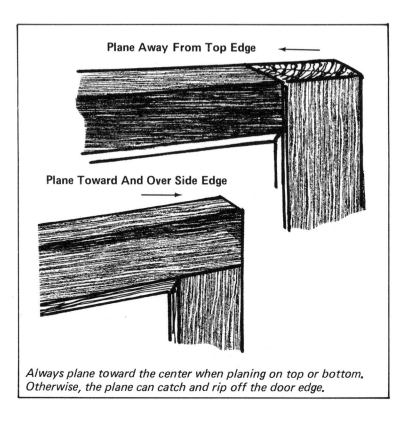

Plane Away From Top Edge ←

Plane Toward And Over Side Edge
→

Always plane toward the center when planing on top or bottom. Otherwise, the plane can catch and rip off the door edge.

frame out of shape.

Usually, the problem is in the hinges. That is very fortunate because it is the easiest problem to fix. The first thing to do is check to see if the screws holding the hinges are still tight. If not, tighten them. If the screws will not stop turning, it shows that the holes have become too large for the screws.

There are some tricky stop-gap ways to tighten the hole. Wrap the threads of the screws with steel wool and reinsert them. The steel wool will take up the slack and allow the screws to be turned down tight. Or, you can wrap cotton around the threads and dip in nail polish, glue, or shellac. The cotton does the same thing as the steel wool, and the adhesive helps set the screw and cotton in place. If you insert a piece of a wooden match or toothpick in the hole, you may be able to give the screw new bite. Finally, you can use larger, longer screws, but the heads must be the

264

same size as the old ones to countersink in the hinge plate.

If none of these tricks work, you must rebuild the wood and start with a new hole. You can put plastic wood into the hole, and when it sets up, you have a new surface to start on. Or, you can drill out the hole to make room for a short length of dowel which you then glue in place. After the glue has set, cut off the stub of dowel sticking out. Use a hacksaw blade without the saw frame.

If the screws are right but the problem is still in the hinge, you have to shim up or recess the hinges to relieve the sticking place. When the door sticks at the top, the bottom hinge side needs to come out some. Put a cardboard (shirtboard is fine) shim between the hinge plate and the jamb. Cut the shim to match the hinge plate, and then cut slots so that the shim can slip over the screws. Loosen the screws on the frame side, and slip the shim in place Retighten the screws, and see if the sticking problem is eliminated. If one thickness of shim is not enough, add more. If the door sticks at the bottom, then go through the same routine at the top hinge.

Deepening The Mortice

IF THE DOOR is tilted, but there is little room around the frame, then you might cut a deeper mortice and set the hinge deeper into the frame. In this case, you move the hinge inward — that is, at the same end of the door as the sticking place.

To deepen the mortice, you must remove the door. Remove the bottom hinge pin first. If the bottom of the sleeve that holds the pin has a hole in it, use a large nail to drive the pin out. Otherwise, use a large screwdriver and hammer to tap the pin out. If the pin is stubborn, shoot a little penetrating oil around it, but be sure to have a rag ready to catch the drips. Remove the top hinge pin and take the door off.

Morticing is done with a chisel, but first use a sharp knife to outline the existing mortice to the desired new depth. With the chisel almost flat, start removing the layer of wood.

Planing The Door

A DOOR that sticks across the top and has plenty of space at the bottom can be corrected by lowering the hinges in the frame. If you diagnose the problem as being swollen wood, you must remove some of the door. But hold it! Does the door just stick occasionally? If so, it may be that extra humidity is doing the damage right now, but when it gets a little drier, the door might shrink

265

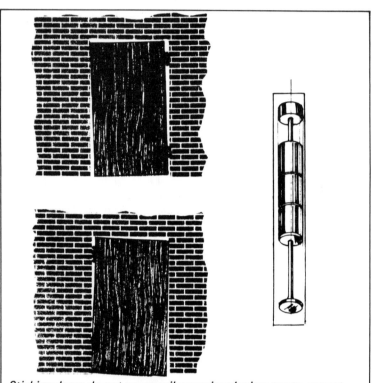

Sticking doors do not necessarily require planing; try to correct any hinge problems before taking off wood. If you must remove the door to deepen the mortice, use a large nail to drive the pin out of the hinge. If pin is stubborn, use penetrating oil.

back to size. If it is just a seasonal problem, live with the door until it dries out, and then seal all the edges to prevent moisture from getting in during the next muggy spell.

If the swelling is not just a passing fancy, you will have to sand or plane. If the door binds at the top, you may be able to remove the excess while the door is still hung. Always plane toward the center when planing on the top or bottom. Otherwise, the plane can catch on the edge of the side rail and rip off a chunk of the door edge.

Coarse sandpaper or a rasp will often take off enough wood, and do it easier than a plane. If you have to take some off the bottom of the door, you may be able to place coarse sandpaper on a

266

stack of shirtboards, and move the door back and forth to remove the excess. As you work, you will have to add padding to raise the sandpaper, and you will probably find that you have to remove the door to really get the job done.

If surface must be removed from the side of the door, avoid planing on the latch side. Most doors are beveled on the latch side to allow them to close without hitting the facing, and you do not want to destroy the bevel with your plane. Plane from the hinge side. You may have to deepen the mortice later, but that is an easier job than putting a new bevel on. When planing along the side, carry your end cuts toward the edges.

When you have finished the planing and have ascertained that your door will once again swing properly, seal the edges where you have exposed new wood. This will keep moisture out and maybe prevent future swelling. Adding a coat of paint to match the door is always smart.

If you find that the problem results from the frame being out of shape, there is very little you can do to the frame. You can try placing a padded 2x4 against the frame and hitting the block with a hammer. Sometimes you can reset the frame just enough to solve the problem. If at first you do not succeed, however, forget it. Go to work on adjusting the hinges or planing off the door to make the door fit the new shape of the frame.

Door Does Not Latch

A DOOR that does not stay latched may be worse than no door at all. You may be lulled into thinking that a closed door means privacy, but such a door can suddenly swing open at any time.

As with most problems, diagnosis is the key to curing the illness. Look at the latch bolt while the door is shut. If the bolt does not come out far enough from the door to engage the hole in the strike plate, it means that either the bolt is hung in the latch or that the door or strike plate needs to be shimmed to move the two closer together. Obviously, shimming out the strike plate is easier, but sometimes you have to shim both strike plate and hinges.

If the latch bolt does not line up with the opening, you must adjust it in some way. You can either file an edge off the latch bolt, or remove the plate and enlarge the hole with a file. If the alignment is very far off, however, you must move the strike plate up or down. This means extending the mortice up or down. Fill in the old screw holes with plastic wood or a plug, and then replace the plate. Be sure to fill in the gap that is left when you move the plate.

267

If everything is lined up and the bolt comes out far enough, but still the door does not latch, the opening is in too far. Usually, it is only a fraction off, and the easiest way to solve the problem is to remove the plate and file to enlarge the hole toward the front. If it is off more than you wish to file, reset the plate farther out of the frame.

Door Noises

MOST DOOR noises result from squeaks in the hinges. All you have to do to stop such noises is to lubricate the hinge pin. Wedge something under the door to prop it up, and remove the hinge pin. The best lubricant is either powdered graphite or silicon spray; both are dry and will not drip on the floor. If neither lubricant is handy, a light coat of petroleum jelly will do. In a pinch, even a very light coat of machine oil will stop the squeak.

The next most common noise is a door rattle, which results when there is too much play between the bolt and the hole in the strike plate. You need something to keep the bolt pushed against the plate. Little felt dots (the ones that are meant to stick on the bottom of ashtrays) placed on the stop have enough give to allow the door to close and latch, but they bounce back with enough pressure to keep the latch tight. Small tabs of foam rubber glued to the stop can also stop the rattle.

Another noise that involves outside doors is the hum that occurs when there is a strong wind. The hum is a sign that your weatherstripping is not quite doing its job. If the weatherstripping is the metal kind, it may just need to be bent to fit tighter.

268

Simple Household Repairs

Weatherstripping Doors And Windows

YOUR DOORS and windows may be fine for keeping out bugs and intruders, but they can be sadly lacking when it comes to sealing out things like wind, rain, cold, and heat. Despite what the commercial says, however, you can fool Mother Nature with a few simple installations. Most moisture and wind can be kept outside by proper weatherstripping around doors and windows. There are several types of weatherstripping, and all are readily available at hardware stores and lumber yards.

Weatherstripping Doors

WE CAN start with doors. An outside door should have a threshold, a raised strip under the door. In times past, all thresholds were made of wood. With all the foot traffic, however, these wooden thresholds would eventually get worn down so much that moisture, dust, and wind could enter the home. The newer type threshold, therefore, is made of aluminum, and comes in a package that contains all the parts and fasteners needed for the complete installation. Actually, these metal units fit over an actual wooden saddle piece that is, in fact, a threshold itself.

The best threshold for ease of installation is the kind with a vinyl flap that sticks up on top. The flap is set in tracks in the aluminum and folded over to form a bubble. The door compresses the bubble when closed, sealing out the elements. You can cut the aluminum easily with a hacksaw, and install the unit with screws

269

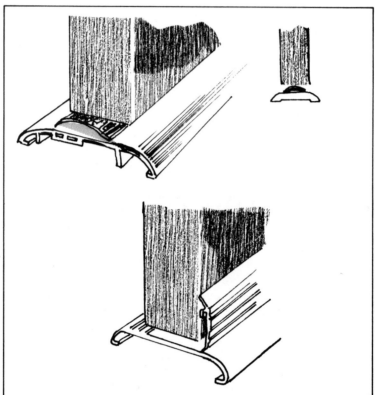

The best threshold for a door is the kind (top) with a vinyl bubble that sticks up to seal out the elements. Two-piece units employ strips of metal to cover the gap between door and threshold.

that are hidden under the flap.

Two-piece units employ a similar strip of metal that attaches to the floor, and a second strip that sticks down from the door to cover the gap. There are even units that have a movable bottom section that flips up when the door is opened to allow you to sweep the carpeting more easily. With two-piece units, however, you often need a certain amount of clearance between the door and the threshold; that clearance may require planing off part of the door. Therefore, the one-piece threshold usually is much easier for the average homeowner to install.

Around the sides and top of a door install the thin spring metal strips that come in rolls. With each roll come tiny brads of match-

270

ing metal for installation. The brads go along the edge of the weatherstripping, making the flange stick up so that it is depressed slightly when the door closes against it.

The installation is easy. Situate the anchored side so that the door closes over it and against the springy part that flares out. In most cases, an outside door opens inward; thus, the flared part faces out. Attach the hinge side all in one strip, but you must cut a small piece to fit behind the strike plate on the other side. Attach the strips above and below the strike plate, overlapping the small strip.

Cut the top strip, and then miter it to allow it to fit over the two side strips without smashing them. Bend the outer edge up slightly — the tip of a screwdriver does this quickly — for a better seal. Be careful not to kink the strips as you work. While this is not the best type of weatherstripping, it is effective if installed properly. If the door ever catches on the metal, the weatherstripping is soft enough that part of the strip can be torn away.

Another version of this type of weatherstripping is the "V"-shaped strip. It works according to the same principle and is installed about the same way as the thin spring metal strips.

A more effective weatherstripping system is the one that employs two innerlocking pieces. One piece is on the door, and the other is on the door frame. Installation is not an easy project because the rabbets must be cut with great precision. Repairs and replacements, however, are easy.

Most need for replacement results from the door getting out of alignment and bending or smashing some part of the metal stripping. You can try to straighten the stripping, but usually it must be replaced. Straightening is best done with a pliers to bend out, and a hammer and block to bend in. If the kinks are bad, however, you should replace the damaged pieces. Replacement strips usually must be adjusted, with slight bends in and out where the two pieces rub together. Be careful not to slam the door until you have made all the adjustments.

Gasket-type weatherstripping for doors is also easy to install. There are pliable types and rigid strips. The pliable type is either of the felt variety or vinyl. Some felt is nailed around the door frame, while another type has an adhesive backing. The pliable vinyl is nailed to the face of the stop, as are the rigid strips (which can also be screwed to the stop). Both are easy to install, but because they are visible they may not look quite as good as the hidden types.

Another piece of weather-fighting equipment for doors is the drip cap. If the door is not covered, rain water can run down the face of the door, and follow the surface on around the corner and

271

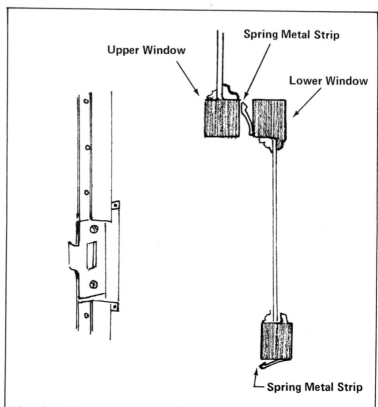

When installing spring strip weatherstripping to a door (left), be sure to cut a small piece to fit behind the strike plate. Metal strips installed on windows (right) exert pressure against the window sash to seal out the weather.

into the house. A drip cap is a piece of curved metal that carries the water out. When the rain gets to the bottom of the cap, it finds no surface to follow and just drips off. The drip cap is often combined with weatherstripping for the bottom of the door. If you occasionally have rain coming in the front door, you might wish to add a drip cap; it is easy to install.

Weatherstripping Windows

JUST LIKE doors, windows also need help in fooling Mother

272

Nature. The three most popular types of window weatherstripping are the thin spring metal strips, the adhesive-backed compressible material, or the vinyl tubular gasket.

The thin metal strips are nailed in place in the tracks, exerting pressure against the window sash to seal out the weather. The bottom strip for the lower sash is best nailed to the sash itself.

Adhesive-backed compressible material comes in either foam rubber strips or felt. All you do to install it is to peel off the backing and press the material in place between sash and stop.

The vinyl tubular gasket weatherstripping can have a hollow tube or it can be sponge filled. Nail the strips in place with small brads. Their big problem is that the strips are so out in the open that they detract from your windows' appearance.

General Hints

AFTER INSTALLING the weatherstripping, you may have to use caulking all around the frame of doors and windows if you spot any separation of the strips from the wall. When all is installed on doors and windows, check the weatherstriping with a hair dryer or a tank type vacuum cleaner with the hose in the blower end. Run the forced air around the outside edges, while someone inside moves a lighted candle around inside the weatherstripping. The slightest leak in your protection will make the flame flicker.

Removing Mildew From Walls

MOST HOUSES today are more air tight than were the homes of previous decades. In summer, air conditioning dictates that the windows stay closed, and in many homes year-round weather control keeps the windows closed all year long. Inside the closed home, however, there are all sorts of moisture producing machines and procedures. Cooking puts steam into the air; people take showers; and dishwashers and automatic clothes washers add to the humidity.

The tight house filled with extra moisture provides ideal conditions for the formation of mildew. Mildew is a fungus. The spores are airborne, and they need dirt, moisture, and heat to get started. Very unsightly, mildew can spread rapidly once it starts. Then, it can create bad odors in your house.

The most likely place in the house for mildew to form is in a bathroom that has no exhaust system. The soap film that collects on the walls provides dirt to feed the mildew, which usually starts between the grout lines or at some other joint. Pretty soon, however, the mildew is all over the place.

Eliminating Mildew

GETTING RID of this type of mildew is a cinch — if you start at the first signs. All you need to do is treat the spots with household bleach. Use a clean plastic squeeze bottle, pour in the bleach, and then squirt the bleach on every mildew spot you can find.

Since chlorine bleach can be a skin irritant, avoid prolonged contact. Working in a closed area like a shower, moreover, is also unwise; the bleach fumes can get to you. Open the windows while you squirt the bleach; then just go away and leave the bleach on the mildewed walls overnight to do its job. The following day, rinse off the area you treated, and the bathroom will probably gleam. If there are any spots that did not go away, try again, but this time scrub the bleach on with a stiff brush.

Even though you have removed the mildew, you are not through yet. You have eliminated the visual evidence, but the spores that caused the fungus are still there. Now you must get rid of the spores or else the mildew will be back in just a few days.

The best home remedy to kill the spores is household ammonia. After rinsing off all traces of the bleach, use a different rag to go over the same area with ammonia. Wear rubber gloves; ammonia is also a skin irritant. The fumes can also get to you. Above all, follow a special rule of caution: Never mix bleach with ammonia! The mixture creates and liberates dangerous chlorine gas.

When the ammonia dries, the spores are dead, and the current crop of mildew is gone.

Preventing Mildew

UNLESS YOU take care of the excess moisture problem, mildew will come back again and again. Since mildew spores just float around, the moist conditions and soap scum will soon invite a new batch. Exhaust fans made especially for bathrooms do a good job, but if excess moisture exists throughout the house, you should consider adding a dehumidifier unit.

Mildew can form on surfaces that might be spotted were you to use bleach on them. For such surfaces, buy some TSP (trisodium phosphate), a strong detergent, from your paint or hardware dealer. Follow the directions for washing with a TSP solution.

Outside walls can also get mildew, usually where foliage prevents the surface from drying. Mix a solution of 2/3 of a cup TSP, 1/3 of a cup household detergent, one quart household bleach, and enough warm water to make a gallon of solution. Scrub the mildewed area with this solution, and then hose it off when the spots are gone. The next time that you paint, use a mildew resistant paint to help prevent the return of the fungus. Many people, however, mistakenly apply mildew resistant paint over a surface that already has the fungus on it. They are surprised when the growth is back in a few months, but paint cannot kill the mildew — you must do that before you paint.

275

Electric Drills

THERE IS no argument about which tool is the world's most popular — the electric drill must be considered a runaway winner. And with good reason. It performs all sorts of work and does it well. Of course, a drill can bore holes. But, it can also make use of a myriad of accessories that turn it into anything from a floor waxer to a hedge trimmer, not to mention all the do-it-yourself projects it can handle — sanding, buffing, sawing, hole cutting, rasping, screwdriving, paint mixing, bevel cutting, knife sharpening, wire brushing, countersinking, and many others.

All these abilities, though, are extras. The tool remains, after all, a drill. Boring holes is its primary job.

Electric drills are called 1/4-, 3/8-, or 1/2-inch models, indicating the maximum size bit that will fit into their chucks. (Chuck-size accommodation is not the limitation it might seem, because you can bore 1/2-inch holes in wood with a bit that has a 1/4-inch shank and hence will fit a 1/4-inch drill.)

Speed Control

ALL SIZES of drills are available with certain extras from which you must make your choice. One such feature is speed control. The

276

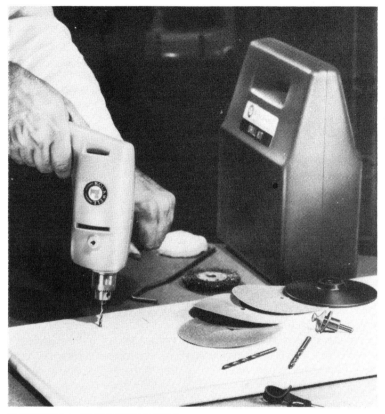

ROCKWELL ELECTRIC DRILL

maximum speeds of drills are as follows:
- 1/4-inch: approximately 1600 to 2200 rpm
- 3/8-inch: approximately 1000 rpm
- 1/2-inch: approximately 500 to 600 rpm

In models with speed control, the maximum speeds can be slowed down to a few rpm, allowing the drills to be used for other important jobs, such as driving wood screws and running nuts.

Speed control is also important in drilling metal. A top-notch job requires a lower spindle speed than most small drills without speed variations will deliver. (When drilling metal, incidentally, the point of the bit should be lubricated with a drop or two of machine oil. Almost any grade will do, even all-purpose household oil.)

Speed variation may be continuous, from 0 rpm to whatever top

277

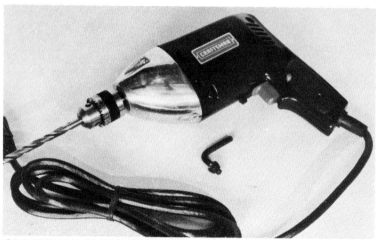

CRAFTSMAN ELECTRIC DRILL

speed the drill provides. Or it may be in switch-selected steps. The control is usually built into the trigger; the more you squeeze the trigger, the faster the drill rotates.

The best kind of speed control incorporates a "speed dial," usually built into the trigger, which you turn to preset the maximum speed you want. Then, when you squeeze the trigger, the speed increases gradually until you reach the preset point. The advantage of this system is that preset speed is literally at your fingertips, and it can be repeated accurately no matter how many times you start and stop the drill.

Where speed control is achieved solely by trigger pressure, you have to feel for the proper speed each time and hold it steady when you find it.

Reverse

THE ABILITY to reverse is not, in CONSUMER GUIDE Magazine's opinion, as important as is variable speed, although undoubtedly it is nice to have. It is particularly helpful when a drill bit jams in the work. Freeing the bit is simple if your drill can reverse. This feature also is important if the drill is used for screw removal to any extent.

Construction Features

NUMEROUS ways are used to put together electric drills, and

278

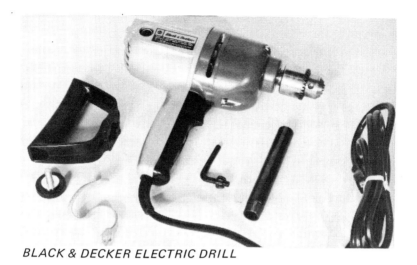

BLACK & DECKER ELECTRIC DRILL

method of construction determines the character of any drill, how long it will last, and how well it will perform. Especially important is physical construction, including the anti-friction and thrust bearings on which everything spins.

There are two basic styles of construction. Which one you are buying usually can be determined by whether the housing is metal or plastic.

In a double-insulated drill, the motor shell — the part that comprises all or most of the tool's body — is almost always plastic. The word "plastic" does not brand a drill "no good." The days when plastic signalled "cheap imitation" are long gone. Today's materials, loosely classed under the name "plastic," are tough, attractive (because they can be colored through and through), and serviceable. If you doubt that plastic can be immensely strong, try to break your telephone.

In a drill (as well as in other power tools) the motor itself is made almost entirely of metals, the bulkiest parts being the armature and the field. This means that the motor must be insulated electrically from the exterior. The simplest way to do this is to make the body shell of plastic, and fasten the motor to it. This is the nature of the double-insulated tool.

You can identify a drill that is not double-insulated by the fact that it usually will have a metal housing. An assembly of metal to metal is more rigid or solid than one of metal to plastic. Therefore, you cannot achieve the same degree of rigidity in the drive-line

279

mechanism of a double-insulated tool that you can with an all-metal tool. The difference is not big; but over the lifetime of the tool, less rigidity will mean more wear. Whether or not wear ever reaches the point where it affects the operation of the drill depends on how much the drill is used.

Bearings reduce friction, thereby keeping wear to a minimum. This makes them critical in determining the quality of an electric drill. But what type bearings should you look for? Most desirable, and most expensive, is a tool with ball and needle bearings throughout. Next best is one with sleeve bearings on the turning parts and a ball-thrust bearing to soak up the pressure of drilling. Last on the quality list are drills with sleeve bearings throughout.

The combination of insulation and bearings that will be found in the drill that is right for you depends on how hard you intend to use the tool. For normal home and shop use, a drill that is double-insulated and has sleeve bearings will stand up well under the kind of sporadic use it receives. For more frequent use, or for heavier duty work, a better drill would be more appropriate. If you expect to purchase some accessories, a larger or better drill is recommended to handle the extra work load.

Double-insulated tools have a convenient characteristic: you do not have to ground them for safety. If the wiring in your house and shop is modern, you have three-prong grounded outlets, and double-insulation will make no difference. But if house wiring is not of the type described, there is no choice; you must have double-insulation.

Horsepower

THE POWER of a drill depends on the current (amperes) it uses, the degree of speed reduction through the drive gears, and the type bearings.

What really matters to the user is the amount of power available at the chuck. Unfortunately, many manufacturers avoid providing you this important information by simply omitting any mention of it — and they will not answer if you ask about it. It is virtually impossible for the buyer to determine effective power at the chuck because of the complexity of factors that determine it. Consider the following analysis of power and you will see why.

Start with an electric motor of a given speed and horsepower. (A motor of greater power will draw more amperes of current.) This power must be transmitted to the drive shaft which will do all the work. At the end of the motor shaft there is a gear that meshes with another gear and drives still another, and so on. The power the motor applies to the motor shaft depends on shaft speed and turn-

280

SKIL ELECTRIC DRILL

ing force. It may be expressed by an abstract number that is the product of multiplying the speed by the turning force.

As the power is transmitted through the gear train, the speed is reduced. The reduced speed means that turning force (torque) must increase.

Saying it simply — as motor speed is reduced by a train of gears, turning force increases.

You can understand how easily a manufacturer can obscure statements of effective power when all these factors are involved in it. And you can also understand why a 3/8-inch drill that draws 2.5 amperes with a spindle speed of 1000 rpm has more torque at the chuck than does a 1/4-inch drill rated the same but with a speed of 2000 rpm.

You may be asking yourself how this relates to variable-speed drills. What happens to their power when you slow them down? Does it remain constant? Is it more, less, or what? To explain what happens electrically would take pages of obscure technical talk replete with formulas and engineering terms. Suffice it to say that there is a loss of power at slower speeds, but there is enough left to drive wood screws easily, and you should not need more than that at such slow speeds.

As for the effect of bearings on power, there is a small loss no matter which kind of bearings are used. However, the loss is larger with sleeve bearings than with ball bearings. Balls roll; sleeves rub, no matter how little. If rubbing has to be overcome, a small part of the power must be utilized to do so. This is dead loss, since the power used never reaches the spindle and therefore contributes nothing to the work capacity of the tool. However, this factor is relatively minor.

281

Guide to Hand Tools

YOU SHOULD never skimp when it comes to buying tools. Good tools are an absolute necessity; you must be able to rely on their ability to do the work for which they were made. A good tool, properly cared for, will last a lifetime. And since the difference in price between an inferior tool and a good one usually is relatively small, an investment in quality will pay dividends for years.

How can you spot quality tools? CONSUMER GUIDE Magazine has researched and tested various tools for you. Hopefully, the information we have compiled will enable you to fill your tool box with the right selection of quality hand tools rather than buy random tools of less worth.

What Tools Do You Need?

THE QUESTION of what hand tools you should keep in your toolbox is as broad as it is long, yet it must be answered. Obviously, there is no fixed formula to determine what you should or should not buy. Naturally, if you intend to use tools only when you absolutely must, your requirements will be far less than if you intend to make a career of do-it-yourself work.

Everyone needs certain basic tools. Among them are a hammer, a screwdriver, a pair of pliers, a saw, a wrench, and maybe a chisel. With this small collection, you can squeeze through a good many kinds of work, but you will never be able to do anything more than barely get by.

And you may run into buying problems even if you are looking for nothing more than these few tools. Suppose you enter a hardware store and ask for a screwdriver. The clerk will not know what you want unless you can be more specific because, as with almost every other tool, "screwdriver" is only a general name for many variations on a basic theme. To fit you with what you want or need, the clerk must have the answers to a host of questions. How large a screwdriver do you need? Must it be for ordinary slotted screws or should it have a Phillips point? Does it require a large handle to give you leverage for heavy work? Do you prefer a round shank or a square one? (With a square-shank screwdriver, one can use the jaws of a wrench to increase leverage enormously in the case of really stubborn resistance.) Do you have to get into a very tight, sharp corner? Perhaps a flexible-blade model is the answer — a screwdriver that actually bends around corners! Do you plan to insert a screw where you cannot possibly reach with your fingers or even with another tool to hold it until the threads bite? If so, you want a screwholding type; but what kind — split-blade or spring-clamp?

So it goes, deeper and deeper into details. The significance of all this is to make it clear that no one except you can tell what kind of tools to buy — or how many varieties of each tool you really should have.

There would be no problem if your tool budget were unlimited and you had plenty of shopping time, but few persons can afford to purchase one of everything. Therefore, it is best first to gather a knowledge of the hand tools available and then assess these tools in terms of your present or anticipated needs.

Hammers

HAMMERS have two main parts, head and handle. Heads are made of steel, handles usually of hickory wood. The steel in the head of a good hammer is a tough alloy that has been hardened by forging; do not buy any other kind. Cheap cast heads have been known to chip or splinter with disastrous results. Forged alloy hammers usually bear a tag identifying them.

Nail Hammers

THE TYPE of hammer most commonly in use is called a nail ham-

283

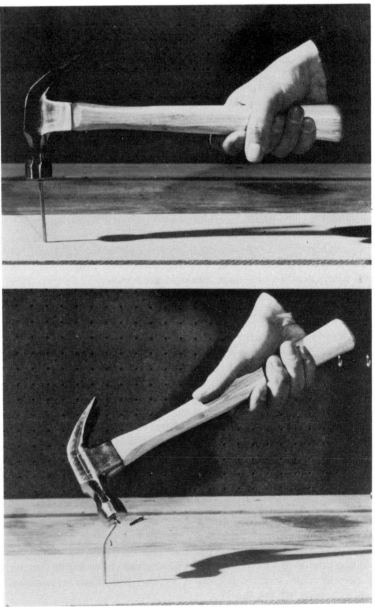

To hammer correctly (top), you must strike the nail squarely; the hammer's face and handle should parallel nailed surface. A glancing blow (bottom) results in a bent or broken nail.

284

mer. It has two main functions: to drive nails and to provide you with the leverage to extract deeply embedded nails of all sizes.

The claws on nail-hammer heads come in two shapes — the sharply curved configuration of the ordinary household hammer which is excellent for withdrawing nails, and the straighter version often called a ripping hammer, which is best for wedging between two nailed boards to force them apart. The straight claw does this job superbly, but it is inferior to a curved claw when it comes to removing nails.

It is also worth noting that the driving faces of nail-hammer heads come in two shapes: flat or belled (convex). In the hand of an expert, a belled hammer drives nails flush without causing even the slightest dimple in the workpiece. It has a further use in nailing up gypsum wallboard, where dimpling is desirable. The belled hammer leaves the nailhead recessed slightly below the board surface, where it later can be covered with patching plaster.

The most useful nail hammer for general use is the 16-ounce size, the weight describing the head. Both larger and smaller hammers are made. The heavier the head, the harder the blow it will deliver. Builders who must do such heavy work as spiking large timbers together often use 20-ounce hammers. But a lesser-weight hammer is often better for driving thin wire nails, because the lighter hammer normally gives you better control. Also, most women will find a lighter hammer easier to handle, although it requires more blows to do a given job.

Hickory Hammer Handles

THERE ARE at least four kinds of hammer handles. Most common are hickory wood handles which are adequate for all but the heaviest continuous use. For do-it-yourselfers, hickory handles should last for years.

Should your hickory hammer handle eventually require replacement, you can install a new one easily and quickly. Most good hardware stores sell handles for a nominal price. Try to purchase one that matches the shape, size, and weight of the old piece. A drastic difference in weight is to be avoided because it will upset the balance of the tool and make it feel completely different when you swing it.

Once you acquire a handle that closely matches the original, here is what to do. If the old handle has not broken off entirely, cut it as close to the bottom of the head as you can get. Use a coping saw or, lacking that, a hack saw. Next, support the ends of the head on the open jaws of a vise or between two bricks, leaving space below the head at the point where the handle is located. Use a chisel or any

285

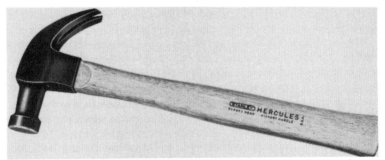

Nail hammers are available with flat faces or with belled (convex) faces. Belled faces are especially good for nailing gypsum wallboard.

other appropriate object that is handy to drive the remnants of the handle out of the head. However, you must drive the broken piece up from the bottom of the head, as the wedges that held it in place will prevent it from going the other way. Once the handle remnant is loose, it comes out easily.

Induce the end of the new handle into the head gently to see how it fits. If needed, sand, file, or shave the end so that you can push it in far enough to have a section about 1/4- to 3/8-inch long protruding from the top of the head. Then, remove the end of the handle from the head and cut a slot in the handle. The slot should parallel the sides of the head when the handle is inserted. The depth of the slot should be about three-quarters of the depth of the head.

From a piece of scrap hardwood, make a thin wedge that fits into the cut and sticks up about 1/4-inch. Put the head on the handle and tap the bottom of the handle on a hard surface to seat the head firmly. Then, place the wedge in the slot and hammer it home. Saw off the wedge and the excess handle on top of the head, leaving about 1/8-inch of handle protruding.

Now, you have to put in the final wedges that lock everything together tightly. Most hardware stores sell these devices in pairs, because you need two for each hammer. The wedges are made of metal, are thin at one end, and are ridged. With a chisel about 1/2-inch wide, you must make two starting grooves in the top end of the handle. Place the chisel so that it is not quite at right angles to the wood wedge mentioned in the previous paragraph, but so that it is not far from 90 degrees. Then, tap it enough to groove the handle end twice. Put the thin end of a metal wedge into one groove and drive it home, then do the same with the other. Finally, cut off that 1/8-inch of handle you left, as well as the wood and metal wedges. (You will need a hacksaw for this.) Finish with a file until the handle

286

and head are flush and smooth. Your hammer will be as good as new again.

This discussion of how to replace a hickory hammer handle illustrates a point we made in the introduction to hand tools. In that introduction we listed a number of basic tools you would need. But for a job as simple as the replacing of a hammer handle, you will already be out of your depth if you limit yourself to the tools described as basic. For the hammer job, you need a hack saw, a coping saw, a vise, a chisel, a file, a saw to cut wedges, and last but not least, another hammer to drive the wedges that fix the damaged one!

Fiberglass Handles

THERE ARE three other kinds of hammers. The best of these, and better than the wood-handle type, makes use of 100-percent re-

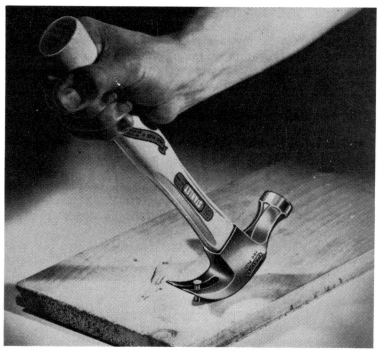

Sharply curved configuration of claw on a household hammer makes it easy to withdraw nails. Claw should be sharp to grip nails well.

287

inforced fiberglass handles. Such hammers are practically inde-structible and will last a lifetime. Their handles are "welded" to their heads by a resin that fills every minute crevice. The bond is immensely strong. Fiberglass handled hammers have the feel of the hickory-handle versions because, like wood, fiberglass has a slight degree of resiliency that cushions shocks from your hand.

The two other kinds of hammers are all-metal. One is made with a steel-tube handle mechanically locked to the hammer head. The other is a one-piece forging — head and handle are a single unit. The handle is covered with a rubber (sometimes leather) cushion to absorb shocks and provide a nonslip grip. The one-piece type is preferable to the tubular.

Tack Hammers

IN ADDITION to claw hammers, there are other types that are quite useful and which should be considered seriously when you decide to expand your tool kit. In no event, however, should you equip yourself with one of these in place of a claw hammer; they are sup-plements.

Such a hammer is the tack hammer. So specialized that it can almost be considered a separate tool, the tack hammer has a head that usually weighs no more than a few ounces, but that manifests a distinctive shape. It is long and slim — almost cylindrical — and slightly curved.

Where you would find the claw on a nail hammer, the tack ham-mer has a split lengthwise; and the split end is magnetized. The pur-pose of the magnetized end is to hold tacks. The tack is placed with the head flat against the split magnetized end; it is then tapped lightly into the target. You then reverse the hammer head and use the nonmagnetic head to drive home the tack.

If you are wondering why a special tool and method are employed for driving tacks, you probably never have tried to drive them. They are too short for your fingers to grip without getting in the hammer's way. Trying to pound them has but one inevitable result — a smashed thumb! A tack hammer is a good protective in-vestment — ask the man who did not own one. Tack hammers also are known as upholsterer's hammers.

Ball Peen Hammers

SOMETIMES called a mechanic's hammer, the ball peen is good for everything but driving nails — and it will even do that in a pinch. Ball peens are made in a very wide range of weights, with heads as

288

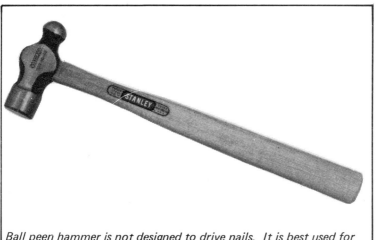

Ball peen hammer is not designed to drive nails. It is best used for inserting replacement rivets.

small as 4 ounces and as large as 40 ounces. For general home and shop use, a 16- to 20-ounce weight is best. In the home, the ball peen really shines at one particular job — spreading replacement rivets. The ball is driven into the rivet to spread it; then the rivet is headed over with either the ball or the face of the hammer.

To the uninitiated eye, it would appear that a ball peen hammer could be used for driving nails just as easily as a claw hammer; but this is not so. You can drive nails with it, but the chances of driving them true are reduced because the face of a ball peen hammer lacks the slight toe-in that characterizes the face of a nail hammer. The toe-in helps match the arc of your swing to the angle of the top of the nail.

Sledge Hammers

APARTMENT DWELLERS will find little or no use for a sledge of any size. But if you are a homeowner, one often will come in handy. Sledges are made in many sizes, the largest requiring real muscle and skill to manipulate. However, a giant sledge hammer has hardly any use in the context of your home unless you intend to spend your life smashing rock or concrete. It is the lighter members of the sledge family that find the greatest use. A small three-pound sledge is useful indeed. Like many other hammers, its handle is made of wood (often hickory), although other hardwoods can be used as

289

Sledge hammers have the weight to do tasks demanding raw force, but most do-it-yourselfers need only a small sledge for household repairs.

well. The head weighs three pounds as the name implies and provides two striking faces.

A three-pound sledge and a cold chisel make child's play of tough jobs. Nothing will take off a rusted bolt quicker and with less effort. Cracks in masonry that must be widened and deepened before patching yield to a few blows. A small sledge is a big help when you are drifting heavy timbers, such as 2x6's, into place for nailing. (Drifting is the process by which one moves an object a little at a

290

time by tapping.) When a heavy job lies ahead, it is time to haul out
the sledge.

Other Hammers

THE AVERAGE do-it-yourselfer can get by very comfortably with
the types of hammers already described. Nevertheless, there are
still other hammers available to him. Many are for such special purposes that they will rarely, if ever, find a place in general use. But
you should consider soft-faced hammers, or mallets, which can be
bought with rubber, plastic, or wood heads. Mallets are useful in
gluing woodwork, for instance. The soft faces will drive a doweled
joint together without marring the wood surface.

Body and fender hammers, always to be seen in auto-collision
repair shops, may be useful occasionally in shaping metal.

Shopping Tips

IT DOES NOT take much knowledge or a microscopic examination
to determine whether you are buying a tool to last a lifetime or one
that will soon have to be replaced. In all hammers with steel heads,
look for a tag or engraving that says "drop forged." Examine the
finish of the head. It should be ground to have a satin look and a
smooth feel.

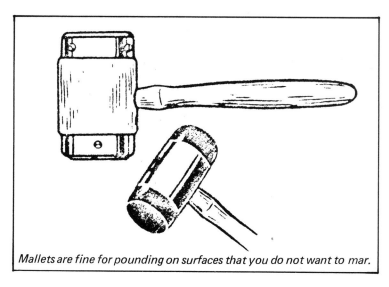

Mallets are fine for pounding on surfaces that you do not want to mar.

291

The edges of the claw should be ground down, almost like an ax blade, into a thin edge that can force its way under a nail head. The vee-groove of the claw should be finished to a smoothly graduated point, and the edges of the vee should be sharp enough to grip the sides of a nail when jammed into it. A groove that does not bite into the nail body is useless for pulling anything but nails whose heads are perfect. Examine the handle and the eye of the head where the handle fits at the same time. There should be no spaces visible, and the handle, if wood, must not have any cracks, no matter how small.

Assuming models of equal weight and quality, expect to pay $4.50 to $5.50 for nail and ball peen hammers with wood handles, and higher amounts as you go up the scale through all-steel types to fiberglass, at about $8 to $9. Four recommended brands are: True Temper, a leader in this type of tool; Stanley and Millers Falls, both of which can be counted on for quality products; and Craftsman (Sears), always a name to consider. These are not the only brand names, by any means, but they are CONSUMER GUIDE Magazine's selections.

Three-pound sledges, wood handled, cost about $5; tack hammers less, $2 to $3. Most of the manufacturers mentioned above also make these types of hammers.

Screwdrivers

THERE ARE more types of screwdrivers than you are likely ever to need. No matter how large your toolbox, you could probably fill it to overflowing with these tools alone. One editor of this publication checked his rather extensive screwdriver collection just for curiosity and counted 31 varieties.

But unless you are a dyed-in-the-wool tool collector, you can get along with a more limited selection.

Sizes of Screwdrivers

THE LENGTH of the blade is what gives a particular screwdriver its size. A six-inch screwdriver, for example, is one with a blade six inches long; the handle is not included in determining the size designation.

Another important dimension to consider is the width of the tip, or blade. The six-inch size, with a 1/4- or 5/16-inch wide blade will be of the most use around the house, and you should start your screwdriver collection with one of these. The 1/4-inch size will be found best for #6 to #8 screws, while the 5/16-inch will fit #8 to #12. Later on, it is advisable to buy two other screwdrivers: a 10-

292

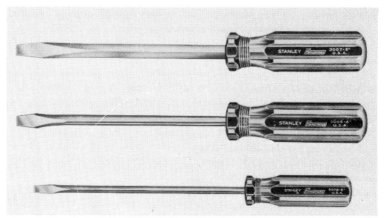

Screwdrivers differ in the width as well as in the length of their blades. You should have a variety for all household tasks.

inch (for heavy-duty work) which will fit #12 to #16 screws, and a pocket size (approximately two inches) for various small applications such as tightening setscrews.

All else being equal, a screwdriver with a square shank is better than one with a round shank. The reason is that you can put a wrench on the square shank to increase enormously the amount of leverage you can apply. A handle with a large diameter is preferable for the same reason — more leverage is possible.

There are good, bad, and indifferent screwdrivers. It is rather difficult to decide which offers the best quality just by looking at screwdrivers because the indications of quality are not readily apparent. And screwdrivers do not carry labels telling the process by which they were made or from what alloy they were crafted.

Nonetheless, there are some things to look for which sometimes can be tip-offs to quality or lack of quality. First look carefully at the blade metal. A satin look is generally an indication of a sturdy alloy such as chrome vanadium. Easier to see is the way the tip was formed. Examine the tip carefully, looking for very fine lines that appear to be ground into the faces of the blade. These may be parallel to the blade or at right angles to it. The latter indicates "cross grinding" and is better because it increases the grip of the blade on the screwhead.

Avoid screwdrivers whose blades appear to have been formed by stamping. The thin sides of the blade should be just as finely finished as the large faces. If they are not, you will not be getting a good tool. Perhaps the surest way to tell the difference is to ask to

293

see an expensive screwdriver and a very cheap one. A careful point-by-point comparison will open your eyes.

Other Screwdrivers

EVERY TOOLBOX should include at least one Phillips screwdriver. This is the type that fits screwheads that have a cross-shaped depression instead of a slot. A four- or six-inch blade is most useful. Larger sizes may be needed if you do much work on your car, where Phillips screws are quite common. Take a look, for example, at the fastenings of the car-door hinges. Chances are, you will find them to be very large Phillips screws.

Offset screwdrivers are a great help when working in tight places. The blade (or blades — some offset drivers have four) is at a right angle to the shaft, and there is no handle in the conventional sense. Offset screwdrivers are also made in ratchet models which allow you to swing them back and forth without removing the blade from the slot. The ratchet feature is exceedingly helpful when you are working in tight quarters.

Screwholding models are perfect for jobs that require you to work in places your fingers cannot get to. These come in various sizes and two common types. The split-blade type is preferable, featuring a sliding collar that spreads the blade wide as the collar is moved toward the tip. As the blade spreads, it locks into the inner surface of the slot, holding the screw fast. The other type of screwholder has a conventional shaft and handle, but also includes a pair of small spring clamps that slide up and down the shaft. The jaws of the clamps grab the screwhead until you get it started in its hole. This type is generally not as efficient as the split-blade version.

Ratchet screwdrivers can save work and time. There is a simple

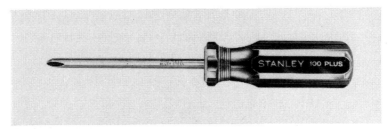

A Phillips screwdriver fits screwheads that have a cross-shaped depression instead of a slot. A four- or six-inch blade is best.

294

ratchet model — it looks rather like an ordinary screwdriver, but you can turn the handle back and forth without removing the point from the slot. The action can be reversed, so you can either drive or withdraw screws.

More useful is the ratchet type known as a spiral screwdriver, the professional carpenter's favorite. This is a long tool — up to 16 inches or even more — with a thick barrel on which a double spiral is impressed.

The blade is placed in the screw slot, and the handle is pushed toward the tip. As it descends, it rotates the blade. At the end of the stroke, the handle is returned to its original position by an internal spring, and it is ready for another stroke. This screwdriver is most useful when many long screws must be driven into wood. It is advisable to predrill the holes though, because the amount of turning force that can be exerted with a spiral screwdriver is not as great as with an ordinary one. However, the speed of driving more than makes up for the time spent in predrilling.

The most common materials from which screwdriver handles are formed are wood and plastic. Both can be found on the very cheapest ones as well as on top-of-the-line models. CONSUMER GUIDE Magazine considers plastic handles better than wood. Wood wears far faster. It may splinter or even eventually work its way loose from the steel shaft, rendering the tool useless. This is not the case with plastic handles, which are molded right around the shaft and are nearly indestructible in normal use.

Proper care for a screwdriver is simple. Use it only as a screwdriver — not as a punch, not as a chisel, not as a pry bar — and it will last for many years in perfect condition. Avoid driving under- or oversized screws. A poor match between blade and slot leads to blade damage, which may eventually necessitate regrinding or filing to restore the tip to proper condition.

Even top-quality screwdrivers do not cost a great deal of money. A fine six-inch standard model should cost approximately $2.50 to $3.00. A low-quality tool of the same size may be about half that amount, but the good one will have far more than double the life.

Pliers

THINK OF pliers as tools that are able to grab things like your fingers do, but with far more strength. The leverage designed into them is considerable, multiplying the strength of your grip many times, and concentrating it in a small area. There are many variations on the basic pliers, but all have a pair of jaws, a pivot point, and handles. Pliers are used for holding, cutting, bending, or reaching into small places where fingers cannot extend.

Slip Joint Pliers

THE MOST common and the most widely used pliers is the familiar slip joint. Even if you do not recognize it by name, you have seen and probably used it countless times. There are two kinds of slip-joint pliers. One has a pair of cutters near the back of the jaw, the other does not. The one with the cutting jaw is called a combination slip-joint pliers, or a combination jaw pliers. It is this type that CONSUMER GUIDE Magazine recommends.

The slip joint that gives the tool its name is a large pivot which fits in such a way that the jaws may move to either of two positions, one better for grasping small objects, the other designed to hold large things. You change the position by opening the handles wide and maneuvering them.

The slip joint's cutting jaws are capable of lopping fairly large, soft wire and small nails. But avoid pressing it into service for bigger cutting chores; even if it works, you may spring the jaws badly.

Despite this warning, slip joints are far from delicate. They are heavy, solid tools that should last a lifetime with minimum care.

When purchasing slip joints, look for a minimum amount of play in the pivot consistent with ease of changing position. Surfaces must be well finished. Jaws should meet precisely and have even serrations. Drop-forged steel is to be preferred. The six-inch size, or slightly larger, is recommended as best for all-round use.

Do not give in to the temptation to use this type of pliers for nuts and bolts. That is a job for a wrench. Plier jaws may injure the nut, or worse yet, the workpiece.

Long-Nose Pliers

THE TWO varieties of pliers already recommended are more or less alike in huskiness and heft, in addition to the way they work. Both are made of thick, heavy steel. A large pair may weigh well over a pound.

Long-nose pliers, by way of contrast, are more finely made and much lighter in weight. They are to be used with finesse, not with brute strength. Excess force may distort the jaws or even snap them off.

Its name notwithstanding, the long nose has an elongated pair of jaws perfect for reaching into tight spots where fingers or larger tools will not go. The jaws of long noses are made in a number of different shapes. One type of jaw, the duck bill, resembles what it is named for. Another type is similar to the duck bill but the jaws are curved, a feature which can be quite handy at times.

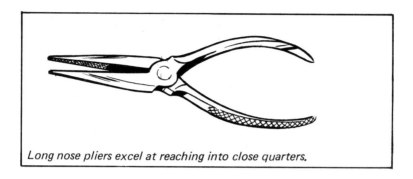
Long nose pliers excel at reaching into close quarters.

The best long nose for general use is the needlenose. It has jaws about one-third to one-fourth the length of its handles, tapering to a small blunt tip. The inside surface of the jaws may have a gridwork of many fine serrations, or the jaws may be ground smooth. The serrated type is best because it grips better, with less slippage.

Needlenoses range in size from less than four inches, mainly useful to electronics technicians or model hobbyists, up to seven or eight inches. The six-inch size is excellent, but you may prefer one a bit larger.

The quality of long nose pliers is easy to check. Rock the handles; there should be no sideplay in the pivot. Close the jaws and examine them end-on. They should meet so squarely that they could almost have been made from a single piece of steel. Pick a pliers that feels comfortable in your hand.

Some brands — Channellock and Crescent, for instance — include long-nose models with molded plastic grips covering their steel handles. They are not only comfortable in hand, but the plastic provides insulation against electrical shock when you are working with house wiring.

A precisely-made pair of long nose pliers will cost about $5, perhaps even slightly more. Many stores have other pliers that are far cheaper. But no matter how low their cost, the too-cheap models are almost worthless.

Locking-Jaw Pliers

MOST do-it-yourselfers find themselves using locking-jaw pliers as often as any other type they have. The unique qualities of the locking jaw make it well worth your while to include one in your toolbox. It can be used as a clamp, a wrench, or a portable vise. You can clamp this pliers on a workpiece and it will stay, leaving your

297

hands free for other duties. Jaws may be smooth or serrated, the former being used mostly for sheet-metal work and not recommended for general use. The serrated type is more adaptable to most home workshops.

Locking-jaw pliers can probably exert far more pressure at the jaws than any other kind of pliers in equal size, because the linkage between jaws and handle produces compound leverage — an extra multiplication of the force exerted on the handle. Take maximum care, therefore, not to deform the workpiece when using these pliers.

The locking jaws are adjustable. That is, you can preset them to the desired opening within the limits of the tool. The adjustment on some is made by means of a large screw that sticks out of the end of one of the handles. The screw also predetermines the amount of pressure the jaws will apply.

One brand — Petersen Vise Grips — is made in a number of different styles for various purposes. All the models in the line are fine tools. Nevertheless, CONSUMER GUIDE Magazine prefers the Channellock brand because provision is made for easy unlocking. The unlocking feature does appear on others, but it is not as conveniently arranged. Once you have struggled to unlock a pair that got a little too much bite, you will know why the unlocking feature is so useful.

The jaw adjustment on some of the Channellocks is spring-controlled, which is easier to set and faster to use than the screw type. Furthermore, the degree of pressure the jaws will exert when closed has its own separate adjustment. The distribution of this Channellock pliers is not quite as wide as that of some other models. If you are unable to locate one, writing to the manufacturer for a local source should be worth the effort. Write to Channellock Inc., Meadville, Pa. 16335.

Other Pliers

THE PLIERS previously discussed will take care of most home workshop needs, and you can probably manage with them alone. There are at least two others, however, that you also may find useful.

The first is the lineman's pliers, also called side cutters. This is a large, sturdy tool with square tapered jaws, and it has cutters on its jaws near the pivot. Some pliers of this type are made with notched cutters, the notches being useful for stripping wire insulation. The eight-inch size is recommended.

The last type of pliers is the diagonal wire cutter, familiarly known as "dike." Extremely useful in electrical work, dikes are also

298

great for snipping small brads or for pulling smallish nails that a claw hammer will not take out. A good pair of dikes can cut a single sheet of paper — not something you would normally do, but nevertheless a good test of how well its jaws work. Try the six-inch size.

Shopping Tips

IT IS easy enough to avoid buying poor-quality pliers. Always ask to see samples in a range of prices. Common sense will make you an instant expert when you compare them carefully. Wobbly pivots, poorly finished surfaces, jaws that do not meet squarely, roughness in the pivot movement — all these are red lights that will warn you to avoid inferior tools.

Some of the better brands of pliers are: Channellock, Crescent, Kraeuter, Diamond, Klein, Utica, Proto, and SK. All of these firms have extensive lines of pliers, although not all make all models in all sizes. Millers Falls and Stanley Tools, both marketers of a more general line of tools, have a number of pliers also. Choice of any of these brands is reasonable assurance that you are buying a good tool that will deliver service for many years.

Saws

IF ANY hand tool can be considered indispensable, it has to be the saw, the most important tool of all. While you can improvise something in place of most other tools if need be, there just is no way to get along without a saw if you have to cut a piece of wood unless you are willing to gamble on hacking it or splitting it with an axe — not the greatest idea to assure a straight separation.

There are several kinds of saws you should possess if you intend ever to do anything more than cut a straight line in a piece of wood.

It is meaningless to try to rate the different kinds of saws in order of their importance to the do-it-yourselfer; there is little doubt that the one you will use most often is the conventional carpenter saw. There are two types of carpentry saws: ripsaws for cutting with the grain, and crosscut saws for cutting across the grain. If you do not do enough work to warrant having two saws, a crosscut saw is better for all-purpose use.

The factors that make a ripsaw rip and a crosscut saw cut cross-grain are the size, shape, and number of teeth per inch. The range is about five teeth for the ripsaw, and about eight to ten for a crosscut. The ripsaw teeth not only are larger but also differences are cut into a chisel-like shape.

A good saw of either kind will cost approximately $8 to $12.

Good saws have blades of tough springy steel. Handles are hardwood.

Look for sturdy, springy blades that will not take a set if bent accidentally. Handles should be of solid hardwood or hardwood plies, comfortable to the grip and fastened securely to the blade often with ornate brass or nickeled hardware. When the fasteners are tight there should be no movement of the handle.

In recent years, saws have been available with blades coated with DuPont's Teflon. This slick, tough material tends to reduce binding, especially in hardwood, and it is also important in deterring rust. There will be an extra cost of about one or two dollars for a coated saw.

Proper storage of saws is more important than for most other tools if damage is to be avoided. Never shove a saw into a crowded toolbox where other steel tools could damage the points. The best way to store a saw is by hanging it either from a nail, through the small hole to be found in some blades, or by its handle. Before storing, wipe the blade clean with an oily rag, removing any residue of sap. Then wrap the saw in clean newspaper to help prevent rust. Should rust occur despite precautions, it may be removed by scrubbing with steel wool, then lubricating with a coat of oil.

Compass and Keyhole Saws

FIRST COUSINS of sorts, compass and keyhole saws are used mostly where conventional woodsaws are too large. Of the two, the compass is the bigger. It can follow reasonably sharp curves and can cut complete circles. The keyhole saw is similar, but can follow much sharper curves and smaller radii. The narrowness of the keyhole saw's blades is what makes this possible.

Both types are used where other saws are too large for the work area or when there are curves to be cut. In making an inside cut, a hole large enough to allow entry of the tip of the saw blade is drilled in the waste area. As the saw is worked back and forth in cutting, it should be guided toward the cutting line. A typical use of these saws would be cutting small holes in wood paneling for electrical outlets.

Compass saws are more commonly available, but the smaller keyhole should be no real problem to locate. CONSUMER GUIDE Magazine suggests that you investigate the value of a "nest-of-saws." This is a single handle sold with two or three interchangeable blades. In a set of two, one is usually a compass blade, the other a keyhole. In sets of three, the third falls between compass and keyhole in size.

Prices for these saws vary widely. Keyhole saws with cast metal handles have been sold for as low as $1.49; a 3-in-1 set for up to $5.

Coping Saws

THE COPING saw performs like no other handsaw can. Its blades are about 6-1/2 inches long and 1/8-inch wide. The saw consists of a steel frame shaped like a "U," and the blade is held in tension across the legs of the U.

A coping saw can follow the sharpest curves of any member of the handsaw family. If you paste a picture to a piece of plywood, you can make your own jigsaw puzzle with it. Its chief purpose, however, is of a more serious nature. It is a prize winner at making what are known as coping cuts; i.e., cutting the end of fancy molding to its own profile so that it fits snugly against an adjacent matching piece. With it, you can also produce scrollwork or scallop the bottom edge of a window valance.

There are two kinds of coping saw frames. One is nothing more than a springy steel bar bent into a U, with a handle attached. The blade is attached by bending the legs of the frame slightly towards each other and slipping the blade ends into simple clamps. The legs snap back when released, putting tension on the blade. This type of frame is inexpensive, $1 to $1.50.

More sophisticated and better made is the more expensive adjustable type. This kind of coping saw allows precise adjustment of blade tension and also permits you to rotate the blade so that the teeth will face any way you want — sideways, upside down, etc. This type sells for approximately $3.50 to $4.50.

Hacksaws

SOONER or later, most people need something that will cut metal — a piece of pipe, electric cable or conduit, or an iron angle. Hacksaws are the tools for the job. Even though made for metal work, they can be pressed into service cutting wood in an emergency. They are fair at cutting hardboard, but not very good for other woodwork.

Hacksaws have two main parts — frames and blades. Frames may be solid, designed for blades of specific length; or they may be fashioned in two parts that lock together, adjustable for blades of different lengths. The single-piece frame is usually adequate for normal use.

Like wood-saw blades, hacksaw blades are made in several grades, the number of teeth per inch varying. The basis for selecting a blade is the work that is waiting. Briefly, the thinner or stronger the metal you intend to cut, the more teeth per inch for the blade. Blades have from 14 to 32 teeth per inch. The rule in blade selection is that at least two teeth should always be in contact with the surface.

In an exaggerated example, it would be wrong to use a 14-tooth blade (each tooth measuring 1/14 of an inch) on sheet metal that is 1/20-inch thick. The spaces between such coarse teeth will be larger than the thickness of the workpiece. The saw blade will simply bounce along the work, tearing not cutting.

Angling the blade across the metal will alleviate this condition to some extent. Nonetheless, for best results, care should be used in selecting a blade. Thin metal also may be clamped to a piece of wood, or sandwiched between two pieces of wood, then cut. This is especially helpful with thin metal.

Here are a few other tips to help you do a better job. A hacksaw is a two-handed tool. Blade teeth point forward, and pressure is put on the forward stroke. One hand pushes on the handle, the other

302

pulls in front. If the width of the kerf (as the cut is called) is not critical, you can speed up your work by putting two blades in the frame, the teeth of one facing forward, the other reversed. When you do this, the saw cuts on both strokes. In any case, avoid excessive pressure; the blades are brittle and snap fairly easily. If you snap one before it is worn out, save the pieces. They are sometimes useful for working in tight quarters — hand-held.

Hacksaw blades do not cost very much. When one gets dull, discard it. Blades are often sold in packets of three or more for about 20¢ to 25¢ per blade. A good adjustable hacksaw frame costs about $6. The fixed type is much less — as little as $2.

As hacksaws are constructed so simply, feel safe in shopping for price. There is not much that can go wrong with any hacksaw you select.

Back, Mitre, and Dovetail Saws

HOBBYIST craftsmen will no doubt want — and use — each of three closely related tools: back, mitre, and dovetail saws. All are indispensable for cabinet working or other fine carpentry. But for the person interested in tools for general use, the hacksaw is the leader.

All three types are similar in appearance and construction; they differ mainly in size and width. Backsaws range from 10 to 14 inches long, 2-1/2 to 4 inches wide, and have about 11 teeth per inch. A typical dovetail saw has 15 teeth per inch, is 10 inches long, and is less than 2 inches wide. The mitre box saw is the largest, with about 11 teeth per inch, 24 to 30 inches long, and 4 to 6 inches wide.

Common to all three is a rigid steel spine attached to the top of the blade and equal to it in length. The spine stiffens the blade, killing any tendency it has to flex. Rigidity is a necessity for these saws because they are designed for making especially precise cuts.

In the home workshop, the backsaw is used most frequently for mitering two boards at their meeting point, as in the corners of a picture frame. The accuracy of such cuts is improved greatly with the use of a mitre box. A simple wooden box (about $6) will suffice for general use. Professional carpenters often buy far more expensive ones (as much as $85). It is with these more professional versions that the mitre saw is used.

The dovetail saw exists primarily for one purpose, the precise job of fitting dovetail joints. If you do not know what a dovetail is, examine a drawer from a piece of fine furniture. The small keystone shaped pieces where the sides of the drawer meet the back are dovetails.

303

Buying Tips

THE THREE top names in saws are Nicholson, Disston, and the redoubtable Craftsman (Sears). Each of these manufacturers offers a full range of models at several price levels. All have fine reputations for quality. Another brand that will be found in a wide selection is Great Neck, but CONSUMER GUIDE Magazine prefers the first three brands. There are also some fine saws from Great Britain and Northern Europe. Their quality is excellent, but their prices are generally high and distribution is limited. It is recommended that you select your saws from our three preferred brands.

Planes

WHEN A PIECE of wood is too large for the purpose you have in mind, it has to be made smaller. The excess amount will determine how you go about getting rid of it. If a board is several inches oversize, the obvious solution is to trim it with a saw. If it is only slightly more than you need, sandpaper might be the thing to use. But when it is too much for sandpaper and not enough for a saw, the plane is the answer.

Cutting down the size of lumber is not the only use for planes, of course. They are invaluable for removing a high spot from a door that is catching on its frame, for instance. The plane has many other uses as well.

Every woodworking plane, regardless of size and type, is constructed similarly. The frame is steel. If you examine one from the front or rear, you will see that the cross-section is shaped like a flat-bottomed U. The bottom surface is called the sole and has a slot through which a chisel-like blade protrudes. Its distance is controlled by a mechanical device atop the plane. The blade or plane iron is fixed against a rigid support so its angle to the sole remains constant.

All planes work the same way regardless of size. On top are two hand holds: a knob in front and a pistol-like grip at the rear. Both hand holds are usually made of hardwood. While some of the smaller planes may lack one or both of these handles, they provide other grips that perform the same function.

Although there are others, two types of planes are most commonly used and are recommended for work around the house — the smoothing plane and the block plane. Smoothing planes are about 8 to 10 inches long. Jack planes are larger versions of smoothing planes with soles extending to approximately 15 inches. Still bigger, but nonetheless of the same type, is the jointer plane which may be as long as 24 inches. All the versions share an identical pur-

304

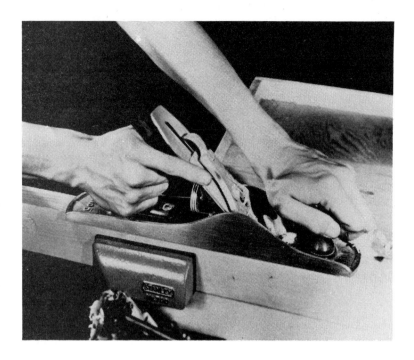

pose — smoothing wood with the grain. The major differences are that the longer models produce better work because they flatten out the movement of the tool, resulting in a flatter finished surface.

To use a smoothing plane, brace the workpiece firmly if it cannot be held in a vise. Grasp the tool with both hands and apply it to the wood in the direction of the grain with steady but not excessive force. Watching the shavings rising through the slot in front of the blade will tell you instantly if the blade is adjusted properly. It is cutting too deeply if the shavings are rather thick and stiff. If the shavings are little stringy pieces, the blade edge is probably not parallel to the work surface, and is not cutting evenly along its width. Or the blade may be dull.

Properly adjusted and used, a plane should remove a thin, continuous, almost flexible curl of wood about as wide as the blade — assuming, of course, that the wood is in fact that wide. The amount of effort you have to expend should be minimal.

As a second plane, CONSUMER GUIDE Magazine recommends a smaller one called a block plane. Its chief function is to cut across grain at the end of a board. In a pinch, it can be pressed into

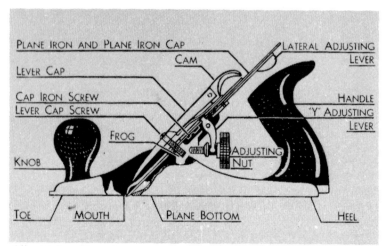

PLANE IRON AND PLANE IRON CAP
CAM
LEVER CAP
CAP IRON SCREW
LEVER CAP SCREW
FROG
KNOB
ADJUSTING NUT
LATERAL ADJUSTING LEVER
HANDLE
"Y" ADJUSTING LEVER
TOE
MOUTH
PLANE BOTTOM
HEEL

All woodworking planes are constructed similarly; major differences occur only in the angle of the blade.

smoothing work as well — but do not expect it to do as good a job as your smoothing plane. When planing cross grain, the tool is handled differently. Short strokes are best. Do not move the plane across the entire board in one stroke. To do so would chip the end at which you finish. Start at one edge, working towards the center. Reverse the board and repeat from the opposite side.

In case the board is so narrow that you cannot follow this procedure, clamp it in a vise between two pieces of scrap that are flush with the surface to be planed. When you use this method, you do plane across the grain in a single stroke, because the scrap will bear the brunt of the chipping and the workpiece will survive unharmed.

Plane Care

PLANES ARE damaged easily if mistreated, but preserving them in good condition is easy and requires only a few simple precautions. Properly cared for, a good-quality plane will never wear out.

Rust is an enemy of all tools, including planes. Therefore, wipe the tool clean with an oily rag after each use. The film of oil that remains on the plane during storage will do much to prevent rust.

If you have been working with wet or sappy wood and some of it has remained stuck stubbornly to the tool, turpentine or mineral spirits may be required to remove the residue.

Never stand a plane on any surface. Place it on its side so that the

306

blade is clear of any contact. If you cannot store it this way, use the blade adjustment to draw the blade into the housing where it is fully protected.

When blades lose their edge, resharpen them promptly. If you do not know how to do it yourself or cannot follow the instructions included with the tool at the time of purchase, take the plane to an expert. Do not attempt to grind it unless you know how. You may destroy the blade's temper if nothing else. If a simple dressing can restore the edge, use a fine-grit oilstone.

Buying Tips

FEW TOOL and hardware shops carry more than one or two planes in stock these days, and the chances are excellent that you will find only those made by Stanley and Millers Falls. Both are fine products which CONSUMER GUIDE Magazine recommends highly. Other sources for planes are the large retail mail order chains such as Sears and Montgomery Ward. Their prices are about average or perhpas a little below the prices in hardware stores.

CONSUMER GUIDE Magazine has not yet discovered imported planes in the marketplace, but if the sales growth of other foreign tools is any indication, they will be here before much longer. Imported tools in the higher-price category seem to be well made and of reasonably good quality — sometimes better than domestic products. But avoid low-priced imports. We have never seen one that impressed us favorably.

Chisels

MOST OF the hand tools any do-it-yourselfer normally uses have an equivalent power tool that does the same basic job. One of the few exceptions to this rule is the chisel (there are some power chisels, but they are expensive professional tools).

Chisels are cutting tools. They come in different designs and can handle everything from delicate woodwork to such rough tasks as cracking masonry or cutting rusted bolts. All the common kinds are alike in that you hold the point against the workpiece and strike the top. But the striking force for masonry may be supplied by a heavy sledge hammer while a gentle blow by the palm of your hand can shave a sliver away from a piece of wood.

Special chisels can be used when turning wood with a lathe. They are held against the spinning workpiece, which supplies the cutting power as it rotates. We are concerned here, however, only with chisels you will need for the day-to-day chores around the house, whether they are for repair, maintenance, or improvement.

307

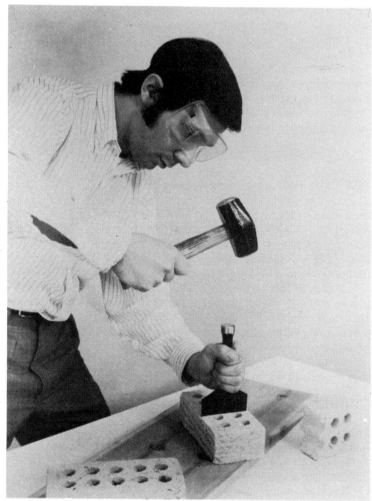

Never use a chisel on metal or masonry without wearing goggles.

CONSUMER GUIDE Magazine recommends two kinds of chisels — one for wood, the other for work on masonry and metal.

Chisels for Wood

WOOD CHISELS are manufactured in various widths and have four main kinds of construction. Since they have to be struck, the most

308

desirable type is one that will not suffer undue damage from the hammer blows. CONSUMER GUIDE Magazine gives the highest rating to the type formed from a solid hunk of steel, which is fitted with a handle. Wood or plastic handles may be used; the latter is preferred. Unfortunately, this type of chisel is the most expensive, as you might imagine.

The least desirable of the three remaining types is a steel piece with a socket on top, into which a wood handle is force fitted. It will deteriorate at two places: the wooden socket will tend to splinter in use, and off-center blows will tend to dislodge or weaken the grip of the socket on the handle.

A similar type of chisel, but a better choice, is strongly reinforced because the pointed end of the chisel (called the tang) is driven into the wooden handle. In another variety, which is still stronger, the handle is made of a tough variety of plastic that resists cracking and other damage. Here, too, the tang is driven into the handle.

Chisels for wood can be bought singly or in sets. The latter represents the best value because you usually save on the unit price when you buy several at a time, and you get a pouch as a bonus. The pouch has little intrinsic value, but it offers safe storage. Chisels are as susceptible to damage as planes, and they should be put away carefully. The pouch solves that problem.

Chisels come in many sizes, determined by the width of the cutting edge. The most useful are the four that usually comprise a packaged set: 1/4, 1/2, 3/4, and 1 inch. Prices range between $6 and $9. CONSUMER GUIDE Magazine advises you to buy one of the better sets if you contemplate any substantial use.

To do their best work, chisels should be kept properly sharp. Most wood chisels have a bevel of 25 to 30 degrees and may be restored by grinding. To touch up or whet the edge, the proper angle is 30 to 35 degrees. Do no overheat the steel in grinding, since that will destroy its temper.

Chisels for Masonry and Metal

THE THICK, heavy, stubby chisels, usually coal black, but sometimes chromed, are the workhorses of the chisel family. They all have a strong family resemblance, despite the fact that a cold chisel may have a blade as small as 1/4-inch, while a brick chisel might be 4 inches wide or more.

A cold chisel is so named because it is made for use in working cold metal. (There is also a hot chisel, but you will not need one for everyday use around the house.) Cold chisels also come in a range of sizes, but CONSUMER GUIDE Magazine recommends only two as standbys — a small 1/4-inch job, handiest for cutting off rusted

309

bolts, rivets, and the like; and another about 3/4-inch, for any heavier work that comes along and for such chores as widening a crack in concrete before patching.

Unlike a wood chisel, whose cutting edge is formed by grinding one side of the blank, a cold chisel is V-pointed, ground equally on both faces. The point of a wood chisel is far keener, but the demands put on a cold chisel could destroy that kind of keen edge in no time.

If you ever plan a project that uses brick as its raw material, you will want a brick chisel. This handy tool makes a moment's work out of cutting a whole brick to the exact size you need.

Safety Tips and Accessories

WHEN YOU shop for chisels, such accessories as safety goggles must be considered. Never use a chisel on metal or masonry without wearing safety goggles to protect your eyes. Flying bits of metal or stone can do as much damage to your eyes as shrapnel can to other parts of your body.

Another safety factor involves the choice of a hammer for striking the chisel. Do not use a nail hammer. A heavy mechanic's or a ball peen hammer is preferred. A small sledge is better yet. Nail hammer heads have been known to splinter when abused. They are not designed for chisel work, and we urge you not to use them for it.

As for the chisels themselves, CONSUMER GUIDE Magazine recommends that you purchase only the best grade. The difference in cost is minor, but the element of protection you get from properly tempered steel is well worth the difference. Buy chisels only of the well-known brands mentioned throughout this chapter.

Files

A FILE is undoubtedly the most simple-looking hand tool of all, and in that respect it is the most deceptive. If you look at a catalog that displays a reasonable assortment, you will realize that there is far more to files than you might have thought.

Although by no means the only manufacturer of files, the Nicholson File Company is the name that comes immediately to the mind of anyone who knows even a small amount about tools. According to an informative booklet, based on a treatise written in 1878 by the founder of this firm, there are so many materials, products, finishes, and working conditions involving the use of files that more than 3000 kinds, cuts, and sizes are required to handle all needs.

310

Fortunately, there is no need to sort out this vast number. Most of them are immediately eliminated because of their specialized nature or size, which makes them of little or no use in the home.

Comparing Files

FILES (and rasps) have three distinguishing characteristics: length; kind, which refers to the shape or style; and cut, which refers to the character and degree of coarseness of the teeth.

CONSUMER GUIDE Magazine considers these basic characteristics sufficient to describe the few files needed to handle general requirements around your home and workshop.

Length

WHEN we refer to a small file, we mean one that is 5 to 6 inches long. Large files are those that are 8 to 10 inches long. These measurements are of the length of the file body only, not including the tang — the pointed end that fits into a handle.

Kind

FILES are available in various types, such as flat, mill, half round, etc. These are further divided into two sub-types; blunt and tapered. A blunt file is one that is the same width from one end to the other, except for the tang. Tapered files gradually become narrower toward the end opposite the tang.

Cut

THE TERMS used to describe the character of the teeth are "single" and "double." (There are also files with curved teeth; but they are not included here.) A further distinction is in the coarseness or fineness of the teeth. The roughest is called "coarse," with the teeth becoming increasingly finer through "bastard," "second," and "smooth" cuts.

Single-cut files are usually used with light pressure for filing metal surfaces or for putting a keen edge on knives, shears, and other cutting implements. Double-cut files are for faster results and where a rougher finish is allowed. Used with heavier pressure than the single cut, they take down metal more quickly. Similarly, the coarser the teeth, the quicker the file will cut — but it will leave behind a rough surface that demands further treatment with a second- or smooth-cut file.

311

Recommendations

CONSUMER GUIDE Magazine suggests that you equip yourself with two files — a large one and a small one of the type called a half-round machinist's file. We recommend the half-round shape because, in cross section, one face is flat and the other rounded; thus, allowing the file to do its work on both flat and curved surfaces. The flat side is always double cut; the rounded side is sometimes single. The single-cut rounded side is preferred because it gives you two cuts in one file. All half-round files are tapered.

A round file about 10 inches long is another handy tool and you may want to add one. It is excellent for enlarging small holes in sheet metal, or for working curved surfaces. All round files are tapered. As a final addition, a small triangular file is best for notching metal and for getting into tight places.

Rasps

A RASP is a file designed for work on wood instead of metal. Fewer rasps are available than files. Rasps have far fewer and far larger teeth than files do and can cut into wood amazingly fast. A 10-inch half-round wood rasp is the best type for all around use.

Using Files and Rasps

MATERIALS on which you use a file or a rasp should be held rigidly, locked in a vise if possible. Hold the file or rasp firmly at the tang end with your right hand (unless you are left-handed), and use your other hand to hold and guide the front of the file, keeping its strokes level, so that your cut is square instead of rounded. Apply enough pressure so that cutting takes place, but not so much that you feel strong resistance.

CONSUMER GUIDE Magazine advises beginners to angle the body of the file slightly with the work; a 75 or 80 degree attitude to the plane of the work is best. Work steadily, examining the object frequently to be sure that no more material is being removed than desired. Finish with increasingly light strokes, to remove filing marks.

Care of Files

TO AVOID rust, be sure to keep files and rasps dry. These tools cannot be resharpened, but they can be cleaned when they clog. Broadly speaking, the softer the material being filed, the faster clogging will occur. Keep an eye on the condition of the file, and clear

312

the teeth as needed. CONSUMER GUIDE Magazine recommends a special device for this purpose, called a file card. Use it as you would a brush.

The steel from which files and rasps are made is extremely hard. Do not toss one in the tool box. It may damage another tool. Files and rasps will last many years with hardly any care, unless abused.

Prices

EXCEPT for some of the more exotic files, these tools are relatively low in price, ranging from as little as $1 for the smaller sizes, up to about $3 for the 10 inchers. At these low prices, you need not overly concern yourself about ruining or misplacing one.

Surforms

A SURFORM is neither a file nor a rasp, but it is capable of doing many of these tools jobs better. The Surform line of tools is a pro-

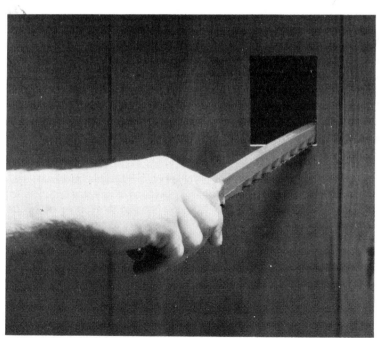

Stanley Surform Mini-file surface forming tool has side cutting action for getting into corners of wood, plastics, and soft metals.

313

duct of Stanley, an old-line name.

A Surform is made of sheet steel that has been formed into a toothy surface resembling a rasp more than a file. But unlike the rasp's solid teeth, the Surform's are merely pressed out of the sheet steel, leaving an equal number of tooth-size small openings. The Surform's teeth have keen edges.

The sheet bearing the teeth is formed into the desired shape and attached to a frame that has a handle. Surforms have been manufactured in all conceivable shapes — from a tubular rasp, to a flat, plane-like tool, to a small drum used with an electric drill for rotary filing.

Surforms have the inherent advantage of being able to take on any shape the manufacturer wants to give them. Equally important, they work superbly. They never clog, because the opening under the teeth permits the passage of sawdust or other material that would clog a conventional rasp. You may find that a Surform is your best bet for woodworking.

Prices are reasonable, in the same general range, or somewhat higher, than rasps. However, since there are Surforms in shapes that no rasp could ever duplicate, there is no solid basis on which to compare costs.

Drills

IN THE COURSE of your home maintenance chores, a drill plays an important part in many projects. Even if you own or plan to buy an electric drill, you should also consider the purchase of a hand drill. Because there are times when a hand drill is a necessity, CONSUMER GUIDE Magazine recommends one as a valuable addition to your tool collection.

Hand drills have the same capabilities as those powered by electricity; they just take a little longer to do the job. They come in two versions — one is similar to, and not much larger than, an eggbeater, for light duty; the other, known as a breast drill, is for tougher work. Both types have chucks similar to an electric drill's and take the same round shank bits.

The light-duty drill has a chuck capacity of 1/4 inch, while the larger breast drill's is usually 3/8 inch. Instead of a handgrip like the smaller drill has, the breast drill is topped by a large curved steel plate. The idea is to push against the plate with your chest or stomach, depending on the position of the drill, thus leaving your hands free for guidance and rotational power.

The breast drill also has a simple but effective two-speed transmission that lets you choose a fast-turning bit for small holes in soft materials or a slower speed for jobs in which the going gets

314

rougher.

You will find that a hand drill is a necessity when you have work to do where no power is available — an outdoor project beyond the reach of your extension cord, for example — or where there is danger of electric shock, as in a soaked or flooded area, or on a boat with water all around. The only alternative we know of is a cordless electric drill, which will certainly do the job, but at a prohibitive cost for the occasional user.

In addition, there is the matter of convenience. If you are in a workshop with all tools and facilities handy, you will turn to your electric drill without hesitation. However, if you need a drill for a few minute's work at a less-convenient site, you will find the hand drill the better choice; and you will find yourself using it more frequently as your confidence in it increases.

CONSUMER GUIDE Magazine recommends that you add the smaller, egg-beater-type hand drill to your collection. The need for a breast drill is normally so infrequent that it does not pay to buy one.

Most egg-beater drills are made with steel gears. Some drills have nylon drive gears, which do not require lubrication, but steel gears should be oiled occasionally and kept clean and rust-free.

Bit Braces

THE OLD-FASHIONED — but extremely useful and versatile — bit brace was invented hundreds of years ago. The form in which it exists today is hardly different in principle from the original.

The bit brace is a steel crank with a knob at one end, a chuck at the other, and another hand grip in the middle. Most chucks are designed for tapered square shank bits. A round shank bit can be used in a pinch, but will give you no more than indifferent success, and then only if you get the bit into the chuck at the right spot and use considerable tightening force. Some models do take both kinds, and you should ask about this when shopping.

The bits for a brace are called auger bits. They have sharp threaded points like a wood screw and work the same way. As you turn the brace, the point of the bit bites into the wood until the cutting edges go to work. Bit sizes range from 1/4 to 1 inch; prices are from $1 to $2 each, depending on size and quality.

When boring with auger bits, take care not to splinter the work piece. The splintering occurs when the point reaches the far side and the cutters begin to come through. You can avoid this by backing out the bit, turning over the workpiece, and boring through from the opposite side to finish the hole.

Larger holes can be made with an expansive bit — an adjustable

315

device capable of boring holes as large as three inches.

A brace has another use that is unique. Equip it with a screwdriver bit, and you will have the most powerful screwdriver imaginable. The enormous increase in leverage over a conventional screwdriver makes the driving and the removal of large wood screws easy. CONSUMER GUIDE Magazine considers this superior to a power screwdriver because the brace gives perfect control.

Brace Buying Tips

PERHAPS TO a greater degree than with many other hand tools, there are major differences between cheaply made braces and good ones. The latter will surely have a ratchet, while the former may not. And even if a lower priced model has a ratchet, chances are that it will be exposed; on the better one it will be fully or partially enclosed, protected from dirt and wood shavings that might interfere with its operation.

An important improvement found only in better braces is ball bearings that allow the end knob to turn effortlessly. A more costly brace will probably have a better chuck, with more precise jaws and smoother tightening.

The price of a particular brace will depend on whether it has all, some, or none of the quality features. The price range is from about $3 to $15. At the upper end, you can expect to get all the features, but check to be sure they are present.

Wrenches

WRENCHES ARE turning tools. Their best-known uses are loosening and tightening nuts. But they can do much more. Without a Stillson wrench, a plumber would be in bad trouble. The assortment of wrenches you can use around the house is tremendous. You can get by with a small set that will cost a couple of dollars — but its abilities will be limited. CONSUMER GUIDE Magazine feels that every do-it-yourselfer should have a somewhat more sophisticated collection.

Materials

THE ARISTOCRAT of the metals from which wrenches are forged is chrome vanadium steel. This tough alloy has the advantage of being lighter in weight than other wrench metals, yet it is almost unbreakable. The chrome tends to resist rust, an ever-present enemy.

Lower down the scale are the molybdenum alloys; at the bottom is carbon steel. A wrench of a given type and span made from either of these two metals will be heavier than one made of chrome vanadium steel because it needs bulk to obtain the necessary strength.

Types of Wrenches

CONVENTIONAL fixed-size wrenches are made in several shapes. The familiar flat (or nearly so) bar with a working unit at both ends comes in two basic types — open or closed, the latter being called a box wrench. Each of these is made either offset or straight. An offset openend wrench is flat, but the opening it turned from its normal position; hence the name "offset."

Box wrenches may be flat or offset in either of two ways. One has a jog in the wrench handle near the box; nevertheless the plane of the box remains parallel to the handle. In the more common type of offset, the handle of the wrench bends slightly (about 15 degrees) just before it reaches the box.

A deservedly popular and most useful hybrid is the combination wrench, which has one open end and one offset box. CONSUMER GUIDE Magazine recommends these wrenches because they combine the advantages of both types. A good starter assortment would be a six-piece set from 7/16-inch to 3/4-inch, made of drop-forged, heat-treated molybdenum alloy. Later, as you need additional sizes, you can add one or two wrenches at a time. You can get them as small as 1/4-inch and as large as 1-5/16 inches.

Some sets can be extremely costly. The reason for the high cost

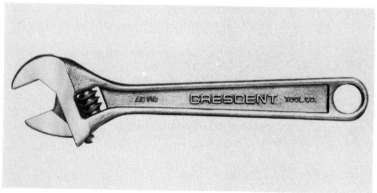

Adjustable wrenches are often called by tradename "Crescent."

317

is that the tools are made of stainless steel — the most expensive alloy of all.

To round out your combination wrench set for the times when you need larger, smaller, or in-between odd sizes, CONSUMER GUIDE Magazine recommends an adjustable open-end wrench. Like the others, it too comes in numerous sizes — from as small as 4 inches long up to 24 inches. A recommended buy is a 10-incher, with a maximum jaw opening of 1-1/8 inches (standard for this size). It is large enough to handle nearly any task you may have. A good quality 10-inch adjustable open-end wrench will cost approximately $5.

Adjustable wrenches have been called "knuckle-busters" with good reason. Take care to set the jaws precisely to the required opening. When you apply force to one of these wrenches, be sure to pull in the direction of the adjustable jaw. Never pull the other way. Turn the wrench over if necessary.

Socket Wrenches

A RATCHET drive and a socket form a formidable combination, giving speed, convenience, and flexibility that most wrenches lack. Their one drawback is that they require extra clearance. When space permits, however, their use is highly recommended.

The accessories available for ratchet wrenches make it possible literally to build your own custom wrench for any given use, whether you have to get into a tight spot or reach deep where other wrenches could never hope to.

Ratchet drives commonly are available in three sizes: 1/4, 3/8, and 1/2 inch. And if you think you will ever need one, you can even find a 3/4-inch drive. For average use around the home, CONSUMER GUIDE Magazine recommends the 3/8-inch size. It is large enough for hard jobs, yet priced reasonably. You can add sockets and accessories as desired.

If you are interested in better wrenches (at higher prices) or are a tool connoisseur, we recommend that you investigate the products of Crescent Tool Company, which manufactures quality wrenches of all kinds as well as other tools. Interestingly, this firm's standing is so enviable, especially in adjustable open-end wrenches, that its brand name, Crescent, is often mistakenly used as the generic term to describe this type.

Wrenches for Plumbing

SINCE PLUMBERS are both scarce and expensive, it is wise to equip

318

yourself with the types of adjustable wrenches particularly suited to plumbing.

The larger of the two is the redoubtable Stillson wrench (properly called an adjustable pipe wrench). The first time you handle one you might think it is broken, because the movable jaw seems loose and about to fall off. It is made this way deliberately to bite into a pipe hard enough to break it loose although it may not have been moved in 50 years. Yet it must be able to shift immediately to another position without your having to reset the jaw opening.

Pipe wrenches must always be used in pairs. The force needed to move a long untouched pipe is so great that, if no precaution is taken, breakage of the nearest coupling or fitting is almost inevitable. The proper technique is to place one wrench on the pipe, and pull it, another on the fitting, and turn it in the opposite direction to "hold back." In this way, the force exerted by the first wrench is transmitted through the stubborn pipe to the second wrench, where it is harmlessly neutralized.

A Stillson wrench with jaws that open two inches should be large enough to handle all but the waste pipe. A good one costs less than $5.00.

You will also need a monkey wrench, which is a special kind of smooth-jawed adjustable wrench. It is the preferred tool for plumbing work where you encounter large nuts that other kinds of wrenches would mar. These are very low priced — about $3.00.

Using Wrenches

CONSUMER GUIDE Magazine offers a word of caution about using any type of wrench. Always place it so that you are pulling the handle toward your body — never in the other direction. If the wrench should happen to slip while you are pushing, there is a good possibility that your hand will smash into something.

When you are pulling, however, your chances of escaping injury are better.

319

Discarded

25¢